ROBERT

PENN

WARREN

AND THE

AMERICAN

IMAGINATION

ROBERT PENN WARREN

AND THE AMERICAN

IMAGINATION

HUGH RUPPERSBURG

The University of Georgia Press

Athens & London

© 1990 by the
University of Georgia Press
Athens, Georgia 30602
All rights reserved
Designed by Richard Hendel
Set in Times Roman
Typeset by Tseng Information Systems, Inc.
Printed and bound by Thomson-Shore, Inc.
The paper in this book meets the guidelines for
permanence and durability of the Committee on
Production Guidelines for Book Longevity of the
Council on Library Resources.

Printed in the United States of America
94 93 92 91 90   5 4 3 2 1

Library of Congress Cataloging in Publication Data

Ruppersburg, Hugh M.
     Robert Penn Warren and the American
     imagination / Hugh Ruppersburg.
          p.   cm.
     Includes bibliographical references.
     ISBN 0-8203-1215-0 (alk. paper)
     1. Warren, Robert Penn, 1905–   —Criticism and
     interpretation. 2. America in literature. 3. Myth in
     literature. I. Title.
     PS3545.A748Z865   1990
     813'.52—dc20   89-20451
                                           CIP

British Library Cataloging in Publication Data available

For Michael, Charles, and Max

And I love the world even in my anger,
And that's a hard thing to outgrow.

Robert Penn Warren
"American Portrait: Old Style"

CONTENTS

ACKNOWLEDGMENTS

I am especially grateful to Max Childers, Robert Cooperman, Rosemary Franklin, and James Kilgo, whose careful reading and criticism of this project were invaluable to me. For their help and assistance, I thank as well Cheryl Abrams, William Bedford Clark, Laurens Dorsey, Glenn Harris, William King, Alice Kinman, Edward Krickel, Warren Leamon, Stan Lindberg, Hubert McAlexander, Rayburn Moore, Patrick Perkins, Karen Orchard, Dana Phillips, Catherine Rogers, Nancy Rubin, Martina Weiss, and my fall 1988 Robert Penn Warren special topics class. I also thank Coburn Freer and the University of Georgia Department of English for providing research time and assistance in support of my work on this book. Finally, I thank my wife Patricia, my sons Michael, Charles, and Max, my mother, and my grandmother.

ROBERT

PENN

WARREN

AND THE

AMERICAN

IMAGINATION

Robert Penn Warren's

American Vision

In Robert Penn Warren's sixty-five-year career the myth of America stands as a central interest and controlling metaphor. The American nation and its land are a chimeric entity in which Warren himself, his characters and personae, firmly believe. Common to that belief is a set of values linked to a particular concept of America emanating from the Declaration of Independence: freedom, individualism, community, "pursuit of happiness." For many of the characters, however, these words hold differing meanings. The America in which they believe, or for which they are looking, often proves far different from the nation prefigured in the Declaration: there America was conceived a dream-like ideal, the fruit of imagination and vision, existing only at the moment of conception, ceasing to exist as soon as it came into being and was cast to the whims of history and human nature, evolving into an entity distinct from what Thomas Jefferson and the other founders envisioned.

Warren perceived America as both a series of related historical events and a company of characters who act out those events. In his foreword to *Brother to Dragons,* his exploration of the gap between American ideal and American reality, he epitomized this relationship in an epigram which might serve as a précis for his entire career: "Historical sense and poetic sense should not, in the end, be contradictory, for if poetry is the little myth we make, history is the big myth we live, and in our living, constantly remake" (*Brother to Dragons,* xiii).[1] In this sense the life of each individual microcosmically subsumes America's existence and history. From his 1929 biography of John Brown to his 1983 narrative poem *Chief Joseph* and the 1985 poems of "Altitudes and Extensions," Warren's work reflects a recurrent, obsessive concern with the representative American individual, invariably a person of stature, a rebel leader or novelist or president or artist or bomber pilot, who personifies the essence of what Warren perceives as American. His three great long poems—*Brother to Dragons, Audubon: A Vision,* and *Chief Joseph of the Nez Perce*—examine such figures. So do a number of lesser poems, including sequences devoted to Theodore Dreiser and Ralph Waldo Emerson, and essays on Dreiser, Herman Melville, Nathaniel Hawthorne, John Greenleaf Whittier, Katherine Anne Porter, William Faulkner, and Jefferson Davis, among others.

Warren was no proletarian. He never apologized for his conviction that history is made primarily by "great" men. On more than one occasion he expressed suspicion of the masses. But his work evinces a deep concern with the common citizens of the nation, the farm woman or frontiersman or cart driver, who embody the same American essences as the Great Men and who contributed significantly to the building of the nation, though perhaps without the conscious intention of the Great Men in whom they believe. The buffalo hunter Willie Proudfit in *Night Rider,* Ashby Wyndham in *At Heaven's Gate,* the woman in the cabin in *Audubon: A Vision* and in *Wilderness,* Elvira K. Tewksbury in *A Place to Come To,* and a host of others as varied as the important historical figures represent aspects of America which remain of great importance, which are perhaps more enduring. Although these men and women may not seek to be a part of history, they nonetheless participate in it, and they possess a capacity for belief in American ideals often quite at odds with the beliefs of the "great" men whom they revere. Over the course of his career, Warren examined with increasing vigor, through his own experience and personae, through the important figures of American history and literature, through the lives and ideals of average citizens, the American individual's place in history. Beginning in 1953 he enriched this exploration with an ever-strengthening interest in the individual's place in modern America and the modern world.

Warren has often been described as a "historical" writer. Three of his novels and his three major poems focus on significant events, controversies, and figures of the nineteenth century. A number of his works set in the twentieth century likewise concern specific historical events, such as the Kentucky tobacco uprisings or the era of Huey Long. Yet he balked at the label of historical writer, though he admitted that history had always been his passion. He specifically refused to apply the label of history to his writings about modern America. Commenting on such books as *Night Rider* and *At Heaven's Gate,* he told an interviewer: "I never did a day's research in my life on these novels. They were coming out of the world I lived in, but not a historical one."[2] History is, he announced in *Brother to Dragons,* "the big myth we live." Yet it is difficult to believe that he did not conceive of his novels and poems about twentieth-century life as also being about events and people which contributed to the making of history, as about the making of a myth which would one day be construed as history. Surely he would agree that although the poem "New Dawn" is about a time (though not an event) through which he lived, it was also about history, and the making of history, for what twentieth-century event bears more historical significance for the future than the dawning of the atomic age? In all of his writing, he explores in one form or another the basic issue of the individual's involvement in time and event. We cannot distinguish in this sense between an overtly historical work such as *Band of Angels* and a contemporary one like *A Place to Come To.* Perhaps the label of history is simply irrelevant. Perhaps Warren resisted it because it implies a writer concerned with the past only for antiquarian reasons, who draws no links between past and present. Those links are always at the center of Warren's writings about history, for he never portrays the past without intending in some significant way to comment on the present and speculate about the future.

Warren repeatedly evinces a deeply felt concern with the quality of life in the modern world and with the modern individual's need for meaning, for a sense of place and identity. These interests are tightly bound to his preoccupation with America, especially modern America and its tenuous relation to the ideals of the founders. He typically portrays his characters in American settings and often presents their search for meaning as a pursuit of the American dream. He addresses the modern individual's plight most openly in *Democracy and Poetry,* which links prospects for the modern individual to the survival of American democracy. These themes are also important in *Audubon: A Vision, A Place to Come To, Incarnations, Chief Joseph of the Nez Perce,* and numerous short poems. But his verse narrative *Brother to Dragons* comes closest to an overt definition of the preoccupation of his career's second half. More intensely even than its interest in Jeffersonian optimism and faltering American vision, this poem considers the need of the modern individual, personified by a speaker named "R. P. W.," to find a way to live, a life's philosophy, in a world which offers little spiritual or philosophical solace. In this sense Warren does not confine himself only to the American past and present. The future concerns him too. Will American democracy survive? Will the individual perish? Will we destroy ourselves? Invariably he turns to the past for answers.

Warren's historical interests are always self-evident. But what do they signify? First and foremost the traditional notion that the substance of the present is rooted in the events and people of the past. The assumption of identity, that quality of being by which we know who we are, is enabled by knowledge of our personal, regional, and national histories. Warren's reiterative concern with what he variously terms the depersonalization or dehumanization of the present is linked directly to the demise of history as a valued form of knowledge in the twentieth century. He explained to Bill Moyers in 1976:

> I don't know how you can have a future without a sense of the past. A real future. And we have a book like [John Harold] Plumb's book, *The Death of the Past*, which is a very impressive and disturbing book. . . .
> He says only history keeps alive the human sense, history in the broadest sense of the word. It might be literary history or political history or any other kind of history. It's man's long effort to be human. And if a student understands this or tries to penetrate this problem, he becomes human. If he once gives that up as a concern, he turns to mechanism.[3]

Warren's repeated accounts, fictional and factual, of events in American history constitute his effort to define a national identity, and a personal identity as well. Part of that effort he directs towards correcting mistaken interpretations of history: a motivating force in his biography of John Brown, *Brother to Dragons, Band of Angels, Wilderness, The Legacy of the Civil War, Jefferson Davis Gets His Citizenship Back,* and *Chief Joseph of the Nez Perce*. An individual with a false sense (or no sense) of history suffers from a false sense of identity. Such a person can misinterpret his own obligation to the past and the present and how he should respond to the crises which confront him.

The Legacy of the Civil War defines one such misinterpretation as the

American Treasury of Virtue. Warren illustrates this Treasury in numerous works from *Band of Angels* to *Chief Joseph*. He contends that Northerners, under the influence of radical abolitionism, came to believe the Civil War was a divinely ordained campaign against slavery. When they won the war, they considered their obligation to the slaves satisfied and turned their attention to the opening of the West and the accumulation of personal and national fortunes. With the collapse of Reconstruction in the Hayes-Tilden Compromise of 1876, the North left the problem of the freed slaves entirely to the South. Southerners then resorted to their own self-deception, the Great Alibi, by which they blamed the Civil War for having caused such great destruction that they lacked the resources necessary to deal with the related problems of racism, poverty, and freed slaves—all the fault of the North.

Warren views American history as a series of periodic evasions of responsibility most often the result of misperceptions of reality and history. This is certainly a major theme of *Brother to Dragons*. Many of the novels explore it as well. Adam Rosenzweig's experience in the novel *Wilderness* stems directly from his romantic expectations about America and the Civil War, while Tobias Sears, the New England officer who marries Amantha Starr in *Band of Angels,* must struggle with his own illusions and ideals.[4] *Chief Joseph of the Nez Perce* portrays Americans as so blinded by an obsessive sense of manifest destiny that they destroy an Indian tribe (representative of all Indian tribes, of all minorities victimized by American expansion) attempting to live according to many of the same values—peace and harmony, family and community, life on the soil—which the growing nation itself believed in.

In *Democracy and Poetry* Warren views the individual's very existence as a separate and self-conscious entity apart from the masses, yet a part of them too, as one of the great achievements of Western civilization. He regards America as a nation which sought to escape the corruption and error of European civilization, which fell victim to its own brand of error and corruption. He thus sees America as a culmination, the last hope of Western civilization, perhaps its last gasp. America offers in this view a powerful metaphor. Its fate portends the fate of the Western world. This is not because Warren believes America has achieved its perfect destiny. He is too much a realist to believe that after eons of evolution and millennia of human history there would suddenly appear a perfect nation immune to the foibles of human character. There are Americans who believe as much, of course. They blame various causes—communism, the federal government, atheism, the Mediterranean fruit fly—for denying their land its ordained destiny. Along with others of his era, Thomas Jefferson believed that human perfection was a realistic goal, that national perfection could be attained. Emerson believed, less practically, in his own brand of utopianism. Warren regards all such notions as dangerous: they can blind us to our own imperfections, permit us to wander unwittingly into brutality against those who do not share our goals. This is precisely the point of Warren's American vision. He offers instead a realistic, often skeptical perspective on the nation's history. For him, the power of the American metaphor resides in the very fact of the nation's imperfections, in the patterns its history reveals.

In its 450-year history America has undergone what Europe and the Mediterranean basin took more than forty-five centuries to experience. American history thus reenacts, after a fashion, world history.[5] But it had, or its founders thought it had, the advantage of hindsight, the chance to avoid past mistakes. This point Warren emphasized repeatedly. He told Bill Moyers: "We had the future ahead of us, and we had this vast space behind us on this continent. We had time and space. We could change the limitations of the European world."[6] This founding illusion seems all the more ironic in light of what we know now: that whether those mistakes might have been avoided, we missed the opportunity, and the mistakes assailed us in their old forms and in pesky new ones as well. From our own vantage point, the disparity between the American vision of 1776 and the American reality of the present glares sharply. Although Warren never seemed surprised that the nation did not become what its founders intended, he did at moments seem profoundly disappointed. He was also deeply scornful that the founders in their blindness fashioned a nation unprepared for its own frailties, a nation which stumbled too easily into the pits of the Civil War, racism, the extermination of the Indians, over-industrialization, commercialism, modern technology, and extravagant national pride. Not surprisingly, Warren's characters are often disturbed and disillusioned at what they find in America. Yet in their conversion from idealism to disillusionment he finds the archetypal pattern of American experience, made no less significant by its being also the archetypal pattern of human experience. Through them, he suggests that although the ideals of the founders might have been beyond reach to begin with, pursuing them is preferable to surrendering to materialism, skepticism, cynicism, or nihilism. That is, unfounded idealism is better than a brazen cynicism which denies the possibility of dignity and value in human life.

As often as he explained and illustrated it in his work, Warren's opposition to the romantic sensibility is not wholehearted. Though he counsels realism, he is in fact a writer of conflicting impulses, of romanticism and realism intermeshed, of understanding founded in a logical comprehension of the world, countered by imagination and vision strongly dependent on the possibility of transcendence. Harold Bloom, professed admirer of Warren's later poetry though he disagrees with it philosophically, has even argued that the late poetry is "uneasily indebted to Emerson": "I cannot recall that Warren ever has written or said a favorable sentence about Emerson. But . . . Warren battles the Emersonian prophecies about the American poet with the sad and formidable inner knowledge that Emerson, like Wordsworth, is inescapable." [7] On another occasion Bloom praised Warren for his "visions of an authentic American sublime." [8] Bloom regards Warren as a romantic poet in spite of himself. Perhaps it would be more accurate to call him a romantic realist, a pragmatic idealist.

That oxymoronic fusion of idealism and pragmatism is the heart of Warren's American vision. It is clearly evident in his treatment of the American landscape. He describes the land for its own beauty, for the moods it inspires, for its reflection of human thought and endeavor. He also makes of it a symbol of the potential for growth and self-realization in the individual as well as the American nation. Two characters most seized by imagination and vision—John James Audubon and Thomas Jefferson (historical figures rendered as poetic characters)—regard the nation's future as inextricably bound to the land. In fact, they regard the American wilderness as an ideal. In *Brother to Dragons* Jefferson envisions the American wilderness as a promised Canaan:

> My West—the land I bought and gave and never
> Saw, but like the Israelite,
> From some high pass or crazy crag of mind, saw—
> Saw all,
> Swale and savannah and the tulip tree
> Immortally blossoming to May,
> Hawthorne and haw
> Valleys extended, prairies idle, and the land's

Long westward languor lifting
Toward the flaming escarpment of the end of day.

(10)

This was Jefferson's vision at the time of the Louisiana Purchase in 1803, when the land's promise was the nation's. Warren offers in contrast the barrens of the Kentucky landscape nearly two centuries later, which shows little sign of the promise Jefferson imagined:

Blunt hills eroded red, stunt-oak, scrag-plum,
The ruined coal-tipple and the blistered town,
And farther on, from shade of a shack flung down
Amid sage-grass by the sun-blasted field
A face fixed at us and the red eye glared
Without forgiveness, and will not forgive.

(12)

Jefferson and the other Founders, according to Warren, fashioned the nation in the image of their humanistic optimism, blinding it to the dangers of human error, the "red eye" which "glared without forgiveness." Audubon himself at last recognized (or so the poem implies) that he lived in a nation whose identity was rooted in society and commerce, not the solitude of wilderness, and that the ideals he sought in the wilderness were unattainable. Still, he never gave those ideals up himself.

Chief Joseph of the Nez Perce contrasts two differing cultural attitudes towards the land. The Nez Perce refuse to believe the land can be owned. They consider it sacred and live nomadically upon it, in harmony with the elements. When the American government orders them to leave, they refuse and resist, for their cultural identity is inherently tied to the lands where they have lived for generations. The United States army and government are intent on possessing that land. It is a commodity to be seized, cultivated, and civilized. They feel no sense of stewardship at all. A hundred years after the Nez Perce lost their struggle for cultural autonomy, their ideals of a life in harmony with nature are alien to the modern-day citizens who live on the land as their successors. This fact alone represents for Warren how far America has strayed from its founding ideals.

Despite his restrained romanticism, Warren refrains from deification of the land or the natural world it signifies. His lifelong aversion to Emersonian nature worship (though late in his career he indulged his own brand) reflects his skepticism. But he is clearly Wordsworthian in his use of nature to reflect and resolve the contents of the human mind. In such works as *World Enough and Time* and *Audubon: A Vision,* nature is a landscape on which human events and conflicts are acted out. Because of the link between American history and the American land, it becomes a particularly American symbol of the failures and ideals of the past, the dilemmas of the present, the uncertainties of the future. In a literal and metaphoric sense, the land's fate mirrors directly the prospects for the American future.

Warren's interpretations of the patterns of American history are not his alone. Other agrarian writers shared them. To an extent they mirror the typical modernist attitude towards Western civilization—that it has disintegrated into fragments, or is about to. America, Warren fears, has fallen too far from the ideals of Jeffersonian democracy and its emphasis on the individual self. Within the individual abide the essential strengths and weaknesses of the Jeffersonian ideal. A strong cautionary note about America persists in Warren's writings, especially since 1953, as if he is convinced that unless certain trends are halted, collapse will occur. At the same time, in such a phenomenon as the civil rights movement he finds reason for hope. Beginning in 1957, with the publication of *Promises,* his poetry turned increasingly to the value of personal experience: to memories, to the inspiration provoked by an important place or event in his life, to historical figures who exemplify individual worth and dignity in the face of forces threatening to dehumanize and destroy. The 1983 poem *Chief Joseph of the Nez Perce* is no anomaly in his career, but a tribute to a man who struggled to preserve his identity and remain faithful to personal and cultural values when confronted by a force he knew would overwhelm him. Ironically, that force is the agent of the United States government, charged with protecting the rights of the individual.

In *Jefferson Davis Gets His Citizenship Back* (1980) Warren expressed a similar admiration for the Confederate president. He regards Davis as a man of integrity (if not competence) who remained true to his personal ideals —the ideals of the South—even though the cost might have been the loss of the Civil War. After the war and Reconstruction, Davis became for the South a symbol of regional identity whose importance grew as forces from within and without the South threatened to burn that identity away. That is, Davis symbolized a Southern individualism which before the Civil War was more American than regional. Modern life, Warren suggests, with its advocacy of conformity and game plans and organization men and women, would confound Davis and his adversaries, who saw nothing good in abandoning the individuality of the personal self to the consuming maws of an amorphous corporate or bureaucratic identity:

> Davis died without rancor, and wishing us all well. But if he were not now defenseless in death, he would no doubt reject the citizenship we so charitably thrust upon him. In life, in his old-fashioned way, he would accept no pardon, for pardon could be construed to imply wrongdoing, and wrongdoing was what, in honor and principle, he denied. . . . suppose Lincoln or Grant should have citizenship thrust upon him by the America of today. Would either happily accept citizenship in a nation that sometimes seems technologically and philosophically devoted to the depersonalization of men? In a way, in their irrefrangible personal identity, Lincoln and Grant were almost as old-fashioned as Jefferson Davis. (*Davis,* 112–13)

Warren is only one of many who have railed against the modern "depersonalization of men." In the particular context of his work, *depersonalization* assumes diagnostic significance. It is the ironic fate of a nation whose Declaration of Independence and Constitution served to *personalize* and empower the individual. And a particular sequence of events and circumstances— the "pattern" of American history—led inevitably to the present perilous predicament.

Warren's patterning of American history inevitably hearkens back to the Jeffersonian ideal of democracy, which, as he explains in *Democracy and Poetry,* envisioned "a society in which free men—of independent self—would exercise their franchise in the light of reason" (4). Jefferson and his contemporaries expected a company of "natural aristocrats," qualified by inborn talent and ability, to assume responsibility for the affairs of their society. The natural aristocrat, or Great Man, plays an important role in Warren's vision of American history. His faith in the Great Man is one of the most anachronistic qualities of his perspective, and he does not apologize for it. But his conception of aristocracy differs significantly from Jefferson's. In an 1813 letter to John Adams, Jefferson wrote: "I agree with you that there is a natural aristocracy among men. The grounds of this are virtue and talents. . . . The natural aristocracy I consider as the most precious gift of nature for the instruction, the trusts, and government of society."[9] The Jeffersonian aristocrat embodies the greatest virtues of his culture. He recognizes its potential and works to bring it to fruition. He serves his society selflessly, though personal gain often comes to him naturally, by merit of his talents. Warren does not believe in the possibility of such a man. Men who rise to serve in his world always possess some selfish motive, though they may be unaware of it and may even believe in their own magnanimity. Senator Tolliver in *Night Rider,* Judge Irwin and Governor Stanton in *All the King's Men,* Senator Cassius Fort in *World Enough and Time,* and Tobias Sears in *Band of Angels* operate with complicating personal stakes—moral, financial, and political—intertwined with their ideals. As Willie Stark tells Jack Burden in some of the most memorable words Warren ever wrote, "Man is conceived in sin and born in corruption and he passeth from the stink of the didie to the stench of the shroud. There is always something" (54).[10] Willie himself is a disillusioned Jeffersonian, a Great Man who answered the call to serve but discovered that good will and righteousness were not required for public service, were perhaps even counterproductive. He does serve his state, at times very well, but often through means hardly graced with Jeffersonian nobility. His discovery of the soul's corruption is the turning point in his career, the beginning of his rise to power and the assumption of his fated identity: it results in his willingness to exploit the moral weakness of others to accomplish noble ends. And he lives in a world where a wholly moral man cannot survive, as Tiny Duffy, Sadie Burke, and Adam Stanton conspire to inform him when he tries to build the state hospital without the corrupt money he has relied on before. (Throughout the fiction, the ideal of a moral man is presented either as an illusion or as simply irrelevant: Willie's lawyer Hugh Miller is one example; Captain Todd in *Night Rider* is another.) Warren puts Jeffersonian idealism to its severest test in *Brother to Dragons,* in which Jefferson himself confronts the presence of evil and imperfection (and selfish motives) in his own life and in the nation he helped found.

Warren gives his clearest definition of the Great Man in *Jefferson Davis Gets His Citizenship Back.* There the proof of greatness is the ability to meet the needs of the moment, to compromise personal principle if necessary to serve a higher principle or greater cause. The Great Man has mastered the art of pragmatism, which, according to John Burt in *Robert Penn Warren and American Idealism,* "allows institutions to develop as the societies they are designed to serve develop, while it attempts at the same time to restrain and direct that development as some principle, not itself subject to pragmatic compromise, would require." [11] Warren finds that mastery in Abraham Lincoln, who understood well what must be done if the Union were to emerge intact from the crisis of the Civil War. The Confederate president Davis did not understand the war's demands, perhaps because he had to deal with different circumstances, also because of personal temperament and health, political philosophy, and less tangible factors. Lincoln had the emancipation issue and the preservation of the Union at stake, and substantial resources to support him. Davis had none of these. Moreover, though Lincoln was a man of principles and ideals, he "saw history not in terms of abstract, fixed principles but as a wavering flow of shifting values and contingencies, each to be confronted on the terms of its context. . . . Davis . . . saw the Constitution as equivalent to the tablets that Moses delivered from Sinai, in contrast to Lincoln, who apparently regarded it in [an] evolutionary sense" (*Davis,* 62). Lincoln could bend or ignore constitutional law for the sake of waging effective war—arresting suspicious men, suppressing newspapers, spending federal money without congressional approval. Davis would not ignore constitutional law and thus limited the South's ability to respond to the crisis of the moment.

Such differences in thinking led to differences in military strategy, Warren suggests. Many Southern military commanders in the Civil War died because they believed they ought to lead their own men in battle. Northern commanders recognized their tactical importance and were more prudent. Sherman's perception of his adversary as a "hostile people" rather than a "hostile army" grew from a similar tactical recognition (*Davis,* 66). Warren does not point out these distinctions between "two societies—one embracing antique values, the other in the process of developing new ones" (*Davis,* 63) in order to criticize either side. He observes that Lincoln acted from a genuine desire to save the Union, that Sherman was well aware of the consequences of his scorched earth policies. Lincoln and Sherman thus understood what they must do to win the war.[12] They were "modern" in their thinking, while Davis "was not a modern man in any sense of the word but a conservative called to manage . . . a revolution. Honor . . . was . . . his guiding star," and honor, with all the disadvantages he faced, was not enough (*Davis,* 68). "Lincoln was a realist," Warren explained in *The Legacy of the Civil War,* "and Davis was not" (37–38). In several instances he suggests that the ascendancy of a Great Man such as Lincoln represented the culmination of Jeffersonian-Jacksonian democracy: "The Jeffersonian dream not only survived, but with the Civil War and the apotheosis of Lincoln in martyrdom, seemed to find vindication in actuality—the common man perfected in artistic sensibility, folk humor, courage, compassion, and humility—the self projected in selflessness" (*Democracy,* 8). In more ways than one, Warren regards Lincoln as a fortuitous product of happenstance, a man who found himself in the right place at the right time, whose vision and pragmatism saved the American union.

Like Lincoln and to a lesser extent Davis, Warren's Great Men are significant figures who helped shape American history and culture. (His historical vision is decidedly patriarchal: his only extended treatments of women are of Katherine Anne Porter and Eudora Welty, literary rather than social or political figures.) They range from men generally esteemed—Abraham Lincoln and Thomas Jefferson, for instance—to more controversial personages—John Brown and Jefferson Davis—to writers and artists—Theodore Dreiser, Herman Melville, John James Audubon—to others whom history and the nation for a time excluded—Chief Joseph and Martin Luther King, Jr., for example.

Warren illustrates repeatedly that such men act out, but do not necessarily control, the events of history. They represent an intersection of the abstractly historical and concretely personal, the impersonal forces of time, geography, and nationalism colliding with the human, the interstitial commingling of the ideal and the actual. They make history, yet also, quite clearly, history has *made* them. In "A Dearth of Heroes," his introduction for Dixon Wecter's *The Hero in America,* Warren finds this contradiction a characteristic trait: "The notion that the hero is a force making history, creating events, and at the same time a mere by-product of history; . . . the folk mind —or, in the end, any individual mind—can entertain simultaneously both propositions, each one representing a profound and compelling need." [13] Warren is not concerned here with heroes as the protagonists of myth and legend but with the Great Men who helped determine the nation's history, whose characters and deeds are significant aspects of the nation's being. Such men are always human first and great second. They are not born into eminence and virtue. More often, to appropriate a phrase from *Brother to Dragons,* they stumble into virtue, and in doing so, more by happenstance than intent, become of service to the nation. But they are most important to Warren not for what they did but for what they were, because of their *selves,* their American identities. They bear meaning symbolic to the nation as a whole, and to Warren personally. Jefferson's struggle in *Brother to Dragons* to admit his imperfections is emblematic of the nation's own struggle, a nation which in Warren's mind has labored too long with its sights set on starry Jeffersonian ideals, too often falling victim to its own frailties. Warren both criticizes and admires Jefferson, a "cultural father" whose virtues are worth emulating, whose mistakes are resented. In *Brother to Dragons* the father of Warren's persona R. P. W. is his personal link to Jefferson. Just as he tries to understand Jefferson's virtues and failures, so must he understand and accept the failure and success of his father:

> The failures of our father are failures we shall make,
> Their triumphs the triumphs we shall never have.
>
> (21)

Observing Jefferson, R. P. W. must consider the substance of his own life, to which his father stands as a "glory and reproach" (21), for the old man has accommodated himself to life's limitations without abandoning his ideals, even in his extremity of age, an accommodation Warren regards as a major victory.

By regarding the historical and fictional figures whom Warren finds important, we regard Warren himself. He suggested as much in "A Dearth of Heroes": "If the hero is the embodiment of our ideals, the fulfillment of our secret needs, and the image of the daydream self, then to analyze him is likely to mean an analysis of ourselves. By a man's hero shall ye know him." [14] Like Joseph, Audubon, and Jefferson, Warren's Great Men hold personal significance for him. This is especially so for the American writers he has eulogized. Inevitably they share a vision of American history similar to his own. They stand in the ranks of the cultural fathers whom he regards as his own literary antecedents. Consider John Greenleaf Whittier, to whom Warren paid tribute in the introduction to his 1971 anthology *John Greenleaf Whittier's Poetry*. Warren was drawn to Whittier for a number of reasons. When Whittier was born in 1807, his family had been farming in New England since the early seventeenth century. They were the sort of independent farmers whom, Warren suggests, Jefferson thought of as "central to a whole society" (*Whittier*, 4). Whittier himself was very much a man of his age. Prideful and ambitious, when by the age of twenty-five he decided that his poetic talents would not be recognized, he turned to politics, specifically to the abolitionist movement to which his Quaker tradition destined him. Unlike such abolitionists as William Lloyd Garrison, whose extremism Warren viewed as antidemocratic and anarchistic, Whittier was a moderate. He was "firm in his belief in political action, that is, in his belief that man is, among other things, a member of society" (21). Though he "never compromised on the question of slavery . . . he steadily insisted on viewing the question in human and institutional contexts" (22). He thus melded his belief in democracy and the Constitution with his opposition to slavery, whose abolition he hoped would "give effect to the spirit of the Constitution" (23). In this sense both Whittier and Warren shared similar political ideologies.

Warren presents Whittier as a poet in spite of himself, who dismissed his youthful literary aspirations as "fancies," who lacked literary taste and had little sense of form or prosody. He wrote volumes of poetry, most of it bad, but on occasion, deeply moved, produced such poems as "Ichabod," "Telling the Bees," and *Snowbound,* the last of which Warren regards as a masterpiece placing Whittier in the "constellation" of "Cooper, Hawthorne, Melville, and Faulkner" (59). Most interesting is Warren's explanation of the force that enabled Whittier to write the good poems he produced: "the memory of the past, more specifically the childhood past, nostalgia, shall we say, for the happy, protected time before he knew the dark inward struggle" with ambition and the outer world (34). At his best Whittier was a poet of personal experience who used the past to measure the present and who made of his own life a representative emblem of the times and the human condition. (In his poetry since 1953, Warren made such an emblem of himself.) In *Snowbound* Whittier dramatized not only his personal sense of the disappearing past of family and childhood but the receding national past as well and his apprehension of the future: "Whittier undertook to see the problem of the past and future as generalized rather than personal, as an issue confronting America, not only himself: furthermore, to see it *sub specie aeternitatis,* as an aspect of man's fate. And he came to see that man's fate is that he must learn to accept and use his past completely, knowingly, rather than permit himself to be used, ignorantly, by it" (56). With all the differences between them, Warren finds in Whittier a partial image of himself. When he observes that "by getting rid of the 'poetical' notion of poetry, [Whittier] was able, eventually, to ground his poetry on experience" (33), he tempts us to consider the profound changes which had occurred in his own work during the decade-long hiatus in his writing of poetry which ended in 1953. But the clearest link between Whittier and Warren lies in their valuation of the past. Both are poets whose moral conscience underlies their visions of the American nation (though in different ways). Warren often seemed to project through the dilemmas of his own life the dilemmas of the nation. He implies that Whittier's sense of exclusion from American society during and after the Civil War combined with his grief over the deaths of his mother and sister to produce such nostalgic family poems as "Telling the Bees" and *Snowbound*. One need only compare such poems by Warren as "Mortmain," "Tale of Time," and "Reading Late at Night, Thermometer Falling" to recognize similar preoccupations. The poems he wrote after 1953 inevitably stress, implicitly or explicitly, his alienation from things modern, if by no other evidence than their growing inward, personal focus, or their concern with the past. Awareness of his kinship with Whittier, especially in *Snowbound,* apparently led him not only to edit the anthology of Whittier's work but also to write the long poem "I Am Dreaming of a White Christmas: The Natural History of a Vision," his own affirmation of Whittier's vision of a vanished personal and, by extension, national past.

Warren sees change wrought by the Civil War as an implicit concern of *Snowbound,* "the new order of 'throngful city ways' as contrasted with the old agrarian way of life and thought" (54). That concern is a significant aspect of the Civil War poetry of Herman Melville, another of Warren's literary Great Men, especially in *Battle-Pieces and Aspects of the War* (1866). Warren is drawn to Melville not by biographical parallels but by similarity of vision. In Melville he finds a conscious analyst of the transformation the Civil War was likely to bring. Like Whittier, Melville was marked by exclusion, having turned to poetry only after the public rejection of his fiction, a victim of the American yearning for adventure and romance rather than art and reality. Melville too, probably more consciously than Whittier, regarded the Civil War as a crucial moment in American history which might irrevocably distance the nation from the ideals and ideology of its founding. In "The Conflict of Convictions," a poem Warren cites both in his introduction to his anthology of Melville's poetry (18) and in *Democracy and Poetry* (9), Melville expresses fear that the war will fundamentally alter the nation's government:

> Power unanointed may come——
> Dominion (unsought by the free)
> And the Iron Dome,
> Stronger for stress and strain,

> Fling her huge shadow athwart the main;
> But the Founders' dream shall flee.

That is, the exertions of winning the war may have so strengthened the government that it will not be able to resist using its power in peacetime, diminishing and even threatening the individual freedoms guaranteed by the Declaration and Constitution. (In *Segregation, The Legacy of the Civil War,* and *Democracy and Poetry,* Warren suggested just such an effect.) Yet the Civil War had for Melville personal import as well. His war poems express his own struggle to discover life's meaning and how to live in the world (both central themes for Warren). Warren argues that the Civil War led Melville "to see that the fate of man is to affirm his manhood by action, even in the face of the difficulty of defining truth. Man to be man must try to comprehend the density and equivocalness of experience but at the same time he must not forfeit the ability to act. This is the tragic split in his fate, but at the same time and by the same token it is the challenge to his nobility" (*Melville,* 25). Although Warren gives much attention to the stylistic elements of Melville's poems, their philosophical dimension most clearly interests him. This rejected poet standing in opposition to his own age—"for which he had little but contempt" (49)—this poet who recognized the import of the war, and of the Gilded Age which followed, to the Jeffersonian Dream, whose search for meaning in a world which held none drove him to the brink of madness, and who ultimately realized that one must search and act on the presumption of meaning, whether it is there or not—this is the Melville to whom Warren was drawn, the Melville who more than Whittier is a reflection of Warren himself.

Warren's attitude towards Theodore Dreiser is considerably more ambiguous. In Dreiser he found a convenient symbol of the Gilded Age, but the sequence of poems and the critical essay in *Homage to Theodore Dreiser* had their true genesis in more than convenience. Warren's lifelong interest in Dreiser stems from his recognition that Dreiser used his art for the same reasons as he: self-exploration and definition, cultural and social analysis.[15] He is especially interested in the parallel between Dreiser's life and art: "The career of Theodore Dreiser raises in a peculiarly poignant form the question of the relation of life and art. The fiction Dreiser wrote is so much like the life he led that sometimes we are hard put to say exactly what Dreiser—the artist—added to what Dreiser—the man—had observed and experienced" (9). When he adds later that "art is the artist's way of understanding—of creating even—the actuality that he lives" (9), he is speaking as much about himself as Dreiser.

More practical considerations also account for Warren's interest in Dreiser. He was, "quite literally, a novelist of the metaphysics of society —of, specifically, the new plutocratic society of the Gilded Age. And this meant that he was, too, the anatomist of the guilt involved in the characteristic ambition of that age as well as the poet of the pathos of success" (32). That is, he was a critical analyst of the same age he embodied, a divided man willing to criticize the robber barons yet capable of idolizing and emulating them as well. Observing a similar paradox in Oliver Wendell Holmes and Mark Twain, Warren suggests that such a division may have been a characteristic trait of the age. Because we know, from such works as *Legacy of the Civil War* and *Democracy and Poetry,* that for Warren the Gilded Age was the age in which America assumed its modern identity, Dreiser thus becomes a symbol of the American artist, torn between a need to criticize the society which fails to value him and the desire to join that society and its materialistic dreams.

Warren consistently viewed the artist as standing outside the mainstream of American life and values. Inevitably his artists respond equivocally to the nature of American life. Whittier, Melville, and Dreiser were all outsiders, for different reasons, though at various times in their lives they attempted to belong to their society. Their exclusion became one basis of their art. The artist for Warren epitomizes the divisiveness of American experience. He enjoys freedom of expression and is even encouraged to believe that it is an inherent part of his individuality, yet he must confront a public which has been conditioned to view individualistic expressions as valueless and even threatening because they do not advance the goals of American enterprise. Those artists most important to Warren have attempted to understand this paradox and the more general contradiction between the illusory principles of the founders and the state of affairs in the modern nation.

Warren's Great Men—whether writers, politicians, or Indian chiefs— are not heroes in any conventional sense. Counterbalanced against whatever nobility they might possess is their flawed humanness. Warren seizes inevitably on Whittier's ambition or Dreiser's duplicity or Jefferson's pride or Lincoln's opportunism to confirm their imperfection. Some of them are "great" only in the highly ironic sense of the main character in Fielding's *Jonathan Wild.* This seems especially true of the fictional Great Men. Senator Tolliver of *Night Rider,* Bogan Murdock in *At Heaven's Gate,* Judge

Irwin, Governor Stanton, and Willie Stark in *All the King's Men,* Cassius Fort in *World Enough and Time,* Tobias Sears in *Band of Angels,* Heinrich Stahlmann in *A Place to Come To*—all strive to attain their goals by methods ranging from virtuous to damnable. Some are consumed by corruption. Others struggle amidst the complicating circumstances of human life to do their best, sometimes stumbling into virtue, like Willie Stark and like Jed Hawksworth of *Wilderness,* other times into error, like Jerry Calhoun of *At Heaven's Gate* and Isaac Sumpter in *The Cave.* Warren insists on the humanity of these men, those he reviles and those he admires. If we are to benefit from their examples, he implies, we must know them for what they are, uncluttered by romantic illusions or hagiography. Then they enable the envisioning of a nation fashioned not by god-like heroes but fallible men and women unaware of their weakness, a nation itself subject to fallibility and the caprice of time, change, and circumstance.

Belief is a crucial component of Warren's Great Men. They must believe in themselves, and the people whom they serve must believe in them as well. In "A Dearth of Heroes," Warren observes that the American hero must always have popular recognition: "In success or failure, in elective office or not, first of all the hero must be, as Wecter says, the 'people's choice.' To be a hero at all he must command, in one way or another, their imagination and acceptance." [16] The "people" hold a prominent if not always esteemed position in Warren's fiction. They often appear as teeming, anonymous crowds; even the nonfiction offers such portrayals (one recent example is the description of the monument dedication in *Jefferson Davis Gets His Citizenship Back*). As a faceless mass, "the people" receive little of Warren's respect. They lack in his view individual conscience and will, are vulnerable to emotional appeal and demagogic sway. They need the organized authority and social unity which a government can provide. They also possess a strong capacity for belief and idealism. They have faith in the Great Men who lead them, in the democracy and the National Dream which they believe those Great Men embody. On the one hand Warren criticizes the contemporary elevation of the common man to heroic stature as "a celebration of (and as an alibi for) the merely average." [17] Yet repeatedly he turns to some common figure in his fiction and nonfiction as representative of characteristic American values and traits. He avoids exalting these figures too highly. The common people remain as human and as subject to error as the Great Men. But because of their typical lack of ambition, sophistication, and pretense (in contrast to the Great Men, who possess these traits in abundance), they often remain closer to those American values than other characters, not merely because they believe in those values, but because they try to live them.

The common folk are eulogized in "Founding Fathers, Early-Nineteenth-Century Style, Southeast U.S.A.," written shortly after the first version of *Brother to Dragons*. The "founding fathers" of the title are the unknown and anonymous men and women who built the nation and who, for the most part, the history books do not remember. They are not Great Men, though many of them aspired to be, and a few, such as Jim Bowie and Sam Houston, approached greatness:

> Some composed declarations, remembering Jefferson's language.
> Knew pose of the patriot, left hand in crook of the spine or
> With finger to table, while right invokes the Lord's just rage.
> There was always a grandpa, or cousin at least, who had been a
>   real Signer.
>
> Some were given to study, read Greek in the forest, and these
> Longed for an epic to do their own deeds right honor.
>
> (NSP, 282)

They were frontiersmen, not politicians or statesmen, not the sort of men commonly designated as founders. They possessed their own ideals and believed fervently in their cause, for which they would die if called to do so. They were "the nameless, of whom no portraits remain, / No locket or seal ring" (*NSP*, 282), the ancestors whose undistinguished and varied lives haunt the American past. "They were human," the poem says of them, "they suffered." In their forgotten and seeming insignificance, they belong to a national tradition, a cultural consciousness. Warren implores they not be forgotten:

> now their voices
> Come thin, like the last cricket in frost-dark, in grass lost,
> With nothing to tell us for our complexity of choices,
> But beg us only one word to justify their own life-cost.
>
> So let us bend ear to them in this hour of lateness,
> And what they are trying to say, try to understand,

And try to forgive them their defects, even their greatness,
For we are their children in the light of humanness, and
   under the shadow of God's closing hand.

(NSP, 283)

By forgetting them, the nation fails to honor them. But by reference to "our own time's sad declension" and "this hour of lateness," the poem implies that the worst failure lies in the gulf between modern America and the values these ancestors embodied. The poem demonstrates the depth of Warren's belief in the importance of the past, not only as a source of identity but of redemption. It demonstrates too, in an almost Whitmanesque way, Warren's all-inclusive vision of the men and women who made, and were made by, American history.

Warren's American characters, from Great Men to newly arrived immigrants to displaced natives of the continent, reflect a vision of history which hinges finally on the experience and perception of the individual. Individual experiences have contributed to the making of American history, itself a continuing struggle to build and preserve a nation which makes individual experience possible. Paradoxically, though the individual cannot restrain the movement of history and is usually its hapless subject, he remains the source of history, for what is history if not the story of millions of individual destinies told from an abstract, generalized point of view? (Consider Fiddlersburg in *Flood*, about to disappear beneath the submerging waters of a hydroelectric impoundment; or Amantha Starr, suddenly transformed from the pampered daughter of a Southern planter to a slave; or Adam Rosenzweig, who steps from the ship which has carried him across the Atlantic into the chaos of the New York draft riots and the American Civil War.) History for Warren is always perceived, experienced, and acted out by the individual. It thus stands to reason that individuals have an obligation not merely to *let* history happen but to do their best to influence it for the good. In *Segregation* and *Who Speaks for the Negro?* Warren calls on Americans to respond appropriately to the moral demands of a historical situation. He makes similar pleas in *The Legacy of the Civil War* and *Democracy and Poetry*. Warren clearly believes that the individual must enter into history, not merely be swept along by it. The narrative perspective in much of his writing reflects this stance of involvement. He never withdraws in his writing from the events he chronicles. His narrative source is often the perspective of an involved individual. Only in the nonfiction, primarily *The Legacy of the Civil War,* does he attempt the kind of panoramic analysis of events which Tolstoy gives in the essay chapters of *War and Peace.*

If Warren regards history as an irresistible naturalistic process—a wind that "blows where it listeth" ("Wind and Gibbon," *NSP,* 77), a flood (in *Flood* and *Meet Me in the Green Glen*), a rock slide (Heinrich Stahlmann's vision in *A Place to Come To*), or a Great Twitch (Jack Burden's metaphor in *All the King's Men*)—he nonetheless portrays it also as a mass of living individuals, tossed along involuntarily, moving with will and consciousness, bearing responsibility for their behavior in the flood which has swept them up. Crowd images in the first six novels clearly suggest this paradoxical notion. It is most emphatically apparent in *All the King's Men* as Jack Burden watches the crowds gathering around the state capitol building, summoned there by Willie Stark, threatened with impeachment by his state legislature. Those people who answer the summons are just the sort of people who voted Stark into the governor's office. He is their Great Man, their representative of the American ideal. Burden describes them with characteristic cynicism, but he cannot disguise the awe they inspire:

> Before noon on the fifth of April there were a lot more wool-hats and red-necks and Mother Hubbards and crepe-de-Chine dresses with red-clay dust about the uneven bottom hem, and a lot of clothes and faces which weren't cocklebur and crossroads, but county-seat and filling-station. . . . I felt like God, brooding on History right there in front. There were the bronze statues on their pedestals, on the lawn, in frock coats, with the right hand inserted under the coat, just over the heart. . . . They were already History, and the grass around their pedestals was shaved close and the flowers were planted in stars and circles and crescents. Then over beyond the statues, there were the people who weren't History yet. Not quite. But to me they looked like History because I knew the end of the event. (157, 161)

In such crowds there is terrible power, as Warren shows not only in the early novels but also in such later novels as *Band of Angels* and *Wilderness,* where raging mobs wreak terrible havoc. Mobs exemplify the danger of the demagogue. They signify the force of history, which sweeps along the hapless individual, as Perceval Munn is swept in the opening scene of *Night Rider.* They conversely suggest the individual's responsibility to resist, if need be, the crowd's movement, to influence its motion, to change the direction of history. Warren's crowds are the literal and metaphoric opposites of his Great Man, whose identity as an individual, a dynamic and identifiable personality, helps explain his power over mobs whose very character issues from the lack of individuality.

Warren's skepticism of the masses, his attitudes towards the past, and his respect for Great Men reflect his essential political conservatism. So too does his lifelong concern with the nature and preservation of political order. Throughout his career he views the state more or less in the classical Greek and Elizabethan sense as city-state or *polis*, a political and cultural entity, a living whole with an organic unity. In his fiction the *polis* exists for the benefit of its individual citizens, to protect them against disorder and the anarchy of the masses. William Bedford Clark explains that "An important *a priori* assumption running throughout the massive Warren canon is the essentially Platonic notion that the *polis*, or social fabric, is the individual writ large." [18] Threats to the state endanger the individual. Warren's first four novels explore historical situations which force the individual to weigh his own desires, or those of a small group, against the greater welfare of the state and its citizens. In each of these novels, to some extent, the government of a democratic state is established as the inviolable ideal against which individuals and events are measured. This is especially so in *Night Rider,* where the Tobacco Association so intently defends its goals that it ultimately condones heinous acts of violence and terrorism—symptoms of a complete breakdown in civil order. The Relief–Anti-Relief controversy in *World Enough and Time* concerns quite simply whether basic principles of civil and constitutional law may be altered to serve the needs of the moment.[19] Though Relief would undoubtedly alleviate the distress of the citizens, it would undermine the stability of government and cause worse problems than it resolved.

The welfare of the state is bound up inextricably with the political and moral health of its leaders and government. The old king's abdication in *King Lear* violates the natural hierarchy. The corruption of the monarchy spreads outward and infects the entire state. Chaos erupts—the physical chaos of the storm, the civil chaos of warfare and court intrigue. The political world of Warren's early novels functions in much the same way. There are no storms on the heath, but Warren offers adequate substitutes. In *Night*

Rider, the gradual change of Perse Munn from a meek lawyer to a ruthless murderer mirrors the decline of conditions across the Kentucky country-side, where the ostensibly innocent demand of tobacco growers for a fair price leads to house burnings, murder, and complete civil disorder. Willie Stark's willingness in *All the King's Men* to exploit human corruptibility weaves a web of intrigue and deceit which entangles the entire state. Bogan Murdock's unethical business practices in *At Heaven's Gate* infect his state with greed and oppression. Numerous people ultimately fall victim. Along with Stark and Munn, he is the cousin of King Oedipus, Macbeth, and Eliot's Fisher King, sitting on the banks of the river with the barren, wasted land stretching behind him.

Warren's classical view of the state is not unaffected by the democratic character of the nation which most concerns him. The Constitution estab-lished the United States government, in Lincoln's words, "of the people, by the people, for the people." This principle alone is the source of much political irony in the early novels, which contrast the ideal implied with the reality of what the nation has become. A leader's character may simply reflect the prevailing political climate which enabled his election to be-gin with. Popular dissatisfaction over corruption and dishonesty is a major factor in Willie Stark's election as governor, and a general atmosphere of boosterism and institutionalized greed makes possible Bogan Murdock's success in *At Heaven's Gate.* The first three novels in particular illustrate how democratic leaders can drift away from the will and values of the people they lead, the people from whom they came. The very process of this drifting can weaken the nation's moral and political fiber. Such a dis-ruption becomes in Warren's fiction the symptom of a democratic leader's fall from the ideals and principles which inspired him to seek office, and, because he was elected by democratic process, the symbol of the nation's fall from the ideals of its founding.

The early novels, and the early biography of John Brown, ex-plore the acquisition and exercise of power on both a personal and political level. Power in these works is linked directly to Warren's conception of the state as *polis*. In a 1981 introduction to *All the King's Men,* he explained: "The issue is between legitimacy and *de facto* power; and here to bring mat-ters up to date, we substitute for the old meaning of legitimacy as heredity and God's will the new meaning of constitutionality." [20] That is, the issue is whether power is wielded in a Constitutional manner, whether it is used to uphold democratic principles, to strengthen and sustain the Union, or to endanger it. The ultimate use to which power can be committed is for the protection of the state and the individuals it shelters. For this reason Warren remained a stalwart Unionist throughout his career: a believer in the mystic concept of unity among the American states, in the ideals and values on which that unity is based.[21]

Had he expressed it in no other form, Warren's belief in the principle of civil order would be sufficiently evident through his portrayals of the emblematic figures who endanger it. The first such individual in his writing is the visionary, self-styled prophet-abolitionist John Brown, the subject of his first book, *John Brown: The Making of a Martyr,* published in 1929. The biography presents Brown as a man so obsessed with a Cause that he loses all sense of humanity and perspective, turns against his government, and murders other human beings in the name of a Higher Good: the abolition of slavery. The evil he desires to purge exists for him in no real context— no relation to history, morality, or humanity.[22] Warren's dislike grows not out of Brown's abolitionism but from his utter indifference to human life and social order, his willingness to foment anarchy if necessary in his battle against slavery. To Warren, Brown was the most dangerous among men. Thirty-four years later, in *The Legacy of the Civil War,* he explained why: "The conviction . . . that 'one with God is always a majority,' does not lend encouragement to the ordinary democratic process. With every man his own majority as well as his own law, there is, in the logical end, only anarchy, and anarchy of a peculiarly tedious and bloodthirsty sort, for every drop is to be spilled in God's name and by his explicit directive" (33). And Warren apparently suspects that Brown consciously exploited Higher Law absolutism to justify his actions.

Brown is the first in a series of social misanthropes in Warren's fiction who sever all ties with humanity in the service of a personal or political cause. Warren portrays Brown as a master of deceit who fools everyone around him, perhaps even himself. An expert in duplicity, he is especially adept at beguiling the leading transcendentalists of the day, those men who made virtue and morality the genuine basis of their professional lives. With more-than-apparent satisfaction, Warren describes Brown's visits to Thoreau and Emerson in Concord, Massachusetts, and cites Emerson's glowing accolade that Brown "is so transparent that all men see him through. He is a man to make friends wherever on earth courage and integrity are esteemed,—the rarest of heroes, a pure idealist, with no by-ends of his own. . . . He believes in two articles . . . the Golden Rule and the Declaration of Independence." Warren observes, "And it is only natural, that Emerson, in his extraordinary innocence, should have understood nothing, nothing in the world, about a man like John Brown to whom vocabulary was simply a very valuable instrument" (*John Brown*, 245–46).

Warren's attitude in the biography towards known figures of American history is the characteristic stance of his career. He rarely stands in awe of them. His recording eye is dispassionate and analytical. Accordingly, we can discern here a theme prominent in the later works, a theme which might seem paradoxical for a writer who so venerates the Great Men of History: the idea that the so-called Great Men of History often had at best only a tenuous link to those people and issues and events which were history's substance. They were, perhaps, spokesmen, commentators, symbols, even, like Brown, exploitative opportunists, relatively isolated from the elements of which history is made. Warren illustrates this notion in a discussion of the Kansas Free Soil disputes:

> "They killed one of the pro-slavery men, and the pro-slavery men killed one of the others, and I thought it was about mutual," an eyewitness told the politicians who, six months later, came to investigate the Kansas affairs. What did Calhoun sitting in his last Senate, or Garrison burning the Constitution, or Webster speaking at Syracuse know of this sort of thing? That generation-long debate between two orders of living, two sets of ideas, two philosophies, was finding strange and brutal repercussions along the frontier country, where men needed peace and all their energies to dig in and live before the harshness of nature. The issues and ideals which to Calhoun, to Garrison, to Webster, were so passionately clear, were very vague here, but what they lacked in clarity was made up for by violence and savagery. Perhaps it is the Gibsons, the R. P. Browns, the Collins', and the Sheriff Jones' [participants in the disputes] who, after all, must settle such issues. It is not a happy thought. (136)

It is not a happy thought because Warren worries that Great Men, and men in general, might in fact exert little force at all over history. They merely reflect it. History itself might churn on unaffected by those who pretend they can affect it, who themselves are its hapless victims. Such pessimism is a major theme of *Night Rider* (1939) and the other early novels, though later in his career Warren evinced muted optimism: *The Legacy of the Civil War*

(1961) at least raises the possibility that individuals can influence history. Warren's pessimism in *John Brown* anticipates a valuation consistently expressed in his writings: the importance of the individual's private self over whatever public persona he might assume. *Jefferson Davis Gets His Citizenship Back* (1980) evinces a clear concern with Davis, Lincoln, Sherman, and other figures of the Civil War as *human beings,* not as shapers of history or wasters of cities. They are identifiable human personalities, with virtues and weaknesses, products of their era and environment. They become great because their society comes to see them as such, or because they come to view themselves as such, not because of innate ability or vision. Such qualities are always acquired in Warren's world.

John Brown is only one of many individuals in American history whom Warren faults for a "private, subjective moral idealism." In *The Legacy of the Civil War,* the transcendentalists, who helped provide a justifying logic to the most extreme among the abolitionists, receive his special blame: arguing that the individual owed allegiance to a Higher Law before any other, they provided reason for ignoring the laws of the land. To be fair, Warren's real concern is with only a particular and small segment of the abolitionists, the extremists, those caught up in blood lust, hatred, and treason. "The cause for which the Abolitionists labored was just," Warren explained in *Legacy.* "Who can deny that, or deny that they often labored nobly? But who can fail to be disturbed and chastened by the picture of the joyful mustering of the darker forces of our nature in that just cause?" (23). He adds that the national atmosphere which prevailed in the decades before the Civil War "did not, to say the least, cement the bonds of society. The exponent of the 'higher law' was, furthermore, quite prepared to dissolve the society in which he lived and say, with [William Lloyd Garrison], 'Accursed be that American Union.' " In the biography itself he observes that "the higher-law man, in any time and place, must always be ready to burn any constitution, for he must, ultimately, deny the very concept of society [and] repudiate all the institutions in which power is manifested—church, state, family, law, business" (26–27). These social institutions insure the order which Warren regards as important.

Through didactic statement and dramatic representation, Warren's writing consistently illustrates that the primary function of government and society is to secure individual rights. It also argues that throughout

American history this function has been served intermittently and selectively. Modern society in particular Warren accuses of depersonalizing and reducing the individual to a faceless cog in a large machine. He attacked the transcendentalists because their thinking in principle denied the social context which protects the individual. Ultimately, he opposed the most extreme among the advocates of Higher Law more for their indifference to human life than for their indifference to society. By 1961 he disagreed with most forms of "civil disobedience" as "revolutionary" acts and "an attack on democracy," but by 1965 he had concluded that laws might be violated for the sake of making society just and moral, improving the lives of the individuals within it.[23] In *Who Speaks for the Negro?* he regards the practitioners of nonviolent civil disobedience as engaged in a struggle for the welfare of the entire nation. Such civil disobedience exists by definition within a social context and serves a social function—its very nature resides in the word *civil,* in a basic respect for human rights and the preservation of social order. When Warren castigates John Brown or Henry David Thoreau, he does so because he believes they ignored the social context. When he commends the participants in the civil rights movement, he does so because they sought to bring justice to society, to strengthen and reinforce it. Indeed, *Who Speaks for the Negro?* speculates in detail (from its 1965 perspective) about the future of the civil rights movement: whether it will continue to use civil disobedience and other nonviolent tactics or will turn to violence, separatism, and other methods divorced from the traditional social context. Warren regarded the movement as a critical moment in American history: it had the potential to strengthen or destroy the Union, depending both on the decisions of those involved as to what course it would take and on the nation's response to the challenges it posed. Paradoxically, in this view, the civil rights movement offered the hope of restoring some of the losses suffered by the individual over the course of American history. It created an opportunity for Americans to seize control of their destinies, to correct moral injustice, to influence the future.

Warren's support of the civil rights movement stemmed both from his advocacy of its essential aim and his recognition that it sought to bring about needed social change. Throughout the second half of his career, he emphasized the inevitability of change and the necessity of adjusting to it, of trying to control and influence change rather than to resist it. Although the Southern agrarians have often been faulted for their stolid resistance to change, their essays in *I'll Take My Stand* (1930) did for the most part recognize its inevitability. In particular, they viewed the incursion of industry into a mainly agricultural South as unavoidable. In the face of such change, however, they advocated maintaining inviolate Southern values, traditions, lifestyles, and customs. These, they contended, gave the South its distinctive identity: to lose them was to forfeit that identity. In "Reconstructed but Unregenerate," John Crowe Ransom observed: "The South must be industrialized—but to a certain extent only, in moderation. . . . The South at last is to be physically reconstructed; but it will be fatal if the South should conceive it as her duty to be regenerated and get her spirit reborn with a totally different orientation toward life." [24] Southern agrarianism thus constituted a rearguard resistance, as its manifesto title implies. Warren was closely allied with the agrarians, but his poetry from the beginning showed an intense concern with time, mortality, and the transience of all things. *All the King's Men* (and the fiction that followed) dramatized the dangers of resisting change and clinging to the past: the result could be an inability to live meaningfully in the present or to prepare for the future. Warren also concluded early on that change confronted the individual with moral as well as cultural obligations. Even in "The Briar Patch," where he argued for a segregated Southern society, he maintained that the quality of life for Southern blacks, especially living conditions, economic opportunities, and education, must be improved not only to prevent their migration to Northern cities but also because such improvement was the moral responsibility of Southern whites.

As a lifelong student of history, Warren recognized that a society caught in the flux of change must struggle to preserve those traditions and values worth preserving, as long as they remain pertinent, to maintain a cultural identity and a distinctive, fulfilling way of life. This was a central theme of Southern agrarianism. But the meaning of "agrarian" as it applies to Warren requires careful examination. There is the meaning associated with the Nashville writers and intellectuals who contributed in 1930 to *I'll Take My Stand,* for which Warren wrote his essay "The Briar Patch." The significance of the Southern agrarians has been obscured by their public image—partially justified—as reactionary, racist apologists for the Old South, a view which hardly allows for objective understanding. "The Briar Patch" itself still enjoys a certain notoriety, and Warren apologized for it on several occasions, most prominently in *Who Speaks for the*

Negro? In fact, however, he rejected outright only one of its tenets: its advocacy of segregation. The essay is important for what it reveals about Warren's agrarianism early in his career, thus for the comparison it provides with his later writings, which demonstrate how that conception changed. It changed very little. Agrarianism is the fundamental philosophical stance of Warren's career, the essential premise on which his American explorations have rested, including his eloquent studies of the civil rights movement. As a crucial document of his early views, "The Briar Patch" merits scrutiny. What are the links between this argument for separate but equal treatment of Southern blacks with such later works as *Segregation* and *Who Speaks for the Negro?*

"The Briar Patch" argued three basic propositions, all of which must be regarded from the perspective of the time and region they reflect: first, that Southern blacks deserved the same rights and opportunities as whites, but within the framework of a segregated society; second, that the arrival of Northern industry in the South would serve only to victimize Negroes and worsen their relations with whites; third, that a rural, agricultural life provided the Southern black with "the happiness that his good nature and easy ways incline him to as an ordinary function of his being" (260–61). The reactionary elements are apparent enough, but they are not so strong as the essay's reputation would suggest. Arguing that a racially separate but equal society was necessary in the South, Warren forcefully asserted that the Southern Negro of 1930 enjoyed few of the rights and privileges to which he was entitled: He "has money in his pocket, but he is turned away from the white man's restaurant. At the hotel he is denied the bed which he is ready to pay for. He likes music, but must be content with a poor seat at a concert—if he is fortunate enough to get one at all. The restrictions confront him at every turn of his ordinary life" (253). Though the essay often reflects a patronizing, paternalistic view of Southern blacks, an occasional willingness to invoke expected stereotypes ("the happiness that his good nature and easy ways incline him to"), it also expressed surprisingly broad-minded attitudes for the time and place of its publication. Donald Davidson even refused to believe Warren had written the essay, accusing it of " 'progressive' implications, with a pretty strong smack of latter-day sociology." [25]

One "progressive implication" must have been the implicit assumption of the equality of blacks and whites. Warren did not treat this assumption as arguable: it was simply fact. And he faulted conditions in the South which prevented blacks from enjoying this equality:

> The simplest issue, and probably the one on which most people would agree, is that of equal right before the law. At present the negro frequently fails to get justice, and justice from the law is the least that he can demand for himself or others can demand for him. . . . The matter of political right carries repercussions which affect almost every relation of the two races, but again the least that can be desired in behalf of the negro is that any regulation shall apply equitably to both him and the white man. (252)

Echoing Booker T. Washington, Warren contended that education was one immediate solution to the "problem," and, asserting that the economic independence of blacks from whites was a crucial means of attaining other forms of equality, he argued that "the most urgent need was to make the ordinary negro into a competent workman or artisan and a decent citizen. Give him whatever degree of education [is] possible within the resources at hand, but above all give him a vocation" (250). Warren did not oppose higher education for blacks, insisting that there was a real need for black professionals but that "so-called higher education for the negro in the South is a small factor in relation to the total situation" (251). That is, he believed the ability of many blacks to perform skilled wage-earning labor more likely to solve the immediate problem of poverty than the availability of higher education for a few.

Here, obviously, Warren faltered, for he did not understand economic independence to mean integration. He argued that opportunity existed for educated blacks in the South but suggested that educated blacks, doctors and lawyers, for instance, ought to be satisfied for the time being with a black clientele and with the right to patronize black businesses equal in quality to those of whites. He did not foresee black doctors treating white patients, or black patrons staying in the same hotels as whites, as likely prospects for the near future. Those who advocated such a form of racial equality were, he averred, "radicals" suffering from (in words he claims Booker T. Washington would have used) "a failure to rationalize his position, from the lack of a sense of reality, and from a defect in self-respect" (254–55). In other words, blacks who desired such "extreme" solutions lacked racial pride, which Warren apparently believed an integrated society would deny them. This was a standard argument in favor of segregation throughout the South. But in "The Briar Patch" it is linked to a sincere concern with the rights and interests of Southern blacks.

Warren also refused to believe that economic independence for blacks was to be found in the arrival of industry from the North, whose promise of relief to impoverished Southern blacks he regarded with skepticism. Industry would provide such relief "only if it grows under discipline and is absorbed into the terms of the life it meets. It must enter in the rôle of the citizen and not of the conqueror—not even in the rôle of the beneficent conqueror" (256). Exactly what does this mean? It means that newly arrived industry must honor Southern values and lifestyles, that Northern industry must heed the state of Southern race relations. If industry exploits the availability of cheap Negro labor, white-black relations might become worse than they already are. Such exploitation would be only another kind of slavery afflicting poor whites and blacks alike. (We see a brand of it in Bogan Murdock's coal mines in *At Heaven's Gate*.) Warren's concern was not only with the possibility of racial discord in the South but with the exploitation blacks might suffer. He found a solution to both concerns in his proposal to organize both black and white labor to insure that blacks would enjoy the same rights in the work place as whites, thus preventing cheap Negro labor from unfair competition with whites.

"The Briar Patch" proposed organized labor (another element Davidson might have found "progressive") as a pragmatic solution to a practical problem. It was intended more to preserve order than to remedy social injustice. It smacks of some slight paternalism as well: protecting "our" Southern Negroes from exploitative Northerners. Yet Warren moved beyond paternalistic pragmatism in his argument that whites must realize that goods and services provided by blacks are not qualitatively different from those provided by whites: "The white mason can learn . . . that color has nothing to do with the true laying of a brick and that the comfort of all involved in the process depends on his recognition and acceptance of the fact" (260). If the white mason doesn't recognize this fact, the Negro bricklayer, who can do his job as well as the white but at a lower wage, will inevitably take the white mason's work away because "in a crisis the employer, whether Northern or Southern, will look at a balance sheet and not at the color of the hand which holds the trowel" (259). Though again one might argue that Warren assumed this position merely to prevent social unrest which might threaten the Southern status quo, it is difficult not to recognize his clear and morally founded insistence on an egalitarianism not limited or confined by skin color.

It seems somehow inconsistent, after advocating the organization of Negro and white Southern labor and the fair treatment of Negroes in the market place, that Warren would then argue that farm life is the life best suited to Southern blacks. But argue he does.[26] Yet it may well be that Warren in "The Briar Patch" advocated an agricultural life for blacks for essentially the same reasons that other writers in *I'll Take My Stand* advocated it for whites: he regarded an agricultural existence as an ideal. This was one of the main tenets of Southern agrarianism. More than a century before, Jefferson wrote in *Notes on Virginia:* "Those who labor in the earth are the chosen people of God, if ever He had chosen people, whose breasts He has made His peculiar deposit for substantial and genuine virtue. . . . Corruption of morals in the mass of cultivators is a phenomenon of which no age nor nation has furnished an example." [27] Rural life, Warren argued, avoids the exploitation of industry and encourages closer relations between the races: "All relations between groups in the city tend to become formalized and impersonal, and such is especially true in those of the two races. . . . With all the evils which beset the tenant system in the South there is still a certain obvious community of interest between the owner and the 'cropper'; profit for one is profit for the other" (262). Such a statement overlooks the fact that owners enjoyed a much larger percentage of the profits than croppers. (Even in *Who Speaks for the Negro?*, Warren continued to suggest that blacks and whites in the South shared a common relation in their closeness to the land.)

Yet Warren's view of race relations in the agriculturally based South did allow for the improvement of conditions for blacks, and it also foresaw problems which that improvement might bring. As blacks became a stronger force in agriculture, he feared the potential for violence which their competition with white farmers might create. Again he urged pragmatism: "If the Southern white man feels that the agrarian life has a certain irreplaceable value in his society . . . he must find a place for the negro in his scheme. . . . In any cooperative or protective enterprise the white man must see that the negro grower receives equal consideration; he must remember that the strawberry or the cotton bale tells no tales in the open market concerning its origins" (263–64).

In its desire to keep Southern blacks down on the farm, "The Briar Patch" was patently naive. It was naive too in its contention that racial problems in the South could be solved solely by pragmatic recognition that equal work deserves equal pay. The struggle towards *that* goal continues today, in North as well as South, for women and Hispanics and other minorities as well as for blacks. In general the essay offered only tentative suggestions about how the South could achieve racial enlightenment. Warren was thus guilty of the same "vague optimism" of which he accused Booker T. Washington (259). He idealized race relations in the rural South of 1930 and glossed too glibly over such forces as the tenant system which produced and sustained it.

Still, for all one might say against it, "The Briar Patch" was not thoroughly racist. One senses throughout a moral conscience refusing to accept that blacks should not receive equal justice under the law, that their work should not be compensated on the same basis as whites, that their crops should not earn a fair price. One senses that conscience too in the assertion that "what the white workman must learn . . . is that he may respect himself as a white man, but, if he fails to concede the negro equal protection, he does not properly respect himself as a man" (260). Such statements, which begin to suggest that racism and segregation are contrary to the very essence of what it means to be human, and American, anticipate both *Segregation* and *Who Speaks for the Negro?*, which made Warren's rejection of racism and segregation unambiguously clear. "The Briar Patch" was one of the most progressive statements of its kind from a white, self-professed agrarian Southerner prior to 1954.[28] It hoped for a racially harmonious South where blacks and whites could enjoy equal rights and privileges— considerably more than other agrarians were willing to imagine. The contradictions on which it falters are the same ones which twenty years later led Warren and other white Southerners to conclude that segregation and racial discrimination were fundamentally immoral and antidemocratic.

Beyond its interests in the racial problems of the modern South, what "The Briar Patch" really concerns is the quality of human life. It argues for the importance of individual freedoms, human justice, and a strong community. It expresses skepticism of urban life and industrialism, forces which to the agrarian mind are indifferent to the humanity of the individual, forces which depersonalize and dehumanize. They are the forces of technology, the defining element of the modern world. As wrongheaded and morally askew as it might in some ways be, "The Briar Patch" confronts fundamentally the same issues Warren explored throughout his career. The concern of *Democracy and Poetry* with the dehumanizing effects of modern technology and science evolved directly from the anxiety of "The Briar Patch" that Northern factories would exploit black workers. In isolation, such a worry might seem merely self-serving, contrived to support the agrarian advocacy of a static Southern rural lifestyle. In the context of his career, however, such a worry proved genuine indeed.

What then were the tenets of Warren's agrarianism in 1930? As a regional phenomenon, Southern agrarianism initially did advocate preservation of a segregated society. For some of the writers in *I'll Take My Stand,* agrarianism remained only a regional issue, a movement to preserve traditional Southern culture against the encroaching North. It contended that human life must center on traditional Judeo-Christian values. Change might occur if it must, they would admit, but if it threatened the temper of Southern existence, it was to be resisted with all urgency. Several agrarians advocated maintaining the South as an enclave against the modern world, a last bastion of resistance which would continue to abide by its own self-contained values, eschewing communality with the rest of the United States or the world at large. In his essay for *I'll Take My Stand,* "A Mirror for Artists," Donald Davidson argued that Southern agrarianism "needs to be defined for the present age, as a mode of life congenial to the arts which are among the things we esteem as more than material blessings. In the emergency it needs, in fact, to be consciously studied and maintained by artists, Southern or not, as affording a last stand in America against the industrial devourer" (59–60). Warren himself concluded in "The Briar Patch" that "the chief problem for all alike is the restoration of society at large to a balance and security which the industrial régime is far from promising to achieve" (264).

Although he never openly renounced his association with the Southern agrarians, Warren's agrarianism ultimately transcended regional boundaries. He continued late in life to speak of himself as a Southerner, as "an old Confederate." [29] Yet he also distanced himself from the regional dimensions of agrarianism. At the Fugitives' Reunion in 1956, he made clear that agrarianism for him was more than a regional phenomenon. His allegiance to it arose from

the sense of the disintegration of the notion of the individual in that society we're living in. . . . It's the machine of power in this so-called democratic state; the machines disintegrate individuals. . . . And the Confederate element was a pious element, or a great story—a heroic story—a parade of personalities who are also images for these individual values. They were images for it for me, I'm sure, rather than images for a theory of society which had belonged to the South before the war. They became images for that only because they are lost.[30]

He added that "for me it was a protest . . . against a kind of dehumanizing and disintegrative effect on your notion of what an individual person could be in the sense of a loss of your role in society" (23). He also more recently described himself as being "in love with America"[31] and as "parochially of the Western World" (*Democracy,* xii), not the confessions of an intense regionalist. His definition of agrarianism as a set of images and values, a way of thinking, not an allegiance to a specific place or region or way of life—as the term is most often applied—is highly significant. Such a "set of values" is an implicit theme of Warren's tenth novel, *A Place to Come To,* in which Jed Tewksbury's spiritual estrangement results not from his physical separation from his home town of Dugton, Alabama, but from his intellectual and (Warren would say) spiritual rejection of all that his home town, his mother, and his father's fabled death represent. Warren himself lived outside the South after the late 1930s and resided in Connecticut and Vermont from the early 1950s until his death. That he continued to think of himself as a Southerner suggests that "Southernness" for him was a state of mind as well: "I can't be anything else. You are what you are. I was born and grew up in Kentucky, and I think your early images survive. Images mean a lot of things besides pictures."[32]

Warren's transformation from regional agrarian to agrarian of the Western world is one of the most significant events of his career. It liberated him from a limiting perspective yet kept him in touch with the values and the region he felt most deeply. In fact, most of his fiction and poetry is rooted in the South. But he is able to view the South from a more critical and objective perspective than he might otherwise have managed. Because the South changed less rapidly than the rest of the nation, he regarded it in a sense as closer to the original ideals of the American founders. Yet because of the change which has confronted it, both following the Civil War and throughout the twentieth century, the South has been faced repeatedly with the questions which to Warren are crucial to the Modern Age: questions of whether and how to change, how much tradition to hold on to, how much progress to encourage, how to preserve identity, how to survive. The South's struggle to preserve its cultural identity and at the same time respond to the moral and economic demands of the modern world (specifically of the civil rights movement) Warren sees as representative of the national struggle (if indeed the struggle continues in the rest of the nation: at moments Warren seems unsure) to cleave to the ideals which underlay the nation's genesis two centuries and more in the past.

Warren's persistent and healthy skepticism, his philosophical eclecticism, his refusal to embrace wholeheartedly any ideology or regional viewpoint are always evident, perhaps most of all in his writings about the South, where willingness to criticize is no less apparent than eagerness to defend. *Segregation,* published in 1956, is a case in point. There he views the civil rights crisis of the 1950s from the perspectives of all participants, committed and uncommitted, segregationists and integrationists. He explains the unwillingness of many Southerners to turn their backs on tradition as a form of "piety," of veneration for the past, their ancestry and heritage (46). At the same time, he admonishes Southerners for allowing themselves to believe that resistance to change is necessarily a good or even possible stance and for their failure of humanity. Rather than remaining passive victims of history, he argues, they should rise to the challenge of the crisis and take history into their own hands, leading the nation towards civil rights for all citizens rather than permitting those rights to be enforced by federal mandate. *Segregation* could never have been written by someone without a deep native loyalty to the region it concerned, or by someone without a moral agrarian base.

More than three decades after it was published, *Segregation* might seem dated. Yet many Southerners, and many Americans, must still confront the dilemma and the moral obligations it illuminates. Perhaps more vividly than any other document of its era, it brings the civil rights crisis to life in intensely human terms. And it illustrates vividly the agrarianism of a Robert Penn Warren who exhorts America to seize control of its destiny, of a writer anguished over the modern individual's plight. It is an agrarianism more forceful and informed than before, more sharply focused and incisive, more broadly encompassing, an agrarianism grown from a fundamentally deep anxiety over the fate of American democracy and the individual, over the survival of civilization. This anxiety is apparent throughout his fiction and poetry after 1950, certainly in Jed Tewksbury in *A Place to Come To,* in the poem "New Dawn," in the call of *Audubon: A Vision* for a "story of wonder, a tale of deep delight." It is the center of Warren's obsessive quest for a means of understanding and redeeming life in the modern world.

Brother to Dragons and

the Sins of the Fathers

The title *Brother to Dragons* succinctly expresses the central issue of this strangely profound poem: the significance of human evil caught in the struggle between Thomas Jefferson's humanist deism and Robert Penn Warren's belief in a fallen, imperfect humanity. In a more abstract sense, the title embodies the tension between philosophical idealism and pragmatic realism which grips the persona R. P. W. as firmly as it holds the wraith of the dead American president. Thomas Jefferson is stricken with horror and repugnance at his nephew's brutal murder of a young slave. To him Lilburne Lewis *is* the dragon, evil incarnate in human form, a fundamental contradiction to the humanist underpinnings of the nation he helped create. More, Lilburne Lewis is his relative, his sister's child and, in that familial sense, a brother. His link to the slave's murderer forces him to confront an additional meaning of the title, one which confounds his belief in human goodness: his discovery that his nephew Lilburne was capable of murder simply because all human beings are capable of evil, as even he, Thomas Jefferson, is capable of it, and therein lies the truth of his role not merely as "brother" to dragons but as the very Dragon itself.

Warren found his title in Job's biblical lament "I am a brother to dragons and a companion to owls" (Job 30:29). Victor Strandberg explains: "It is most revealing that Warren's attention is focused not on Job's suffering and loss and endurance, but upon the one thing [Jefferson] could not endure— his loss of pride. Being a brother to dragons . . . is a fate singularly unde-served for a man who had always (like Thomas Jefferson) walked 'upright and perfect . . . and eschewed evil.' " [1] In the poem's first section Jefferson seems deeply wounded and horror-struck at his nephew's deed, which he is much interested in blaming on anyone but himself. He berates his sister Lucy for not having killed her son at birth. When she begs him to take her son's hand in forgiveness and kinship, he refuses sanctimoniously: "Look—blood's slick on that hand! You'd have me compound the crime?" (*Brother to Dragons* [1979], 116). He readily recognizes the contradiction the murder poses to his former humanism. But he refuses to acknowledge the possibility of his own guilt, of any connection at all with the crime, which he likely fears would render his life's achievement hollow. Yet the acknowledgment of blood-guilt, of his nephew Lilburne's essential humanity, his kith and kin, is the event towards which the poem moves him.

The central conflict of this poem develops out of the apparent fact that Jefferson never in his lifetime mentioned his nephew's murder of the slave. In his foreword, Warren cites one historian's speculation that "Jefferson could not bring himself to discuss—or perhaps even to face—the appalling episode." Admitting that "further research" might disprove this fact, Warren stubbornly insists that the absence of comment is nonetheless "convenient for my poem; but the role of Jefferson in the poem, or in history, does not stand or fall by the fact. If the moral shock to Jefferson administered by the discovery of what was possible in his blood should turn out to be somewhat literally short of what is here represented, subsequent events in the history of our nation, which he helped to found, might amply supply the defect" (xii). He thus takes the absence of comment as a sign of psychological and philosophic horror. And to make doubly certain there is ample reason for the spectral president's despair, Warren provides him with ample knowledge-after-death concerning some of the unhappier events of American history. The cause of Jefferson's horror thus becomes the subject of *Brother to Dragons*.[2] Warren chooses thematic over historical accuracy. It is not important that Jefferson's lack of comment cannot be proven, or that details of the murder have been altered. Rather, it is important that Warren uses such speculation as a metaphor for the essential issues of the poem, which itself he has calculated to deliver certain substantive judgments on the nation's history. (Shortly after the new version's appearance, he characterized the poem as "all one large metaphor").[3] The point is, as he states in "Wind and Gibbon," that "history is not truth. Truth is in the telling" (*NSP*, 77), or, as he assures us in the poem's introduction, that "if poetry is the little myth we make, history is the big myth we live, and in our living, constantly remake" (xiii). The destruction and recreation of myth —American myth—is a central purpose of *Brother to Dragons*. Jefferson's problematic despair merely sets the stage for the real interest and significance of the poem, its symbolic and anagogical dimensions. Jefferson is the emblem of the American republic and its humanist foundations. He is, according to William Bedford Clark, "a symbol embodying Warren's critique of America's history and his hopes for America's future."[4]

In 1957 Warren explained to Ralph Ellison, then editor of the *Paris Review,* what he regarded as the unique circumstances of the nation's genesis:

> There's another thing in the American experience that makes for a curious kind of abstraction. We had to suddenly define ourselves and what we stood for in one night. No other nation ever had to do that. In fact, one man did it. One man in an upstairs room, Thomas Jefferson. Sure, you might say that he was the amanuensis for a million or so people stranded on the edge of a continent and backed by a wilderness, and there's some sense in that notion. But *somebody* had to formulate it . . . and we've been stuck with it ever since. With the very words it used.[5]

Brother to Dragons incorporates this version of Jefferson as national amanuensis. Early in the first section Jefferson suggests not only that in composing the Declaration he acted as an agent of national will but that in that genetic national moment he fell victim to the same flaws of pride and blindness to the past which would plague the nation's future:

> So seized the pen, and in the upper room,
> With the excited consciousness that I was somehow
> Rectified, annealed, my past annulled
> And fate confirmed, wrote.
>
> (8)

Jefferson thus represents in a formal, even ritualistic fashion not merely the nation but also the paradox upon which Warren contends the nation was founded: the paradox of an imperfect human nature called on to satisfy the requirements of a form of government which demands of its citizens essential goodness.

No theme in American history and literature has proved so fundamental. To Ellison's question about "themes which are basic to the American experience," Warren responded:

First thing, without being systematic, . . . would be that America was based on a promise—a great big one: the Declaration of Independence. . . . When you have to live with that in the house, that's quite a problem. . . . America is stuck with its self-definition put on paper in 1776, and that was just like putting a burr under the metaphysical saddle of America—you see, that saddle's going to jump now and then and it pricks.[6]

As he makes clear, especially in *Democracy and Poetry,* Warren considers democracy the form of government most congenial to the individual and to a meaningful existence. He endorses the Jeffersonian ideal of "a society in which free men—of independent self—would exercise their franchise in the light of reason" (*Democracy,* 4). Yet he seems to believe also that though democracy might be well suited to human nature, human nature is not well suited to democracy. In his view our national history has been an arduous struggle to achieve the ideals of a founding philosophy and a national dream which lie beyond human grasp, which have slipped further from grasp as time has passed. The consequences have been devastating: slavery, civil war, the destruction of the continental wilderness, the brutal mistreatment of the American Indian, urban violence, racism—all of which *Brother to Dragons* specifically mentions. They alone might dishearten the Jeffersonian idealist. Jefferson himself seems grievously daunted in the poem and cites these consequences in explanation. Yet the poem urgently opposes despair as a response to the nation's failures. It advocates instead the alternative of pragmatic rationalism, a mode of perception somewhere between the impassioned idealism of eighteenth-century Philadelphia and the nihilist cynicism of the modern age. But the assumption of such an attitude, for Jefferson, for the persona R. P. W., for Warren the poet—and, the poem implies, for the nation as a whole—may come only after difficult struggle.

As a poetic creation, historical figure, and national leader, Jefferson provides a complex yet fitting emblem of that struggle. He is the essence of the American paradox. Proclaimer of human equality and author of the most eloquent of documents of human liberty, he owned slaves and in his old age, as R. P. W. notes, depended on their labors for his livelihood. In *Notes on Virginia* he argued for their intellectual inferiority. He believed in the nobility of his species, yet his own nephew committed heinous murder. The democratic nation he helped establish began drifting away from his noble ideals even before his death and soon bogged down in warfare and materialism, strangely blind to its own self-deceptions. In the poem Jefferson casts back a pitiless, skeptical eye on his life and philosophy in light not only of Lilburne's murder of the slave but of all that has transpired in America since his death on July 4, 1826, the fiftieth anniversary of the signing of the Declaration. As he assesses the damage, so too does R. P. W., acting on behalf of the nation as a whole. What we have then in *Brother to Dragons* is a relentless evaluation of American past, present, and future.

As many readers know, *Brother to Dragons* exists in two distinct versions, one published in 1953 and another, revised and recast, in 1979. (*The Georgia Review* published a dramatic version in 1976.) The earlier version has earned a substantial reputation and considerable critical attention. Yet Warren made clear his preference for the later version. His foreword notes his "dissatisfaction with several features" of the 1953 poem and argues that the 1979 version is a new and rewritten poem (xiv). In a 1980 interview he suggested that those who regard the 1953 version as better "are dead wrong"—the later version is "vastly improved in general poetic quality" with "a much more fluid and natural verse movement now than it was before." [7] Thematically the two versions are similar, almost identical. Except for minor details, the story in both is the same. Rather than attempt with inevitable confusion to discuss both versions, I will consider the one which seems to me the better of the two and allow it to stand for both. The 1979 *Brother to Dragons: A Tale in Verse and Voices, A New Version* in my opinion is the better poem. More characteristic of Warren's style since 1950, it fully and clearly explores the themes which lie at its heart. Authorial intention should by no means always be honored in such matters, but with *Brother to Dragons* there seems no good reason not to respect Warren's judgment. [8]

The 1979 poem is more dramatic, less didactic, and less polemical than the original. Jefferson remains the main character from the past, but he shares the foreground with other characters who were of minor importance in the 1953 version. Meriwether Lewis in particular becomes a significant aspect of Jefferson's recovery from cynicism and despair. His increased presence strengthens the wilderness theme and in general emphasizes the relevance of the meat-house murder to American history. Warren seems less concerned in the revision with picking at Jefferson's philosophical bones, more intent on illuminating crucial elements of the American and human condition—as if in the revision he has forgiven Jefferson his folly, forgiven himself the unctuous righteousness with which he sought in 1953 to excoriate the dead president. This change in attitude is evident in a comparison of the opening lines from both versions. The opening of the 1953 poem:

> JEFFERSON: My name is Thomas Jefferson. I am he
> Whose body yet under the triple boast,
> On my green mountain—
>
> R. P. W.:   Yes, I've read your boast
> Cut in the stone where your body still waits
> On your green mountain, off in Virginia, awaiting,
> I suppose, whatever fulfillment of the boast
> May yet be.
>
> (5)

The 1979 poem begins more aggressively, yet indirectly, throwing focus not merely on Jefferson but on the issues which obsess him. Where before Jefferson introduced himself with arrogance and pride, now he expresses suffering and bitter humiliation:

> My name is Jefferson. Thomas. I
> Lived. Died. But
> Dead, cannot lie down in the
> Dark. Cannot, though dead, set
> My mouth to the dark stream that I may unknow
> All my knowing. Cannot, for if,
> Kneeling in that final thirst, I thrust
> Down my face, I see come glimmering upward,
> White, white out of the absolute dark of depth,
> My face. And it is only human.
>
> Have you ever tried to kiss that face in the mirror?
> Or—ha, ha—has it ever tried to kiss you? Well,
> You are only human. Is that a boast?
>
> R. P. W.: Well, I've read your boast
> Cut in stone, on the mountain, off in Virginia.
>
> (5)

This new Jefferson is more human, more fully realized than the earlier man. He assumes from the beginning the proportions of a tragic figure, repelled by the thing—humanity—he dedicated his life to exalting. The earlier Jefferson seems in comparison almost pasteboard, pumped up with vanity and ill-conceived notions, ripe for R. P. W.'s cutting pronouncements. Because of the president's deepened humanity in the revision, R. P. W. is less compelled to attack his failings (though he still does so), more able to contemplate fully the murder's implications for Jefferson's life, his own life, and the nation's history. He also engages in considerable self-criticism. His own role is more prominent, an important change since he himself must interpret, act on, and be influenced by what the poem reveals. As Margaret Mills Harper has remarked, "R. P. W. in the 1979 version more clearly parallels, rather than leads, Jefferson in his search for knowledge."[9] Certain now of his attitude, Warren feels less obliged to explain and preach, and he has omitted much of the abstract apostrophizing, focused on the concrete, and effectively clarified the meaning of the events for American history. The resulting poem approaches closer to the dramatic epic form which the original version strained less successfully to attain. The result is also, I think, better poetry. Above all, the poem shifts in focus away from smug cynicism to the philosophical concerns which were always at its heart.

Brother to Dragons explores the delusions underlying American civilization. A number of critics have suggested a similarity in theme between the poem and Joseph Conrad's *Heart of Darkness* and other writings, and it is true that Warren had written an essay on Conrad (" 'The Great Mirage': Conrad and *Nostromo*") while he was working on the poem.[10] But the themes of *Brother to Dragons* grow directly out of the historical characters and events it concerns. Its themes are endemic to American literature. In fact, they are endemic to Warren's career. They include concern with a national and individual identity, the opening up of the frontier, the exploitation and ruination of the wilderness, and slavery. Foremost above them stands the corruption of the American Dream in the nineteenth century as the nation moved inexorably away from the ideals of the Declaration and the Revolution. Warren returns to this theme repeatedly in his work, but in this long poem he presents it clearly for the first time. In *Brother to Dragons* he seeks to uncover the root causes of the Dream's corruption, and he finds them centered in the emblematic figure of Jefferson, who recognized the nation's potential for greatness and was most fatally blind to its potential for blunder. This is not to say that Jefferson is made to bear responsibility for the Dream's ruin but that as the self-conscious American philosophe, political architect, and national leader, he embodies the forces which left the nation vulnerable to its own corrupt nature.

Of Warren's fictional protagonists, Jefferson most resembles Jack Burden of *All the King's Men* (by Jefferson I mean Warren's literary creation, the figure modeled on but not always faithful to the historical man). Like Burden, Jefferson first appears a broken idealist, mired in disillusionment over what turns out to be his own sense of failure. He began his career as a proponent of reason and the goodness of humankind. Shocked by his nephew's crime, the decline of his own fortunes, and the turn of events in the nation he helped found, he for a time abandoned his ideals and abjured all that he once found noble. Like Burden, Jefferson must struggle to comprehend and accept his place in the imperfect human world. Burden reaches such an accommodation when he recognizes his role in the suicide of Judge Irwin, who turns out to have been his father, and accepts his complicity in the deaths of his friends Willie Stark and Adam Stanton. Jefferson arrives at his own accommodation when he is confronted, near the end of the poem, with the fact of his own vanity, his partial responsibility for the suicide of Meriwether Lewis, whom he called his son, and his own capability for the sort of murderous violence exhibited by nephew Lilburne. Accepting his human limitations, the limitations of the world, he begins to nurture a small restored faith in the *possibility* of his species and in the value of pursuing ideals which remain always beyond reach, whose pursuit invests life with whatever small meaning it can possess.

Few characters in Warren's fiction ever achieve such an acceptance, though all consciously or unconsciously struggle for it. Perhaps Jediah Tewksbury of *A Place to Come To* is the only one to realize it fully. John James Audubon and Adam Rosenzweig approach it. Amantha Starr in *Band of Angels* and Bradwell Tolliver in *Flood* do not achieve it, though again it perhaps lies within their eventual grasp. For all these characters, the challenge of acceptance and adjustment requires a particular mode of perception, a way of seeing and understanding the world. *Brother to Dragons* argues that romantic humanism blinded Jefferson to certain inevitable aspects of human character and reality. So too, it argues, has America been blinded by belief in its own exalted cause to the possibility of its own error, corruption, and even malicious intent. From the beginning this poem has been viewed as an attack on Jefferson's enlightened humanism. That it is. But this aspect has been so overemphasized that other, more important dimensions have been neglected, until recently at least, and the poem as a whole has suffered from the distorted image of a polemic against what Cleanth Brooks has called "some of the liberal secular ideas of our time." [11] What it is, in fact, is a plea for philosophical moderation and understanding, for pragmatism, for stubborn belief in values and ideals which the world of "naturalistic considerations" may prove illusory but which are important nonetheless and which empower the individual to recover from the characteristic despair and disillusionment of the modern age.

Jefferson is not alone in his disillusionment. Virtually every character in *Brother to Dragons,* including R. P. W., the persona separate from but closely related to the poet (the dramatis personae identifies R. P. W. as "the poet"), suffers and must struggle to overcome it. Some, like Lilburne's brother Isham, are too limited in talent and vision to comprehend their condition or to name the despair they feel, so they fail ever to transcend it or even to recognize the need for transcendence. Others, primarily Lilburne, have fallen too far for recovery by their own powers, though the denouement of the fifth section suggests (not too convincingly) that human love and forgiveness can rescue him. Most, however, stand in hope of recovery. A proper way of perceiving the world is the resolution towards which they move. Their groping is a communal effort. But the success of all depends finally on Jefferson, who stands for each a shattered ideal by which they once measured the significance of their lives, whom they now blame for their failure. Ultimately, their struggle is a metaphoric drama in the mind of the poet/persona, and their progress is a lesson he must take to heart as his own.

The poem thus illustrates and explains the essential pattern of idealism, disillusionment, and readjustment which for Warren is the archetypal pattern of American history and the central pattern of his own literary career.

Jefferson's despair as the poem begins reflects his conviction, rooted in the meat-house murder, that he has lived his life for naught, that his America was founded on a delusion. He enters the poem repeating to himself with sardonic grimness that his face "is only human" and that "You are only human." He continues so to remind himself throughout the poem. During his own lifetime humanity was a source of optimism. Now it brings him grief, for being "only human" he interprets to mean evil and imperfect, unworthy of the ideals by which he once measured his kind. Paradoxically, he still admits "in senility / And moments of indulgent fiction" his willingness to "defend my old definition of man" (5), but he does so sheepishly, fully convinced of the falsity of his former convictions. He now believes that the nation was conceived in a moment not of vision but of blindness. "We were only ourselves," he says of himself and the other Founders,

> Packed with our personal lusts and languors, lost,
> Every man-jack of us, in some blind alley, enclave,
> Crank cul-de-sac, couloir, or corridor
> Of Time. Or Self.
>
> (6)

By "only ourselves," Jefferson means "only human," thus imperfect and corrupt. The "blind alley" blossoms into a metaphor which he applies to himself and the nation: he suggests the founders were wandering in a labyrinth, unaware of the menacing evil, the Minotaur, lurking beyond some dark turn, "hock-deep in ordure, its beard / And shag foul-scabbed, and when the hoof heaves— / Listen!—the foulness sucks like mire" (6). On the one hand he means simply that the founders lacked the vision and foresight necessary to determine their destinies. But he also means that, unaware of humankind's evil nature, they wrote a Declaration of Independence and Constitution which left the new nation unprepared for the hazards to come.

 The figure of a humanity wandering in labyrinthine darkness must be particularly irksome to Jefferson, who believed that by reason and will the individual could control human fate. Among his many roles in life were those of architect and engineer. He designed Monticello, the original buildings of the University of Virginia, and the state capitol building in Richmond—archly Greco-Roman structures, in the style of the Maison Quarée he later extols. Their style proclaims his faith in human reason and vision. He is thus presented in the poem as a modern-day Dedalus shocked to find himself responsible for the labyrinth of democracy, at the end of whose intricate maze of deceit, compromise, and brutality lurks the human beast, the Jeffersonian beast. Wandering "hock-deep in ordure" is not at all what he considered himself to be doing in his life, he who once envisioned himself standing in glory, prophetic, "From some high pass or crazy crag of mind," gazing out over the expanse of his nation. Out of the labyrinth flow despair, confusion, and doom, not what the designer intended. In the end Jefferson concludes that dark and labyrinthine uncertainty is one condition of life, that each person (and the nation as a whole) must stumble through as best he can. But he comes to that conclusion as a triumph of sorts, in a context considerably at odds with the despair which opens the poem.[12]

Lilburne Lewis's murder of the slave John is the paradigmatic episode of *Brother to Dragons*. It is responsible not only for the former president's disillusionment but eventually for his recovery. Jefferson refuses until the end to acknowledge his human and familial relation to Lilburne. He also refuses to regard the murder's implications for him personally. He is quick to condemn Lilburne as a murderer whose hands drip with blood, by extension to castigate the entire human race for its evil. Himself he excludes, refusing to concede his communal link with the rest of humanity. His reaction to the murder is bitter and raw, emotional rather than intellectual, as if he is repressing some dimension of meaning that he wishes to evade.[13] He condemns without pausing to understand. This is part of the reason for his despair and cynicism, for he isolates himself from the human race and denies himself the understanding he must attain before his spirit can rest. The poem struggles towards this moment of peace. Because most of its characters are disembodied spirits who have been dead for more than a century, it is difficult to know precisely what "finding peace" will mean for them. Perhaps their own peace is not the issue.

Throughout *Brother to Dragons* looms the American wilderness. Jefferson among the nation's founders was most eloquently aware of its rich potential. He could claim responsibility for the Louisiana Purchase in 1803, and he sent the Lewis and Clark expedition to survey the land acquired. Lilburne Lewis, of course, finds the wilderness overpowering in quite a different way. In the poem's present time, the absence of wilderness points to a larger emptiness in the nation as a whole. In the "no time" in which the characters converse, however, wilderness stretches in an immediate geographical sense three thousand miles from Monticello, Virginia, to the Pacific breakers of the Western coast. Wilderness in this sense is a source of pure wonder and inspiration. Meriwether Lewis recalls his journey west with an ecstasy verging between delirium and nightmare:

> And we suffered the rigor of seasons,
> White dew and sun-heat, and the time
> When hibernants are withdrawn to the only comfort
> In the iron world. And snow on the far peak glared blue

In excess of light, and no track of beast on the unruffled
White of the high plain, no wing-flash in high air,
And in that glittering silence of the continent
I heard my heart beating distinctly, and I said,
Is this delight? Is this the name of delight?

(111–12)

This is wilderness as immensity of space, a vastness the human imagination must endeavor to embellish and fill. For Jefferson the wilderness is a
mirror of dream-like ideals which he and Meriwether both misinterpret.
Jefferson links the wilderness directly to his conception of the American
nation, specifically to his faith in the new nation's potential for growth and
greatness. He regards it too as evidence of his own accomplishment. He
speaks of the land gained through the Louisiana Purchase as his personal
domain bequeathed as a gift to the nation:

> My West—the land I bought and gave and never
> Saw, but like some Israelite,
> From some high pass or crazy crag of mind, saw—
> Saw all. . . .
>
> (10)

Wilderness here reflects Jefferson's attitude towards the nation, its people,
and its future. His interest is at least in part proprietary, and his likening of
himself to Moses perhaps a reflection of his unconscious self-image not only
as a leader but as a prophet, a philosopher with some more-than-human relation to the world. More bluntly, the Mosaic allusion specifically suggests
a large degree of pride and vanity.

Meriwether Lewis willingly assumes the role of Jefferson's emissary into
the wilderness (Warren called him a "true 'light-bringer' ")[14] because he
shares the same faith in the power of civilization to redeem the untamed
land. It is an odd faith. It stems for Jefferson from his conception of man
as a being who has moved inexorably through history towards perfection,
gradually sloughing away animal imperfections. Man is, in his mind,

> the towering
> Definition, angelic, arrogant, abstract,
> Greaved in glory, thewed with light, the bright
> Brow tall as dawn.
>
> (8)

The natural world this sublime creature inhabits Jefferson sees as a place of harmony, and the evil he encounters there he at first explains away as a necessary part of the equilibrium. Unlike his successor Emerson, he does not hesitate to acknowledge evil in nature or the human race. But he deems it

> merely shade
> Of the old lubricity and Gothic night,
> Flotsam and frozen foam
> Of an ebbed disturbance in Time's tide.
>
> (28)

That is, the product of natural random chaos and disorder, of humanity's bestial origins, of brief lapses in the progress of civilization up from darkness. Civilization is a redeeming force, and when Jefferson speaks of man in this idealized sense, he means civilized man. He explains that because man "Carried the shadow of the forest, [I] therefore thought / That man must redeem Nature, after all" (26–27). Because man struggles towards perfection, an earthly divinity, his mission is to redeem, or civilize (which in Jefferson's time meant something positive and virtuous, the opposite of what it came to mean for such a writer as Conrad) the wilderness and its inhabitants. Civilized man's knowledge of darkness better endows him with the wisdom needed to redeem the land. Thus Jefferson sends Meriwether "To redeem the wild land to the Western Shore" (26–27). But "redeem" is ambiguous. Meriwether and Jefferson and many others of their time believed civilization a virtue. Hardly could Jefferson or Meriwether have paused to consider that civilizing the wilderness might do it harm. But "redeem" also means (especially from the poem's retrospective view) appropriation, seizure for one's own use. To "redeem" in this sense can mean to assess the profitability of, to exploit. Likely neither Jefferson nor Meriwether fully understand this connotation, but it is there nonetheless, and its consequences become painfully evident later in the poem and in the nation's history. They were neither the first nor the last civilized men to camouflage material motives with such concepts as redemption and virtue.

Jefferson chooses Meriwether as his emissary not merely for his competence, but also because the younger man believes in him. What is just hinted at early in the poem, and stated more strongly later, is the notion of a Jefferson as much enamored of his own vision as of the land his vision encompasses. For Meriwether the wilderness is something more—proof of the human world's virtue—and his explorations convince him for a time of the possibility of democracy. Under Jefferson's influence, his misinterpretation of the wilderness effectively renders him unable to cope with the civilized world. Both he and Jefferson are blind to the darker meanings of wilderness—its association with chaos and darkness. Wilderness seduces Lilburne to murder and self-destruction, stripping away the repressive controls of civilization and unleashing the flaws of violence and imperfection which bode ill for the nation's future. (These are "flaws" only from the perspective of one who, like Jefferson, believes that virtue is the natural condition of humanity; they are more accurately termed the "realities" of human character. As Freud observed in *Civilization and Its Discontents,* "Civilization has to use its utmost efforts in order to set limits to man's aggressive instincts and to hold the manifestations of them in check." Without those limits, anarchy and chaos ensue.)[15]

Only Jefferson and Meriwether find true reason for hope in the wilderness. Others discover darker potentialities. Charles Lewis seeks an escape there from his failures in Virginia. His retreat to the Kentucky frontier provides a parable, in a sense, of the settlement of the American nation, for he fled to Kentucky to escape personal disappointment, to escape himself, to begin anew. He is thus doomed from the start, since such evasions of responsibility are impossible in Warren's conception of the world. Charles himself senses the impossibility. His desire to set up life in a vacuum isolates his sons from the sustaining, stabilizing forces of a more civilized Virginia. The results are especially evident after the death of Lucy, the last ideal, the final vestige of order and meaning in Lilburne's life. Though Charles understands the folly of his efforts to escape, he prefers pretense to reality:

> *Fled*—that's the word. Fled the intolerableness
> Of a world that I had made. And had made me.
>
> .   .   .   .
>
> So fled,
> Sought new world, new birth, tension and test, perhaps terror.
> Said I'd renew, if for an instant only,
> The dear illusion, lost in youth, of being
> Some part of human effort, and man's hope.
> Said I'd redeem the wild land, set blossom by the stone.
> But knew it was illusion. Knew that I fled,
> Not as redeemer but the damned.
>
> (11–12)

Although he admits some slight responsibility for the meat-house murder, Charles also reveals the same desire to evade blame characteristic of others in the poem. He regards the "madness" which drove Lilburne to murder as hereditary and wonders "was I the vessel, vase, and propagator / Of madness? Or was it she [Lucy, his wife]?" (11). He exerts no control over heredity and need bear no responsibility for it, especially if Lucy provided the offending genes. Blaming heredity, he absolves himself. Once again he evades reality, as before he fled Albemarle and, after Lucy's death, the Smithland mansion. His absence there at the crucial moment is a critical factor in the events which unfold between his sons Lilburne and Isham, and for the slave John. For Lilburne the wilderness becomes a malicious, sentient force which saps his civilized self and reduces him to savagery. In fact, wilderness is merely a projection of changes occurring within him, precipitated by his mother's death and his isolation in the Kentucky forests. This aspect of the poem seems parallel in a number of ways to Conrad's *Heart of Darkness*. Lilburne Lewis is not the civilized paragon that Mr. Kurtz was, but he shares many of the same implicit assumptions about civilization and its virtues, and he falls for the same essential reasons.

In this poem where ways of perceiving and understanding the world are of major concern, the wilderness is a blank space which holds whatever meaning the perceiver wishes or needs to find there. It is one of the "naturalistic considerations" in the poem, with no inherent meaning of its own, subject to the intellectual, spiritual, and emotional manipulations of the perceiver. Attempts to understand it, to redeem it, to discern within it some comprehensible and coherent force can be painfully frustrating or fundamentally catastrophic. The wilderness is simply what it is, wilderness, nature. But its very immensity compels the perceiver to search for the meaning it does not hold. Jefferson and Lilburne at first construe it in strikingly dissimilar ways. The brief third section of the poem brilliantly and frighteningly evokes the wilderness in winter. On the one hand it expresses the horror of a wilderness which Lilburne Lewis has begun to realize was not designed for his pleasure or is even conscious of his presence. On the other it presents an image of nature wholly stripped of subjective or anthropomorphic interpretation. The key passage describes a "big channel-cat" floating motionlessly "in the interior of that unpulsing blackness" beneath a foot of winter ice. The fish has attained harmony with its surrounding:

But there is no sensation. How can there be
Sensation when there is perfect adjustment? The blood
Of the creature is the temperature of the sustaining flow:
The catfish is in the Mississippi and
The Mississippi is in the catfish and
Under the ice both are at one
With God.

Would that we were!

(61)

The catfish recalls the image earlier used by Charles Lewis, "The shell the shellfish spins from the slick slime / And deliquescence of itself to fend / That self, and its poor palpitation, boxed in dark" (11). It suggests as well Warren's poem "A Way to Love God," where the eyes of sheep staring into "nothingness" are "round and stupid like the eyes of fat fish in muddy water" (*NSP*, 165–66) and epitomize an unquestioning mindlessness which is the purest and only satisfactory form of religious faith (that is, unquestioning faith is unnatural, less-than-human: the human condition dooms us to uncertainty and doubt on all levels of knowledge). The compulsion to find meaning drives on many of Warren's characters. It is an essential human need. An individual who accepts and surrenders to the world's nothingness, such as Percy Munn in *Night Rider* or Jeremiah Beaumont in *World Enough and Time*, dooms himself at least to alienation, if not obliteration. Yet the compulsion to find meaning is riven with pain. It is a paradox of the human condition. The insensible animal mindlessness of the channel catfish, or the ungazing sheep, might be preferable to the state Lilburne Lewis finally reaches. Like the grieving Rider in Faulkner's "Pantaloon in Black," Lilburne just can't stop thinking.

Wilderness is more than pastoral setting or symbolic national potential. It is more even than a philosophical vacuum demanding to be filled. It represents a failure of national responsibility and stewardship. The present-day fate of the national wilderness, alluded to in *Brother to Dragons*, is the result of a lack of foresight in the Founders, of a specific incompatibility between their vision of the future nation and the reality the nation became. (Jefferson envisioned an agricultural America, yet by the end of the eighteenth century, industry and commerce were already playing an important, increasingly controversial role in national affairs.) When Jefferson and

Meriwether first describe the great western wilderness, they seem unworried that it one day might be encroached upon or even destroyed by the men who settle it. Meriwether recalls with wonder how he "Saw the sad bison lick the outstretched hand, / And on the western rocks, wracked in wild clang and smother, / The black seal barks and loves us, knowing we will come" (10). William Bedford Clark observes, "Jefferson's ecstatic vision of the west presents it as the familiar Garden of the World, but his reference to the bison and the seal, inevitable victims of America's westering, points towards the withering of both the Garden and the Jeffersonian Dream." [16] The nation expanded westward convinced that wilderness bounty was endless, there to be taken. Taken it was, with a rapacity that left little remaining in its wake. (In *Night Rider* Willie Proudfit, describing his days as a buffalo hunter, recalls the enormous size of the herds and of the slaughters: "Fer as a man could see, hit was buffalo. They was that thick. No pore human man could name their number, only the Lord on high. That a-way, and no man to say the end. But I seen 'em lay, skinned and stinken, black-en the ground fer what a man could ride half a day. A man couldn't breathe fresh fer the stinken. And before you knowed hit, they wasn't no buffalo in Kansas" [410].)

In the poem's present or "any time," Jefferson knows what has transpired in the years since his death. At least he refers to the Battle of the Wilderness in the Civil War, to the Haymarket Riot of 1886 and the brutal opposition to unionization in 1937 by the Ford Motor Company and "Henry's goons" (86)—all unhappy episodes in the history of a less-than-perfect republic. R. P. W. himself well knows how wilderness has fared in modern America. As a contrast to Meriwether's pastoral descriptions of the buffalo and the booming mountains, he offers the "sun-bit" Kentucky landscape of the modern day: "Blunt hills eroded red, stunt-oak, scrag-plum, / The ruined coal-tipple and the blistered town" (12). As several readers have noted, this passage describes a modern American Waste Land whose need for redemptive and life-bringing water R. P. W. can satisfy only with the patter of urine on "parched soil" (13).[17] The sunbit Kentucky landscape is what has become of the "shining land" Jefferson and Meriwether envisioned. That land is no more, the obligations it conferred long forgotten, the promise it once held superceded by profit motives and progress. In the town of Smithland, suggests William Bedford Clark, Warren portrays "the ironic culmination of its founder's materialistic ambition, and they stand as burlesques of Jefferson's sense of national destiny." [18] In his second trip to Smithland, Warren notes the small town's prosperity and links it to the Korean War, for which he hints American expansionism was also at least partially to blame:

> Who would begrudge such solvency?
> And who's to blame if there's a correlation
> Between it and the dark audit of blood
> In some Korean bunker, at the midnight concussion?
> Yes, who's to blame? For in the great bookkeeping
> Of History, what ledger has balanced yet?
>
> (127)

The questions are rhetorical, but Warren does not mean to leave them unanswered. The ledger is the crux of the metaphor. History is a natural force, impersonal, indifferent, beyond human control. No one is to blame for the course it takes. The ledger converts all moral and ethical considerations into mere financial statistics. If the ledger balances, nothing else matters. At least, Warren suggests, this is the motivating logic of the modern age, and the burning irony of the passage makes clear his contempt for such logic. What he calls for here is individual and national responsibility, no matter that history may be beyond human control. The assumption of responsibility he regards as a matter of human identity and dignity, part of the meaning of "civilized." The ravaged land of the present day reflects just such a failure of stewardship. Meriwether describes the wilderness as immortal and unchanging, an idyllic land to which he can return if he ever chooses. To him it lies outside the world of men and politics and time. Jefferson probably would assume a similar view. Yet the wilderness falls victim to American expansionism just as do the Indians. Although this failure is not a major focus of *Brother to Dragons,* it looms significantly in the background as an additional consequence of the failure of humanity, reason, and imagination which the poem does concern. Later works, primarily *Audubon: A Vision* and *Chief Joseph of the Nez Perce,* explore specific aspects of the failure more fully.

Unlike his uncle and Meriwether Lewis, Lilburne finds in the Kentucky wilderness not a source of light and inspiration but a darkness which gradually, inexorably drains away his civilized being. His decline is a cruel process of disillusionment, abandonment, and isolation. He begins as an idealist naively expecting the best from life, and he is disappointed at every turn, by every person and event. His wife turns cold to him, his mother dies, his father flees, his mother's china and silver begin to disappear. Alone in the Kentucky wilderness, denied the love of mother, wife, or father, he is left to fashion his own moral standards. And the standards he fashions only confirm the darkness and savagery he senses within himself. Lucy understands this process well enough and believes she had a part in it. She grieves that if she had lived

> My love somehow might have sustained my son.
> It might have been to him like a hand stretched out.
> And little Isham—oh, Ishey—love might
> Have at least been some light against the ignorant torpor
> That breathed from the dark land. Yes,
> If I had loved,
> Loved well enough to live, the tiptoe horror
> Had not come sly, to insinuate
> Itself in my name to Lilburne, my son.
>
> I saw the dark land creep into my house.
> I saw the dark night creep into my bed.
> I saw the river-dark swim in my cup.
>
> (17–18)

Life and reality disillusion Lilburne—human mortality and the world's imperfections. The "dark land" offers no sustaining authority or meaning, no reassurance that things are not as empty and brutal as they seem. Perhaps even more he is disillusioned by what he discovers in himself. He finally begins to relish what he regards as his own degradation. His wife Letitia, incapable of confronting reality but secure as long as others shelter her from it, becomes one of his victims. He exalts her as "an angel from the sky" but immediately turns on her, warning

> If you're an angel,
> Then I simply give you one piece of advice:
> Go!
>
> .   .   .   .
>
> Go back to Heaven if you can,
> And if you can't, then try the Other Place,
> For . . . even Hell would be better than this sty.
>
> (47)

Soon after, he returns from town drunk and apparently sodomizes her. Letitia herself cannot describe the act:

> And it was an awful thing
> I didn't even know the name of, or heard tell—
> I'd plain forgot—
> It was so awful that folks could do so awful.
>
> (49)

The thing's "awfulness" perhaps resides as much in her husband's manner as in the act itself. But however shy and sheltered she might be, the act is one of brutal violence, of rape, and she views it as the negation of the precious adoration she needs and regards as love. She is willing to forgive him until he forces her, the next day, to admit that she enjoyed the act. Then he gloats:

> "But, Angel," said Lilburne, "just yesterday,
> You were an angel and your hair was gold,
> And golden stars in it, I put them there.
> But now—
>
> .   .   .   .
>
>   now I see when angels
> Come down to earth, they step in dung, like us.
> And like it."
>
> (52)

After this episode, Letitia rejects Lilburne. But she does so in a way characteristic of her inability to face reality, for life and sexuality repulse her. Lilburne, who seems incapable of love to begin with, has used her to prove to himself that all he holds dear is sordid, fallen. As for Jefferson, the discovery of the fallen world overwhelms him. (Both Lilburne and Jefferson represent their disillusionment with the world in an image of dung.) Lilburne cannot readjust to the new reality. He has discovered that he is "only human," that human failure and inadequacy penetrate the world, that nothing endures forever. He revels in what he takes to be the world's and his own empty horror. Though Jefferson does not resort to the same extreme means of confirming the horror, his surrender to it is just as great. Like Lilburne, he becomes alienated. And if we assume that the essential problems which he and Lilburne experience—disillusionment, despair, alienation—are those too of R. P. W., then we begin to see why the ghostly figures and issues of this poem so concern the persona of the present time.

Lilburne takes his mother's death as conclusive proof of the world's meaninglessness. Yet he is partially to blame for it. Early in the poem Lucy expresses her belief that if she had better loved her husband and sons, she would not have died, and she might have averted the tragedy which followed. (Though her belief seems foolish, she is the only person in the poem to accept from the beginning responsibility for the events which happen.) In fact, a failure in compassion together with her love for Lilburne is what really seems to kill her. She dies shortly after finding herself unable to help the slave John, whom Lilburne has beaten. She is shocked not only at his cruelty, but at her own inhumanity. She cannot bring herself to touch the slave's bloodied face ("To touch it," she says, "and the terribleness / Of knowledge" [53–54]; "That blood—why, I knew it was only a dream!" [54]). Blood signifies her son's brutality, thus her own failure as a mother: she raised him up to be what he became. More significantly, blood signifies her responsibility to and kinship with another human being—the slave her family owns and for whose health and welfare she is accountable. Her failure to help him makes her aware of her responsibility for his enslaved and vulnerable condition, that condition which allowed the brutality that has wounded him. It informs her of her moral as well as physical weakness. Her inability to respond to his suffering is perhaps more terrible to her than her son's brutality. She wants to help the slave ("Oh, God! / I will go back and endeavor anew / The blessedness of the human obligation" [55]), but the shock of her weakness prevents her. Throughout the poem blood symbolizes guilt, violence, familial and communal responsibility—the failure of human responsibility on every level. Like her brother at Monticello, Lucy Jefferson Lewis cannot bring herself in life to confront the significance of blood, though in death she is more reconciled to it than anyone else.

The slave John, whose suffering and death are a source of blood, also symbolizes guilt and responsibility, especially as they pertain to slavery. He is a metaphoric conscience for the characters in the poem and for the nation, though he never speaks, except in three lines expressing his sense of being overwhelmed by forces beyond his control or understanding:

> I was lost in the world, and the trees were tall.
> I was lost in the world and the dark swale heaved.
> I was lost in my anguish and did not know the reason.
>
> (118)

His bloody face informs Lucy of her son's brutality and of her own moral weakness. His identity as slave signifies to Lilburne his own failings, his links to and separation from the human community. If John were not a slave, Lilburne might reason, then I could not mistreat him, and because he is a slave, I did mistreat him, and so my mother died. John is thus a reminder of the condition of slavery, of the owner's responsibility for enforcing and maintaining it. He is another sign of guilt, individual and communal guilt. R. P. W. speaks of the "intolerable eye of the sly one, and the sibilant / Confabulation below / The threshold of comprehension" (70). Literally he means the trickery and subterfuge which were a necessary defense among slaves against their condition. But he refers also to an unconscious awareness in the slaveholder's mind that the existence of slavery makes the subtle revolt and insubordination inescapable. The very fact that slaves are slaves makes their owners aware, "below the threshold of comprehension," of their moral and social responsibility for the evil that slavery is. John is, in this sense, Lilburne's "darkest self" (116), the sign of his own moral failure. And the historical reality which John as a slave represents, the dire extremes to which he would drive Lilburne as an individual and the nation as a whole, was too grim and dark for Jefferson or his contemporaries to acknowledge.

Lucy Lewis's death severs Lilburne's last link with the civilized, secure, and ordered world he once knew, confirming his assessment of the natural world as "this sty." Her death frees him from the restraints of that world too, for bereft now of wife, father, and mother, he has only himself to please. The only remaining vestige of the old world, of social convention and responsibility, is John. John depends on him for food, shelter, and life. Such dependency infuriates Lilburne. Even Isham, under his brother's sway, half-sensibly resents it. When Lilburne orders John to fetch the pitcher from the kitchen, Isham exclaims:

> Now things get queer. I never hated John.
> Before, I mean. Him just another nigger.
> But now to see him standing there so weak,
> And frail to fall, and how his eyes were rolling,
> It looked to me there wasn't a thing but hate
> Inside me, and to hate that nigger John
> For being so God-damn mean-weak was nothing
> But sweet joy.
>
> (79)

Lilburne hates John for the same reason he kicks his favorite hound; both depend on him and are weaker than he. They constitute a social and human obligation which he is unable and unwilling to fulfill. (In *Wilderness* Adam Rosenzweig comes to resent the black army deserter Mose Talbutt for the same reason.) Jefferson too is aware of the black man not only as a social conscience but as a being whose very existence brings into question the nature of civilized authority and personal morality. But he expresses this awareness in a way which makes him seem as paranoid as Lilburne:

> Their feet come soft,
> Come softlier than silence,
> And innocence will avail nothing—I tried
> To be innocent, but the eyes—
>
> (70)

What is it about the eyes? What do they suggest? Perhaps Jefferson sees in them deceit, hostility. But they mean something else as well. Like the confabulation, they make the white owner aware of slavery's injustice; they express silent reprobation and thus become another source of guilt. Perhaps they remind Jefferson that the presence of slavery in his republic contradicts the principles of freedom and inalienable rights on which it was founded. Is that why he cannot feign innocence? The eyes, and the human minds behind them, are a social and moral conscience for Jefferson, the reminder of a failure and an inconsistency whose magnitude he cannot acknowledge.

R. P. W.'s description of the eyes seems to accord with Jefferson's, yet like the former president he cannot fully confront their significance:

> Who doesn't know down home
> The intolerable eye of the sly one, and the sibilant
> Confabulation below
> The threshold of comprehension.
>
> . . . .
>
> Always nothing, but always something,
> And in the deep vessel of your self now the dark
> Dregs are disturbed, uncoil now, rise
> To murk the rational ichor of innocence.
> No use to say you've dealt justly with individuals
> Or held the most advanced views on the race question.
> Do you think the Dark Inquisitor can be deflected
> By trivialities like that?
>
> (70–71)

The conflicting impulses R. P. W. presents here are the source of Lilburne's fury against John. The "confabulation" of the slaves constitutes a threat to the master's authority, intended to deceive in the guise of faithful obedience. Such a threat would be naturally infuriating. Even more infuriating is the master's realization that his dominance over the slaves, his ownership of them, enables their insubordination to begin with. Lilburne is the source of his own torment, and to punish that torment, to punish the slaves, he can torment only himself, for deep down within "confabulation" translates belief in the social good of slavery into confirmation of its evil. Lucy explains that in killing John, Lilburne was defending

> but himself against the darkness that was his.
> He felt the dark creep in from all the woods.
> He felt the dark fear hiding in his heart.
> He saw the dark hand set the white dish down.
> He saw poor John as but his darkest self
> And all the possibility of dark he feared.
> And all he wanted—
>
> (116)

John's enslavement—owned by Lilburne, wholly subject to his control—makes Lilburne aware of his potential for savagery. He thus becomes for Lilburne the absolute opportunity for freedom, the irrevocable escape from the restraints of civilized control. He confirms Lilburne's discovery of the world's depravity and becomes its concrete symbol. When Lilburne first strikes John for breaking his mother's china, the other slaves begin misplacing and breaking silverware and china, their only available means of asserting themselves against him. The more aggressively he tries to suppress these small acts of rebellion, the more frequently they occur. The disappearance of his mother's belongings signifies the vanishing of the world he fears he has already lost. His decision to kill John and halt the disappearances is hardly so much a desire to preserve civilization as to hasten its disappearance, to confirm and even relish his own submergence in the violent and horrible animal self he has discovered. Had he known of its existence beforehand, he could have steeled himself against it, summoned the necessary restraint. But with no prior knowledge of the Minotaur within, he submits entirely. As his victim, John represents American slavery's ironic significance to the ideals of the nation's founding.

The poem's treatment of slavery parallels Query VIII of Jefferson's *Notes on Virginia,* which points out the degrading effect of slavery on the slave-holder: "The whole commerce between master and slave is a perpetual exercise of the most boisterous passions, the most unremitting despotism on the one part, and degrading submissions on the other. . . . The man must be a prodigy who can retain his manners and morals undepraved by such circumstances." [19] Lewis Simpson suggests that Jefferson in this passage metaphorically expresses the "complex tension between the precept that slavery is morally wrong and the pragmatic historical experience of the world the slaveholders had made." That is, though they felt slavery to be morally wrong, they also found it essential to the building of a strong and lasting society. And they were willing, if only half-consciously, to do what was necessary to preserve their positions. Simpson observes:

> Jefferson may suggest that the self, seeking its identity, uses the rational mind as an instrument to end its captivity to, its suppression in, the old hierarchical order, but rejects all rational constructs, obeying only the need to exist in its own image; that the self, expressing its will to self-dominion through the illiterate slave . . . is capable of any act of violence required by its will to identity—of committing in the name of the will to freedom any act necessary to fulfill the will to identity.[20]

Lilburne is not much concerned with maintaining his social or political position, but he clearly intends to preserve his independent self against the threat the slaves represent for him. The obliteration of self is what he seeks to prevent, yet the murder he commits is a conscious severance of his links with the past, with civilization, with the social obligations that slaveholding entails. His murder of John is, then, an act of suicide.

The meat-house murder is the emblem in *Brother to Dragons* of the American capacity for inhumanity and violence. Such a capacity is innately human, of course, but American democracy, predicated on Jeffersonian humanism and its belief in original virtue, was defenseless against its existence. Unprepared for the inevitable human reality (as Lilburne was unprepared for his inevitable human self), unwilling even to admit its philosophic possibility, the nation was left defenseless against its own brutal impulses. Thus Jefferson explains that,

> as history divulged itself,
> I saw how the episode in the meat-house
> Would bloom in Time, and bloom in the lash-bite

And the child's last cry, down in the quarters when
The mother's sold. And for another joke,
Ask the Christian Cherokee
How the heart bled westward on the Trail of Tears.

(85)

Slavery and the mistreatment of the American Indian were two manifestations of brutality whose moral implications the nation was unprepared to
confront. (Slavery, of course, long predated the Declaration of Independence, but once the Declaration was signed and the American republic with
its promise of freedom created, slavery became a burning and inexplicable
contradiction.) But the supreme consequence of the "episode in the meat-
house," Jefferson argues, was the Civil War, where "vanity, greed, and
blood-lust may obscenely / Twine in the excuse of moral ardor and crusade" and whose Battle for the Wilderness, with its crackling forest fires,
produced the odor of burning human flesh "That so reminds you of the
odor in the meat-house" (86). The consequences extend further, through
the nineteenth and into the twentieth century, in labor riots and prejudice
against immigrants and the poor and in numerous other episodes:

But a few more items from the ample documentation—
Pittsburgh and Pinkerton and the Polack bleeding
In some blind alley, while the snow falls slow,
And Haymarket, Detroit and Henry's goons—
Oh, that's enough—and how much since!

(86)

The murder represents not merely the invalidation of Jeffersonian humanism
but the American republic's failure to honor the ideals its founders meant it
to embody and their repeated violation throughout its history.

       Lilburne's murder of John only convinces Jefferson of the fool-
ishness of his former ideas. It does not provoke him to amend them. He
abandons them. It estranges him from the human race, which in the "any
time" of the poem he holds in contempt. He refuses to see in the murder
any evidence of blemish in his own character. It remains for Meriwether
Lewis to convince him of his bond with humanity, his complicity in communal human guilt. Earlier, when Jefferson described himself as the Israelite

who would never see his Promised Land, Meriwether was placed in the role of Aaron who led the Chosen People into the Promised Land. He also willingly, if half-consciously, assumes the role of Jefferson's son. When Meriwether makes his second appearance in the poem, Warren develops the relation of the two men more fully. At first we knew only that Meriwether stood fully in thrall of Jefferson's "towering greatness," that when the younger man returned the proffered affection, Jefferson's face "was suddenly turned away" (10). Meriwether believes that when he stood accused of fraud and incompetence as governor of the Louisiana Territory, his former benefactor deserted him. He probably also means that Jefferson's high judgment of humankind suddenly seemed to him false and hollow.

Meriwether Lewis's experience parallels Lilburne's. Yet Jefferson stands closer to Meriwether than to his nephew. Jefferson proclaims the link. And he is surprised to be called betrayer by the man who so admired him, especially when he feels himself betrayed by the other "son" Lilburne. Jefferson regards Meriwether as a representative of "the level-eyed / And straight-browed ones to come" (9), of the future settlers and citizens of the American wilderness. In his own place he sent Meriwether to explore the western half of the continent, "I said I cannot go, / But my own blood will go / To name and chart and set the human foot" (9). If Jefferson is the symbol of civilization, then Meriwether enters the wilderness as his emissary of light and progress, of the redemptive powers of civilization. Meriwether deeply believes in this role. He is indifferent to the savagery he encounters, for he realizes his separateness from it: he believes he is separate because he is civilized. As a civilized man of civilized virtues, a believer in the goodness of men, he feels impervious. "The world trusts you, my son," Jefferson had said to him in farewell, and for a time Meriwether believed that promise, trusted in other men to recognize the goodness of his character and respond appropriately. His travels reinforced his trust in humankind, for he remembers fondly the men with whom he traveled. He tells Jefferson:

> for one brief moment my experience
> Seemed confirmation of all you had said, for in
> My imagination the voice remained of the night ocean,
> And I thought that I knew
> How men may long travel together, as brothers.
>
> (113)

Yet the civilized world does not trust him as his mentor had promised, and he suddenly encounters the illusion under which he has labored. Like Charles, Lilburne, and Jefferson, he reacts with bitterness to the discovery:

> Then St. Louis, and I broke bread with civil men.
> Well, I had seen
> The savage tear the steaming guts,
> And blood streak the cheekbone,
> And would that I had wallowed and remained there!
>
> (113)

Jefferson's optimism prepares Meriwether for what he thinks he has found in the wilderness. The harmonious company of men, the struggle against nature, the savagery of the Indians—these do not suggest to him that he has been misled. He knows his own exaltation. The wilderness confirms what Jefferson had bequeathed him. But the civilized world denies it entirely. He is thus unprepared for the human world, and he blames his mentor:

> Had I not loved, and lived, your lie, then I
> Had not been sent unbuckled and unbraced—
> Oh, the wilderness was easy!—
> But to find, in the end, the tracklessness
> Of the human heart.
>
> (114)

Though Meriwether believed in his own goodness, he was instead merely naive and possessed of his mentor's vanity. In his opinion, Jefferson's "lie" betrayed him. ("Lie" is too harsh. Throughout the poem Warren opposes such extreme terms, even when R. P. W. uses them, for they imply self-righteous moral blame for a simple human error in understanding.) By convincing Jefferson that the deception left him unprepared for the world and finally drove him to suicide, Meriwether and Lucy move Jefferson towards acceptance of his kinship with humanity. Yet in blaming him for betrayal, Meriwether himself is seeking to evade responsibility for his own failure to see truth.

Like others in the poem, Meriwether Lewis must be redeemed from cynicism and despair. Once he stood as Jefferson's successor, sharing the same egalitarian vision of "How men may long travel together, as brothers" (113). In this spirit he accepts the governorship of the Louisiana Territory.

When his fortunes fall, when he is falsely accused of corruption, he loses trust in humanity and the president who befriended him, but he retains his faith in the wilderness. Thus, at the end of the poem's fifth section, he leads the incantatory chant which represents the restoration of the visions and ideals the spirit-characters had lost.

Because the climax of *Brother to Dragons* hinges on nothing more than the characters' acceptance of a certain philosophical attitude and on Jefferson's acceptance of his humanity—hypothetical acceptances, of course, since all but one of the characters are dead and cannot put their new attitudes into action—the end of the fifth section is disappointing. From the start the poem has moved towards absolution of guilt, the purgation of despair. When that moment arrives, it is a passionless, bloodless ritual, the fulfillment of an ordained pattern, the sort of contrived literary resolution characteristic of Eliot's lesser plays, of the closing act of Faulkner's *Requiem for a Nun*. Still, the restorative chant thematically resolves on a historical and national level the philosophic issues of the poem, calling for the fusion of Jeffersonian ideals with acceptance of the limitations of human nature, a sort of pragmatic idealism:

> Dance back the Shining Mountains, let them shine!
> Dance into morning and the lifted eye.
> Dance into morning past the morning star,
> And dance the heart by which we must live and die.
>
> (120)

Here imagination and vision, the power of ideals, belief in human potential, are restored. But they must be tempered with knowledge of history and human nature. "All is redeemed, / In knowledge," Meriwether says, to which Jefferson answers "But knowledge is the most powerful cost. / It is the bitter bread. / I have eaten the bitter bread" (120). The message here is paradoxical and not wholly encouraging. The poem argues for a continued pursuit of the ideals of the country's founding, tempered by knowledge that they are unattainable. The governance of human nature by reason was one of the ideals of the Declaration, and Jefferson wished to see it as a governing principle of the nation. Yet he mourns the loss of that light, relegating it almost to the status of dream: "But can it—can it be that we are condemned / To search for it?" (119). Yet without that search we forfeit our humanity, become wraiths like the figures in the poem, or lose ourselves in the mire of "naturalistic considerations" without hope or vision, like the shellfish described by Charles Lewis, exuding the illusion of its own civilization "from the slick slime / And deliquescence of itself to fend / That self and its poor palpitation, boxed in dark" (11).

The need to pursue those ideals is the most important message the poem has to deliver, if we judge by urgency of presentation. The message contains an element of pessimism, for it takes the form of an Indian ghost dance acted out by the spirit-characters. Warren found the ghost dance sufficiently powerful as a metaphor to use it on at least two other occasions: in the Willie Proudfit section of *Night Rider* and in *Chief Joseph of the Nez Perce*. In a note following *Brother to Dragons,* he explains that the "religion of the Ghost Dance" appeared "when the Indians of the West were in their last paroxysm of resistance and despair." Its promise of destruction for the white oppressors, of restored ancestral lands and power, attracted numerous Indians desperate for the slightest hope of defeating the white man and driving him from their lands. Yet the hope which the ghost dance offered was hollow. Through it Warren demonstrates that the restoration of meaning to the spirit-characters is essentially a sham, an act, a literary ritual. Only the living character, R. P. W., can glean some benefit from it.

Brother to Dragons advocates the adoption of a particular mode of perception, a philosophy of life, which eschews illusions and rigid patterns of understanding that prevent one from grasping the true reality. Such a perspective permits one to confront life and its responsibilities unburdened by illusion. Paradoxically, the poem also advocates pursuit of ideals which it recognizes as elusive and unattainable. Not surprisingly, Warren takes pains throughout the poem to uncover modes of perception which distort reality. Each of the major characters in some sense exemplifies the dangers of romantic idealism. Meriwether Lewis is unprepared for the civilized world's corruption. Charles Lewis is humiliated by his failures. Letitia is so horrified at her husband's emotional disturbance (and perhaps too by her own sexuality) that she abandons him and withdraws from life entirely. But Lilburne Lewis provides the prime example. Through him the meat-house episode demonstrates that idealism leaves one ill prepared to confront the evils of the world and human character. Jefferson himself suggests that the circumstances which blinded him to the possibilities of the meat-house murder led directly to the Civil War and the corruption of nineteenth-century America. Warren in other places warns against the dangers of "self-righteousness and phariseeism" (*Legacy,* 64), of the virtuous smugness which can blind one to the presence of evil or imperfection and the necessity of dealing with it (note his discussion of the Northern Treasury of Virtue in *The Legacy of the Civil War*).[21] There is an element of the didactic in this poem, one purpose of which is to call attention to how the nation stumbled into certain errors in the past and to suggest a realistic, rational mode of thinking and of regarding history which can make such errors less likely in the future. As he explained at the Fugitives' Reunion in 1956, "The past is always a rebuke to the present. . . . And that is a much better rebuke than any dream of a golden age to come, because historians will correct, and imagination will correct, any notion of a simplistic and, well, childish notion of a golden age. The drama of the past that corrects us is the drama of our struggles to be human, of our struggles to define the values of our forebears in the face of their difficulties." [22]

Among the figures in the poem, R. P. W. is most concerned with modes of understanding and perception. He insists to a fault on fact and truth, on reality unblemished by subjectivism. Near Smithland, when he first ascends the hill where the ruined Lewis mansion stands, he encounters the black snake, "old *obsoleta,*" and is tempted to see in it a symbol of the "evil" which once transpired nearby. But he dissuades himself, recognizing the snake as "no spirit, symbol, god, / Or Freudian principle, but just a snake" (25). (Despite this denial, the snake does *symbolize* evil—no one who knew the history of the place could fail to recognize that meaning, even if later discarding it.) R. P. W. takes a similar view of the New Madrid earthquake which struck on the night of John's murder:

> Yes, God shook out the country like a rug,
> And sloshed the Mississippi for a kind of warning—
> Well, if God did, why should he happen to pick out
> Just Lilburne's meanness as excuse? There'd been God's plenty
> Of such excuses, and they multiply
> Right now in Old Kaintuck, without any earthquakes
> Nor Year of Wonders
> To scare the homefolks with appropriate omens.
>
> (90–91)

Superstition is not the only perspective with which the poem takes issue. With satiric irony R. P. W. mimics the objection which Marxist and other

critics of overt ideologic agenda would voice to the notion that slaves might
have loved their owners:

> if the word *love*
> Sounds too much like old Thomas Nelson Page
> To sit easy on our stomachs salivated with modernity,
> Then we can say that in the scale of subordination,
> The blacks, those victims of an obsolescent
> Labor system (we can't, you see, just say
> "Immoral labor system," for that
> Wouldn't be modern, except for people
> Who want things both ways)—well, the blacks
> Had been conditioned, by appeals to the ego,
> To identify themselves with the representative
> Of the superordinate group, i.e., the mistress.[23]
>
> (68)

Such reasoning, whether from moralistic or Marxist perspective, dehuman-
izes the reasoner and prevents understanding of human beings caught in
human situations. Even as R. P. W. struggles to accept the human while
avoiding the hazards of romanticism and skepticism, Lucy Lewis has, in
her own way, achieved that perspective. Despite the evil her son committed
—evil she does not deny—she still loves him. Though she does not ask that
he be excused, she does ask that he be understood, because he acted as only
a deluded and driven being can act. She also demands that her brother try
to recognize the human motives underlying his own behavior, especially the
vanity which she argues helped motivate his friendship with Meriwether
and the optimistic humanism of the Declaration. Vanity is a human trait
to which Jefferson will not admit. To do so would convict him of being
human, imperfect. "If I believe you," he asks her, "what is left for me?"
(117). He fears that a less-than-noble motive might sully those deeds he
considers the crowning achievements of his life. But she assures him,

> Your dream, dear Brother, was noble.
> If there was vanity, fear, or deceit in its condition,
> What of that? For we are human, and must work
> In the shade of the human condition.
>
> (118)

Only by accepting the human, with its risk and promise, can he or the nation ever hope to realize any aspect of the "dream" expressed in the Declaration. Cleanth Brooks observes: "It is a great Jefferson who emerges at the end of Warren's poem, a Jefferson who has, in giving up his more callow hopes in man, actually strengthened his basic beliefs in man's potentialities. At the end of the poem Jefferson is a chastened though not a disillusioned man." [24]

The perspective the poem urges, and which R. P. W. finally achieves, is a paradoxical fusion of "naturalistic considerations" with human illusions, ideals, and virtues. The two extremes may seem mutually exclusive. Yet both are necessary to human life and identity. As R. P. W. considers his aging father, the failures of his own life, and the prospect of his inevitable mortality, he questions the value of "philosophic" wisdom in the face of senescence and death:

> We wonder, even as we consider their virtue:
> What is wisdom and what the dimming of faculty?
> What kindliness, and what the guttering of desire?
> What philosophic wisdom, and what the fatigue of the relaxed nerve?

But he concludes: "still, despite all naturalistic considerations, / Or in the end because of naturalistic considerations, / We must believe in the notion of virtue" (21). If life has no meaning, if its only end is oblivion, we must find a way to create meaning, and to live by it. Belief in virtue, in ideals, in transcendent patterns of understanding, insulates the self against reality, asserts the worth of human identity and the beliefs on which it is built against the naturalistic void of the world. Again we recall Conrad's *Heart of Darkness,* where Marlow's lie to Kurtz's Intended is his concession that civilized illusions are preferable to reality. Marlow considers this discovery hideous, more "dark" than the darkness of the corrupted man he discovered in the jungle. R. P. W. finds it not so dark at all. It simply provides a fulfilling way of living and confronting the world, a source of meaning and importance, of identity and kinship with the human race.

It is R. P. W.'s burden to discover and accept the philosophical perspective which the poem favors. Though in many of the short poems, and in *Chief Joseph* and *Audubon: A Vision,* Warren and his persona are indistinguishable, such is not always the case here. In the first and seventh sections R. P. W. clearly *is* Warren, recounting anecdotes about his father and their two trips to the ruins of the Lewis mansion near Smithland, Kentucky. But in the central sections with Jefferson, Lilburne, and the others, R. P. W.

strikes the modernist pose of a time-wearied cynic, skeptical and contemptuous of visions and ideals, clunkily mired in the mundane realities of an unimagining twentieth century, eager to debunk and ridicule Jefferson's optimism. When Jefferson remembers with awe the perfect dimensions of the Roman Maison Quarée in France, R. P. W. derides the edifice as "a heap of organized rubble . . . thrown up by a parcel of those square-jawed looters from the peninsula" (29).[25] Later he denies that Lilburne could have loved his mother. It is Jefferson who correctly diagnoses him:

> JEFFERSON: What I lack, my friend, is the dream
> Of joy I once had, and that,
> From the way you talk, I doubt
> You ever had.
>
> R. P. W.: All right—for it is scarcely
> The most fashionable delusion of my age, and I—
> I simply never had it.
>
> (34)

R. P. W. has lost the quality of human compassion and the possibility of vision. The events of the poem—ranging from the moment of composition in the Philadelphia attic of 1776 to the murder in the meat-house in 1811 to the modern-day visits to Smithland—confront R. P. W. with the essence of the human, its grandeur and ignominy. Trying to understand Lilburne's murder of John and Jefferson's reaction to it, R. P. W. must reconcile himself to the meaning of humanity and human values, specifically to love and compassion and forgiveness. Clearly, his criticism of Jefferson's humanism parallels Warren's own opinions. Just as clearly, his cynical rejection of the human as anything more than a series of animal impulses marks a modern way of thinking that Warren finds dangerous and reprehensible. (Consider Jack Burden and the Great Twitch in *All the King's Men,* or Jeremiah Beaumont's nihilistic despair in *World Enough and Time*. Warren surely did not advocate these attitudes. Nor should he advocate them in a persona with his initials.) R. P. W.'s struggle to grasp the value of the human makes him a far more compelling figure than Jefferson. R. P. W. is a living being. The figures with whom he converses are spirits, figments of his imagination. He stands to gain in the living world from his struggles. They can profit nothing. James Justus aptly remarks that their redemption "is not for the ghosts' benefit but for those who preside over their calling up."[26]

The figure through whom R. P. W. at last comes to achieve his own redemption is his aging father, who accompanies him on two trips to the Lewis mansion. The poem offers a number of father-son pairings: Lilburne and Charles Lewis, Jefferson and Meriwether, Jefferson and Lilburne, as well as R. P. W. and his father. In a sense, R. P. W. also regards Jefferson as a father figure whose failings he considers a personal betrayal. (Warren once termed himself a "Jeffersonian Democrat.")[27] In each case the father in some way fails the son, by falling short of the ideals the son associates with the father or by revealing his own weakness or corruption. If R. P. W. finds corruption in his father, he does not remark it. Instead he is concerned with his father as a human figure, pathetic in some ways and admirable in others, a man who has had to confront the failure of his life's material ambitions. With wistful pity R. P. W. describes how his aged father once tried to teach "some small last Latin to a little child . . . and she would say / The crazy words, and laugh, they were so crazy" (22). Warren observes:

> There's worse, I guess, than in the end to offer
> Your last bright keepsake, some fragment of the vase
> That held your hopes, to offer it to a child.
> And the child took the crazy toy, and laughed.
>
> I wish you could tell me why I find this scene so sweet.
>
> (22)

During the second trip to Smithland, his father tells a story from his child-hood. The story at first seems to have no point: the old man recalls how *his* father, whose grave has disappeared in the Kentucky woods ("the oak-root has heaved down the headstone" [126]) would gather his sons together each spring and dose them with percoon:

> "It's old-folks talk, but then they held it true,
> My father said how winter thicked boys' blood
> And made 'em fit for devilment, and mean.
> But he'd sure fix that. Percoon would wry your tongue."
>
> (127)

R. P. W.'s father does not even remember what "percoon" was: "Why, Son, / I just don't recollect. But it's percoon" (127). This tale is part of "that land and the weight of its mystery . . . the mystery of years and their logic" (127), a small fragment of one man's existence in a certain place and time. It is also the story of a father who sought to care for his sons, who thinned their blood with percoon to keep them away from devilment and meanness, and who, through whatever failures or successes, held on to certain values and handed down a tradition, as R. P. W.'s father has passed one down to him. This is why he tells the story. He stands near the end of his life still holding to what he values, be they old memories or dead languages, despite whatever evidence experience might have offered that life has no meaning, that its only end is death and the naturalistic consideration of animal oblivion.[28]

The father is a standard, the weight of tradition. In him R. P. W. glimpses the pattern of human life, the ideals and disillusionment, the will to go on. In his pride, the son might hope to avoid the father's mistakes, the pitfalls of the past. Yet he knows that whatever triumphs his father has enjoyed can never be his own. He will always feel inferior. He must make his own way in the world:

> The failures of our fathers are failures we shall make,
> Their triumphs the triumphs we shall never have.
> But remembering even their failures, we are compelled to praise,
> And for their virtues hate them while we praise.

(21)

Warren later paraphrased these lines in "Reading Late at Night, Thermometer Falling," addressed to his recently dead father: "And I, / In spite of my own ignorance and failures, / Have forgiven you all your virtues" (*NSP*, 204). R. P. W.'s father stands in *Brother to Dragons* as a flesh-and-blood contrast to the spirits who grapple over the meat-house murder. Though he is an old man "who has filled the tract of Time / With rectitude and natural sympathy, / Past hope, ambition, and despair's delectable anodyne" (21), he clings to the beliefs and possessions that have given his life meaning. He contrasts with R. P. W. as well. His presence in the poem, suggests Richard G. Law, is "symbolically a rebuke" to R. P. W., for against him the son must measure his own success and failure. The image of the father "is an emblem, not merely of the burden of piety which the son must carry . . . but of the '*fact* of the past,' the cornerstone of reality, the prime meridian, of any world the son may live in, or dream of."[29] In his 1988 reminiscence "Portrait of a Father," Warren's account of his father is consistent with the poem's image of the old man as an ideal of integrity, sacrifice, and self-denial who did not hesitate to lay aside personal ambitions when the demands of family crisis called and who survives in the son's imagination, and in the poem, as a standard by which the poet must inevitably measure himself.[30]

While R. P. W. is not trapped in the limbo of grief, humiliation, and disappointment which entraps the other characters, he stands at a significant point in his own life. He is struggling with the meaning of "naturalistic considerations" as they pertain to matters of human endeavor. He is old enough to foresee his own mortality. He is forty, and he seeks his own glory ("the only thing in life is glory"):

> Oh, remember
> Now your seeding and the world's magnificence
> To which your heart must answer if it can.
>
> (16)

"Seeding" is one's personal ancestry. Warren considers the example of his father's own life "a story told, / Its glory and reproach domesticated" (21). But "seeding" also suggests a cultural and national heritage. The meathouse murder belongs to that heritage. Its mysteries and contradictions are what R. P. W. seeks to understand, for by coming to understand them, he can accept his place in the world. As Jefferson must struggle away from the despair which grips him in death, so must R. P. W. forge an attitude which fuses acceptance of naturalistic considerations with the capacity for imagination and vision. This fusion he achieves in the final section, where he accepts the human need for philosophical illusion ("Who is to name delusion when the flesh shakes" [129]) as a necessary cost of the "joy" of life:

> I raised my eyes
> And thought of the track a man may make through Time,
> And how the hither-coming never knows the hence-going.
> Since then I have made new acquaintance
> With snow on brown leaves.
> Since then I have made new acquaintance
> With the nature of joy.
>
> (129)

The image of "snow on brown leaves" signifies the new philosophical perspective: snow symbolic of the pure ideal, contrasted against the brown leaf, product of life and mortality, which will endure, in some form, after the snow melts away. One further philosophical gesture R. P. W. makes here: recognition and acceptance of his complicity in the events of human history, "the glory of the human effort." Whatever fame an individual might achieve in his lifetime, greater glory lies in the recognition of his place in the human world:

> We have yearned in the heart for some identification
> With the glory of the human effort. We have devised
> Evil in the heart, and pondered the nature of virtue.
> We have stumbled into the act of justice, and caught,
> Only from the tail of the eye, the flicker
> Of joy, like a wing-flash in thicket.
>
> (131)

The great and continuous process of life and history, and R. P. W.'s vision of his place within it, is the joy which concludes the poem. The poem itself is a source of joy, stemming from the poet's discovery of a perspective which gives his life meaning and identity. Like Warren's two other long poems, *Audubon: A Vision* and *Chief Joseph of the Nez Perce*, *Brother to Dragons* seeks from the past a glory which will restore meaning to a diminished present. Though most of the poem occurs in the past, occasional glimpses of the present, of the scarred Kentucky landscape and the "comics, and headlines of the world's disaster" (22), suggest the present day's diminishment. Smithland is an emblem of that diminishment, its inhabitants typical citizens of the modern world who must search for glory in books, or in drink, or by killing a goose strayed south from Canada, "Lost from its constellation that bestrode, / Star-triumphing, the icy-altitudes, / While the hoots moved south" (15). History itself is glory. Yet history, as the poem demonstrates, is a human story, a series of human events subject to the distortions and misinterpretations which tellers, historians, and poets may give it. R. P. W. recognizes his capacity for distortion when he returns to the ruins of the Lewis mansion for a second time and sees that the trees and ruins are not so magnificent as he had recalled: "I had plain misremembered / Or dreamed a world appropriate for the tale" (128). History stands as an ideal in which one may believe, the ideal of Jefferson and the nobility of men and the Declaration of Independence. It may stand as well as a human story in which mistakes are made but where vision and imagination and belief in the human effort, however insignificant, hold some decisive sway. Finally, history is merely history, the past. The demands of the present are what we must confront, and though history may help prepare us for those demands, we ultimately have only our own knowledge of the world and human nature to guide us.

The events of *Brother to Dragons* shadow forth the birth and growth of the American nation. Here and there in the poem Warren invokes the reality of the nation's history, of the anonymous men and women who struggled to realize the visions which people such as Jefferson conjured up. There is Jack Boyle, for instance, who owns the hill on which the ruined Lewis house stands, who, like other Americans, is "a man of decent ambitions, country hopes, [who] did his best, / Mortgage and weather taken to account / And minor irritations flesh is heir to" (20). Strung out in time behind him are others who helped build the nation, who floated on the river of its history, the keelboat man who "shook the shallows" with his boast (13), and all those who

> Had moved on that broad flood—the good, the bad,
> The strong, the weak, the drawn, the driven,
> The fortunate, the feckless, all men, a flood
> Upon the flood. . . .
>
> (129)

In his biography of John Brown, Warren suggested that these are the citizens who truly settle the basic issues of history, who live out the issues which politicians in Washington only debate.[31] In one form or another they have played a prominent background role in most of his novels and in many of the poems.

Despite the brilliant moments and the undeniable significance of its subject, *Brother to Dragons* lacks the scope and pure vision of either *Audubon: A Vision* or *Chief Joseph*, which nonetheless grew from the same concerns as this predecessor. Even in the superior 1979 version, there are moments too forced and deliberate, passages which lack the conviction and spontaneity of the other long poems and many of the shorter ones. There lingers a degree of what Harold Bloom has termed "ideological ferocity," didacticism, narrative polemic calculated as much to argue philosophical and political attitudes as to make an artistic statement. Calvin Bedient finds the poem "too morally earnest": "Its vice of tone is a certain pompousness that wears no clothes, a straining for virtuous wisdom in the incertitude of the void."[32] To be fair, Warren never held that polemic and art are exclusive. In *Democracy and Poetry,* he discussed the "therapeutic" function of poetry, which

> more often than not . . . brings to focus and embodies issues and conflicts that permeate the circumambient society, with the result that the poem itself evokes mysterious echoes in the selves of those who are drawn to it, thus providing a dialectic in the social process. The "made thing" becomes, then, a vital emblem of the struggle toward the achieving of the self, and that mark of struggle, the human signature, is what gives the aesthetic organization its numinousness. It is what makes us feel that the "made thing" nods mysteriously at us, at the deepest personal inward self. (69)

Art is, he added later, "the process by which, in imagining itself and the relation of individuals to one another and to it, a society comes to understand itself, and by understanding, discover its possibilities for growth" (76). *Brother to Dragons* in this sense seeks to diagnose and explain certain of America's ills and blindnesses. A similar purpose underlies *Chief Joseph.* But the polemical mission of *Brother to Dragons,* the sporadic stentorian dogmatism, occasionally interferes with the poetry, and there is sometimes the suspicion that Jefferson is allowed to resolve his problem primarily for the sake of driving the lesson home. Moreover, when Jefferson can at last accept his human self without forfeiting entirely his former ideals, what in human terms does it matter? The poem has made its point, but Jefferson, in the poem and in life, is dead. His acceptance of the human matters only for R. P. W., who *is* alive, a fact elevating him to the protagonist's role, though he occupies that position only in the opening and closing sections. In *Audubon,* the relationship of the contemporary persona and his historical subject is reversed. The persona there lives through the naturalist's struggle with his artistic ideals—it is a resolved struggle, a thing to be contemplated in its wholeness, an intact source of inspiration for the poet, who presents himself, by implication, as immersed in a similar but unresolved struggle. In *Chief Joseph* there is a corresponding imaginative identification between the poet and his historical paradigm.

The most eloquent passages in *Brother to Dragons* remain those focused on R. P. W., especially the introductory and concluding narratives of his trips to Smithland with his father. Meriwether Lewis's dream-like account of his journey through the American West is nearly as moving. These sections, coupled with the undeniable artistry and power of the rest of the poem, make *Brother to Dragons* a distinctive achievement. There is hardly another work like it in American literature. Its struggles with philosophical issues at the heart of the nation's life and history make it one of the most self-consciously *American* poems ever written.

CHAPTER 3

Audubon: A Vision and

the American Imagination

The central figure in Warren's 1969 poem *Audubon: A Vision* is considerably less a historical personage even than the Jefferson of *Brother to Dragons*. He is a construct of the poet's imagination, a fusion of historical fact and imaginative vision where vision seizes precedence. In the poem's fifth section, "The Sound of That Wind," the poet seems almost to struggle to recall the envisioned Audubon from history, to place him in the real world. He quotes from Audubon's journals and cites brief facts about his life ("He dreamed of hunting with Boone, from imagination painted his portrait") as if to enforce a substitution of the real for the imagined. But vision inevitably prevails, appropriating the Audubon of history as the poet's personal symbol of his struggles in the world, of creative passion, of the American nation's struggles, especially through the nineteenth century, with its own ideals. *Audubon: A Vision* eulogistically renders the naturalist Audubon as he exists in the poet's mind, and as the poet would place him in the American imagination. He comes to signify the poet's relationship to a historical and cultural past. The poem also seeks to define Audubon's mythic significance in history and literature—to influence his image in the national imagination, to participate in the shaping of national memory.[1]

Warren's Audubon engages in a lifelong struggle for identity. His struggle is peculiarly American, akin to the dialectic of idealism and pragmatism which for Warren is the shaping pattern of American history. Its outline is clear enough: Audubon, practically an orphan, seeks to lose himself in an Edenic American wilderness. He desires merger with nature, the loss of

AUDUBON: A VISION   79

self, transcendence to an identity larger than his own—nature's.[2] He learns in the forest that such a merger is unattainable: he inhabits the real world, of which the wilderness is one part. His thwarted desire for merger transmutes into a desire to preserve the wilderness of his vision in artistic form. Art becomes his means of merger, of transcendence. Throughout his life he clings to his vision with an integrity and fidelity Warren extols. If his life is something less than a success, at least in its failure to achieve the goals he set, in a more important sense Warren presents it as a victory of imagination which in the final poem becomes the source of inspiration. Audubon's life and art thus testify to the integrity of the human spirit and imagination, which cling stubbornly to the ideals of the wilderness despite the world's temptations to abandon them. It is finally the ideal which matters, not the facts of a natural world which undermine it nor the failure and compromise of the life to which the ideal gives meaning, purpose, and vision.

Warren presents Audubon's life as a dual vision. First there is Audubon's vision of the American wilderness. In the forest he glimpses a timeless existence uncorrupted by human presence. Warren embodies this realm in the images of the heron and bear of "Was Not the Lost Dauphin" and in other images of nature scattered through the poem. He contrasts these images, often quite deliberately (as in the fourth poem), with details and artifacts from the corrupt, civilized world of men. Though Audubon desires union with this pure and natural realm, he ultimately discovers in "The Dream He Never Knew the End Of" his human self, whose corrupt nature will always prevent such a merger. But there is also the discovery that the woods are mortal, bound by time, and inferior to the ideal he envisioned. The sordid realities of the mortal world and his own human frailty constantly undermine his ideal. Only through art can he reconcile his vision of the timeless Edenic wilderness with the physical world's realities. The distinction between the ideal and the world is the selfsame distinction between life and art. Through art Audubon is reconciled to life. His identity is deeply rooted in his "passion" for the American wilds ("what / Is man but his passion?" [213]). His life is a struggle to preserve that identity against the lures of civilization—fame, fortune, domestic happiness. If in life he finally succumbs to those temptations, in art he does not: he remains true to the passion that defines him. In the imagination of Warren the poet, Audubon's life is a monument to pure passion, complete devotion to an artistic ideal. His wilderness vision, its single-minded transubstantiation into art, Warren celebrates in his own vision (admittedly personal, subjective, ahistorical) of the man and his life.

Part of what makes Audubon significant to Warren, and what Warren wishes to impress on his readers, is the absence of wilderness from the modern American landscape. No longer a vast, inescapable frontier, wilderness is relegated in modern America to the status of (at best) venerated curiosity. Congress argues its fate, and it is banished to the corners of American consciousness as national forest, hunting preserve, wildlife sanctuary. The very meaning of *wild* has vanished. No longer a sign of potential growth and prosperity as in *Brother to Dragons,* wilderness today is more often viewed as a hindrance. The identity of eighteenth- and nineteenth-century Americans, their individual and communal consciousness, was rooted in awareness of wilderness, if not as an overwhelming physical force, at least as an immanent symbolical meaning. The modern individual has no such awareness. Audubon's passion is Warren's case in point. It could not *be* in modern America. The poem is predicated on its impossibility. Warren thus turns to the American past—when nature and wilderness *were* significant presences—and to Audubon for the images which can provide inspiration and identity. He invokes them specifically in the final poem, "Tell Me a Story," which calls for "In this century, and moment, of mania . . . a story of deep delight." The past thus becomes a wellspring of meaning and significance for the empty present.

The brief prose prologue to *Audubon: A Vision* establishes the artist/naturalist as a symbolic orphan who chose to keep the facts of his parentage obscure even after he knew the truth. (His real mother's identity became known only early in the twentieth century, though he apparently knew it himself from an early age.[3]) Audubon's identity—the product of his father's and his own deceptions—is thus an immediate issue. Also an issue is why, as Warren notes, Audubon helped purvey in the public mind a false "version" of his origins "along with a number of flattering embellishments." The prologue, with its emphasis on identity, suggests that the poem which follows will provide needed explanations for these mysteries. It does not. In fact, the poem and its prologue stand curiously at odds: the prologue is straightforward and seemingly factual, a brief, objective account of Audubon's early life. The poem is fragmentary, subjective, and not consistently concerned (on its surface) with Audubon. The prologue ends by noting that Audubon "was, indeed, a fantasist of talent, but even without his help legends accreted about him." The most famous such legend identified him as "the lost Dauphin of France, the son of the feckless Louis XVI and Marie Antoinette," a legend which did not surface until after his death in 1851. The poem discounts this rumor in its first line ("Was not the lost dauphin") but immediately substitutes the legend of another fabulist—that of Warren himself.

Audubon emerges in the opening poem as an Ishmael wandering in search of identity, a penitent Adam seeking readmission to a wilderness Eden. Identity is the central issue—identity rooted in passionate involvement with nature (and, by implication, estrangement from humanity). Clinging to a version of the past which he knows to be false, he exists in a vacuum and must create *ex nihilo* a self which can truly be *him*self. If he was not the lost dauphin, then who was he? Whom did he become? He

> was only
> Himself, Jean Jacques, and his passion—what
> Is man but his passion?
>
> (213)

Passion quite literally defines Audubon and is the source of the problems which plague him (and the poet) throughout the poem. It has several pertinent meanings. Although devotion to nature is synonymous in the American literary and historical imagination with Audubon's name, his passion denotes separation from nature as well. He studies nature out of a desire to merge with it, to abolish his own self completely, to achieve an identity separate from the human world. Passion thus denotes unsatisfied desire. Throughout the poem we remain aware always of Audubon's separateness. This is the element which most struck Warren about Eudora Welty's 1943 story "A Still Moment," in which Audubon appears as a character. In his 1944 essay "Love and Separateness in Eudora Welty," he remarked the irony of the fact that in order to paint the heron, to " 'know' the bird as well as 'love' it," Audubon must kill it so that he can study it feather by feather: "Here, too, the fact of the isolation is realized: as artist and lover of nature, [Audubon] had aspired to a communication, a communion, with other men in terms of the bird, but now 'he saw his long labor most revealingly at the point where it met its limit' and he is forced back upon himself." [4]

Inherent in the separateness of Warren's Audubon is his suffering, the cost he must pay for his passion. The dawn sky in part one of the poem is the "color of God's blood spilt" and "redder than meat." A heron flies across an "inflamed distance" of sky. Calvin Bedient finds that this imagery colors Audubon's vision with "the divine pierced by the hardness of the world. This seeing discloses a divided sphere where power and sacrifice, beauty and violation, love and suffering, mingle terribly. . . . The dawn thus perceived is a portent of passion's transgressions, oblation, and pain." [5] With suffering we also find the passion which redeems. But redemption is not at hand. Audubon's relation to nature is antagonistic, not harmonious. In the first poem the heron and bear, emblems of the wilderness ideal, enforce his separateness. Warren reduces the heron to a series of abstract identifying gestures which denote Audubon's estrangement from the scene he beholds:

> And the large bird,
> Long neck outthrust, wings crooked to scull air, moved
> In a slow calligraphy, crank, flat, and black against
> The color of God's blood spilt, as though
> Pulled by a string.
>
> (213)

The bird's flight is gracefully evoked, though the "slow calligraphy" and the string metaphor render it forced and artificial. Almost *too* pure. Audubon's alienation becomes further apparent in his reaction to the bird:

> Moccasins set in hoar frost, eyes fixed on the bird,
> Thought: "On that sky it is black."
> Thought: "In my mind it is white."
> Thinking: "*Ardea occidentalis,* heron, the great one."
>
> (213)

He first distinguishes between the ideal image of the bird in his mind and its actual appearance against the morning sky. To recognize the ideal in the actual is the artist's purpose. He must reconcile these opposites through artistic representation. Yet Audubon takes an additional step in his catalog of names: "*Ardea occidentalis,* heron, the great one." Here he acts as naturalist, compelled to place the bird in the scientific schema of the natural world. Yet even in this one line, where he struggles to define the bird precisely, he cannot remain dispassionate. He immediately follows the scientific name with the common one—heron—and then with the subjective, mystic "great one," perhaps an Indian name, certainly an expression of awe. This brief list of names suggests his intense involvement, his demand for scientific objectivity and clarity, and his separateness. He describes and redescribes, names and renames, as if to convince himself that the creature moving through the sky is the same one contained by his mind and imagination. Moreover, he must resort to this repetitive naming and describing as a way of trying to penetrate through to the core of the nature which the bird inhabits.

Audubon's wildlife paintings seek to do the same. They are precise and accurate to a fault, especially those in *The Birds of North America,* his best work. But they are emotionless and cold. They depict beautiful static creatures which do not *live* on canvas.[6] Precision and detachment are the characteristic traits of Audubon's art. But art is not Warren's main interest here. He is concerned with the passion which spawns art. The very existence of Audubon's paintings is also evidence of his passion to achieve the merger for which he lived his life. Had merger been possible, he would not have needed to paint. Yet he is constantly reminded of the impossibility of merger. Even the blueberry-eating bear and autumn's last humming bee— more engaging images than the heron—remind him of "How thin is the membrane between himself and the world." However thin, it is impenetrable. This inability to penetrate to the heart of the Real is the same paradox mourned by Keats in "Ode to a Nightingale" and "Ode on a Grecian Urn" and by other romantic poets of the nineteenth century. In this sense Audubon's passion is a romantic obsession, but his ultimate means of living his passion is not.

The heron conveys Audubon's separation from nature. We can see how by comparing this section of the poem with William Cullen Bryant's "To a Waterfowl" (1815). Audubon's bird, moving in its "slow calligraphy, crank, flat, and black" against the morning sky "as though / Pulled by a string" (213), suggests especially this stanza from Bryant's poem:

> Vainly the fowler's eye
> Might mark thy distant flight to do thee wrong,
> As, darkly painted on the crimson sky,
> Thy figure floats along.

The resemblance, intended or not, is ironic. Bryant draws comfort from the bird's flight, in which he finds reassuring proof of divine guidance, of

> He who, from zone to zone,
> Guides through the boundless sky thy certain flight,

> In the long way that I must tread alone,
> Will lead my steps aright.

In Warren's poem, nature is devoid of any comforting Guide who marks the way. Bryant's nature has no integral existence except in relation to the human observer, who is free to explain or sentimentalize it as he will. Audubon recognizes in the heron nature's integral existence that Otherness which frustrates his desire for merger, more extreme and intense than the Wordsworthian or even the Emersonian ideals. He cannot pierce the "membrane." He remains always the Alien, too conscious, too humanly aware. He thus confronts the sad knowledge Emerson describes in his essay "Experience": "It is very unhappy, but too late to be helped, the discovery we have made that we exist. That discovery is called the Fall of Man. Ever afterwards we suspect our instruments."[7] Audubon never suspects his instruments, but his discovery in the second poem that he inhabits a fallen world, that he himself is fallen, is the central moment of his life.

In distinct contrast to the wilderness ideal of "Was Not the Lost Dauphin," "The Dream He Never Knew the End Of" presents the wilderness of the real world, marred by the presence of human inhabitants.[8] The coarse, rank imagery—frequently of disease and decay—contrasts markedly with the sublimity of the first poem. The difference seems consciously calculated to illuminate the gap between Audubon's idealism and the realities of the world. The time is winter, the "Shank-end of day." A "spit of snow" covers the ground. The cabin Audubon encounters is "a huddle of logs with no calculation or craft," "a wound rubbed raw in the vast pelt of the forest":

> Smoke,
> From the mud-and-stick chimney, in that air, greasily
> Brims, cannot lift, bellies the ridgepole, ravels
> White, thin, down the shakes, like sputum.

> (215)

Here lurks the humanity Audubon has come to the woods to escape. He knows precisely what to expect: "his nostrils already / Know the stench of that lair beyond / The door puncheons." Even the Indian's presence violates his expectations. Neither noble savage nor accomplished hunter, simply human being, the Indian has recently lost an eye to an arrow which "jounced back off his bowstring. / Durn fool—and him a Injun." Every detail of the scene seems calculated to disillusion, to foil any impulse to romanticize.

If Audubon expects to discover his ideal in the wilderness, the human presence in the cabin fulfills his worst nightmare, one which, Warren suggests, he recalls from early childhood. The woman at the door looms at his nightmare's center. He seems almost to recognize her, "What should he recognize? The nameless face / In the dream of some pre-dawn cock-crow—about to say what, / Do what?" (215). The woods hag is, we might imagine, the opposite of his wife Lucy, though later he feels attracted to her exactly as he might to Lucy. He may sense in her too the face of his mother, whom he has never seen, whom he searches for in every woman he meets. His loss of her, which he may interpret as abandonment, may be implied in his "dream of some pre-dawn cock-crow," a possible allusion to Peter's denial of Christ the night of his arrest in Gethsemane. Indeed, this woman too will betray Audubon, her guest, when she plots to rob and murder him. Yet in strange ways she compels him to feel guilt for having betrayed her, though why he should feel so remains unclear until the second poem's end. (Calvin Bedient calls his guilt Oedipal.[9]) Guilt of betrayal is one of Audubon's characteristic emotions, one the reader must often feel for him—his betrayal of Lucy, of his ideals, of the wilderness.

If Lucy is Audubon's ideal woman, the hag in the cabin is his reality. Warren insists on her ugliness, imbues her with depravity if not real evil, portrays her as a witch, the obverse of the ideal human form:

> The face, in the air, hangs. Large,
> Raw-hewn, strong-beaked, the haired mole
> Near the nose, to the left, and the left side by firelight
> Glazed red, the right in shadow, and under the tumble and tangle
> Of dark hair on that head, and under the coarse eyebrows,
> The eyes, dark, glint as from the unspecifiable
> Darkness of a cave. It is a woman.
>
> (216)

Once again, as with the heron in the first poem, Audubon seeks to identify and place the phenomenon he observes in the realm of the real world. Once again he seeks to identify the Ideal within the lineaments of the Real. But his discovery of the Real threatens to undermine the Ideal. It congeals the image before him and occupies the center of his consciousness. His recognition in the hag of the same womanhood he has known in Lucy, his ideal, disturbs and perplexes him. He is particularly disturbed by her transformation as she examines his gold watch. What other, unlived life does she imagine?

Hand reaches out. She wants it. She hangs it about her neck.

And near it the great hands hover delicately
As though it might fall, they quiver like moth-wings, her eyes
Are fixed downward, as though in shyness, on that gleam, and her face
Is sweet in an outrage of sweetness, so that
His gut twists cold. He cannot bear what he sees.

Her body sways like a willow in spring wind. Like a girl.

(216–17)

She is a profound contradiction: ugly, unkempt, essentially uncivilized, yet her rough form is the form of woman, the sublime ideal. Warren foreshadowed this opposition earlier by identifying the cabin's inhabitants as "The human filth, the human hope." At first Audubon cannot reconcile these opposites, their intellectual and emotional significance: "His gut twists cold. He cannot bear what he sees." He is attracted to, entranced by, the basest of forms. That attraction betrays the purity of his devotion to the woods, to his wife Lucy, to his art. It belies the unreality of the life he has sought to lead. Its importance becomes clear the next morning as the men who prevented her from killing him prepare to hang her and her sons. Again she entrances him, this time by her dispassionate acceptance of fate:

And in the gray light of morning, he sees her face. Under
The tumbled darkness of hair, the face
Is white. Out of that whiteness
The dark eyes stare at nothing, or at
The nothingness that the gray sky, like Time, is, for
There is no Time, and the face
Is, he suddenly sees, beautiful as stone, and

So becomes aware that he is in the manly state.

(220)

Audubon undergoes here the same process of perception he experienced as he watched the heron: the particular becomes the abstract, the Platonic ideal. The very nature of the woman's dying emphasizes her ideality. She achieves "a new dimension of beauty." Yet her beauty is like stone, cold and impenetrable, purchased at the cost of death, a beauty she could never have possessed in life.

The woman's beauty is also the allure of death, of mortality, an image of highly charged eroticism. She is a wilderness siren, a Circe who entices victims with her sexual attractions (to Audubon the attraction of death, the loss of self), then devours them. She possesses this death-dealing, sex-giving quality from her first appearance at the cabin door. Yet her embodiment of the ideal is also apparent from the first. Her physical imperfections camouflage the ideal, but they are proof of her human self, and fused with the ideal they attract Audubon. The night before, the contradictions she embodied perhaps accounted for his paralysis, his willingness to lie passively waiting for her spit-honed knife. Yet now for a moment, aroused sexually by the hanged woman who died so effortlessly, "without motion, frozen / In a rage of will, an ecstasy of iron, as though / This was the dream that, lifelong, she had dreamed toward," he achieves reconciliation and can enter into life, at least one version of the life he had sought to live.

Audubon's attraction to the woman has the equally important effect of rescuing him from his obsession with death. "The Dream He Never Knew the End Of" makes clear that his desire for merger with nature is a retreat from life. Nature for him is a series of frozen moments, a static rather than progressive and evolutionary process. He observes the woman's preparations to kill him with the same detachment with which he observes wildlife. What he sees seems to him only "the tale / They told him when he was a child . . . the dream he had in childhood but never / Knew the end of, only the scream" (218). This childhood nightmare suggests that he believes his fate to be predestined, beyond his control. It suggests that he searches in the woman's face for the image of his lost mother. The prospect of his death both entrances and paralyzes him:

> And he, too, knows
> What he must do, do soon, and therefore
> Does not understand why now a lassitude
> Sweetens his limbs, or why, even in this moment
> Of fear—or is it fear?—the saliva
> In his mouth tastes sweet.
>
> "Now, now!" the voice in his head cries out, but
> Everything seems far away, and small.

He cannot think what guilt unmans him, or
Why he should find the punishment so precious.

(218)

There is a curious though superficial similarity between Audubon's passive acceptance of what promises to be his death and the woman's stolid, aggressive acceptance of her execution. (In him, passivity is weakness; in her, will.) She refuses whiskey ("What fer?": she feels no need to numb herself). She refuses to pray, skeptical of God's existence and the world he made ("If'n it's God made folks, then who's to pray to?" / And then: "Or fer?"). When the moment arrives, she seizes it:

> The affair was not quick: both sons long jerking and farting, but she,
> From the first, without motion, frozen
> In a rage of will, an ecstasy of iron, as though
> This was the dream that, lifelong, she had dreamed toward.

(220)

Her death is an integral part of her life, an assertion of identity. It is her active engagement in this final moment that so provokes Audubon. Through her final expression of self she achieves what seems to him "a new dimension of beauty." It empowers him with a similar will to seize his own life, to pursue the existence he has wanted to live, to take aim at his own destiny, to squeeze the trigger (the metaphor for certainty of self in the fourth poem, "The Sign Whereby He Knew").

The woman approaches her death, as her life, with a fatalistic acceptance of what must be. Desire for her guest's gold watch made his murder seem worth the risk. She would have succeeded in her plot had intruders not interfered. When she is foiled, she receives the consequences without flinching. She is, quite simply, a living inhabitant of the living world which Audubon has sought to ignore. Still, he does not understand why she has moved him. His numerous unanswered questions make clear his confusion. He asks "What has been denied me?" and realizes "There is never an answer," that "The question is the only answer." That is, uncertainty of self, of destiny, of life's inexplicable imbalance, will likely plague him to the end of his days, but the search for self, for purpose, will provide him with meaning and significance.

"The Dream He Never Knew the End Of" closes with Audubon's return to the forest. We are left with images of falling snow and the crow which will soon arrive to scavenge the hanging corpses. Both are agents of time and decay, and their inevitability hastens Audubon's departure. He does not wish to observe the moment

> when snow thatches
> These heads with white, like wisdom, nor ever will he
> Hear the infinitesimal stridor of the frozen rope
> As wind shifts its burden, or when
>
> The weight of the crow first comes to rest on a rigid shoulder.
>
> (221)

Perhaps this moment would be too much to bear. It would provide the ultimate proof of mortality. Though he will not see decay begin, he can imagine and comprehend it well enough, for through his experience in the old woman's house, and through her death, he has discovered the truth of the world he inhabits. He enters into that world not prepared to abandon his dream of merger with nature but ready to pursue it by different means than before. If he cannot achieve his ideal, then at least he can envision it in his art.

In "The Dream He Never Knew the End Of" Audubon discovers his place in the world, his purpose in the wilderness. Liberated from his obsession with the source of his self, he can relish the prospect of what the self is to become: "We are only ourselves, and that promise. / Continue to walk in the world. Yes, love it!" (222). In one sense he has been defeated. He has discovered that the world in which he wishes to live does not exist. In a more important sense he is victorious: not only has he escaped death, but he has kept his vision intact. He confronts directly the reality of a world which contradicts and confounds vision, yet he senses in the contradiction a larger unity, a reconciliation of opposites which, rather than negating vision, sustains and propels it. Still, this reconciliation is anti-Emersonian. It allows for the existence of evil and death in the world, and it denies the possibility of transcendence beyond the physical realm.

The short third poem would seem vague and fragmentary if removed from the context of the poems surrounding it. Within that context, it serves as a bridge between the experience of "The Dream He Never Knew the End Of" and the rest of the cycle. It is another anti-Emersonian, anti-transcendental statement which reinforces the previous poem, suggesting both the limitations of human insight ("We never know what we have lost, or what we have found") and potential ("We are only ourselves, and that promise"). Audubon continues "to walk in the world" because it is his nature to do so, because he knows nothing else, because his passion endures all, circumscribed though it may be by the limitations of his human self and the natural world. Existence is its own reward, its own transcendence, and in the process of coming to be the self one is destined for, existence is its own source of joy ("Yes, love it!").

"The Sign Whereby He Knew," the fourth poem, contrasts Audubon's desire for transcendence against the dull realities of the life and responsibilities which inevitably hold him down. The poem opens by stating the compromise, the failure, which Audubon's life came to be, at least when measured by the ideals he hoped to attain:

> His life, at the end, seemed—even the anguish—simple
> Simple, at least, in that it had to be
> Simply, what it was, as he was,
> In the end, himself and not what
> He had known he ought to be.
>
> (223)

The fatality here is not that of failure but of human and mortal inevitability. Audubon's humanity doomed him to fail, to be less than what "He had known he ought to be." Yet still against such inevitable compromise there looms "The blessedness!," the hope and desire of living one's life precisely as one would live it, without compromise or qualification. Warren couches this ideal in a hunting metaphor:

> To wake in some dawn and see,
> As though down a rifle barrel, lined up
> Like sights, the self that was, the self that is, and there,
> Far off but in range, completing that alignment, your fate.
>
> (223)

Such surety, such total and complete control of destiny, is not possible. It "is not a dimension of Time"; it belongs to the unattainable. The ideal must remain forever beyond reach. In the world of the real the hunt for one's fate has always an uncertain outcome. It is never clear what quarry will lift "its noble head." Yet again the hunt itself, the quest for the unattainable, remains significant. The contrasts which make up the fourth poem illustrate the tensions between Audubon's life and his art, the compromises he was forced to make, yet which did not deter him from the pursuit of his ideal through the creation of art.

The poem's second section paradoxically illustrates these tensions by reflecting another image of harmony, one the human observer can perceive only obliquely. As in the first poem, "tension" suggests separation from nature:

> If you stare into the water you may know
>
> That nothing disturbs the infinite blue of the sky.
>
> (223)

The sky is the Infinite, at which Audubon can stare only indirectly. He can sense it in its reflected image on the water's surface, where sky is "reflected below in absolute clarity." The circular spring "surrounded by gold leaves" is an image of natural perfection and harmony. The "gloss / Of the surface tension" is disturbed by "Not even a skitter-bug." In the perception of such an image, Audubon glimpses for an instant a measure of the relationship with nature he once sought. But again there is no transcendence. He remains separate from the Infinite whose reflection he studies. The water's surface, its tension, is another impenetrable membrane.

The cost of such brief moments is separation from hearth and home, from human society. The times were ripe. Audubon could have succumbed easily to opportunity, the allure of house, wife, children, and social prominence. Warren bluntly lists the possibilities:

> Keep store, dandle babies, and at night nuzzle
> The hazelnut-shaped sweet tits of Lucy, and
> With the piratical mark-up of the frontier, get rich.
>
> (224)

Such opportunities are not to be taken lightly, nor are those men who succumb to them necessarily to be seen as failures. The social logic of the day ascribed Audubon's own failure to get rich to "weak character." He was simply a different run of man, dedicated to his "passion," embodied in the "great trumpeter swan" which rises at dusk from the pond's dark surface to "fight up the steep air where, / At the height of last light, it glimmered, like white flame" (224). This is clearly an image of the natural ideal, an image sufficiently powerful to separate him from his wife Lucy, however much he might love her. The final image of the section epitomizes his self-imposed isolation: "After sunset, / Alone, he played his flute in the forest" (224). This is, perhaps, the poem's strangest image. The flute produces music, a source of pleasure to player and hearer. It suggests the pipes of Pan, as if Audubon achieves in this moment some sort of pastoral ideal. Yet only he can hear the music he plays. The flute symbolizes his self-containment, his aloneness in nature, and his dedication to his life's purpose. Yet the image does not imply narcissism. Rather it suggests the purity of Audubon's passion and, by extension, the purity of Warren's admiration for it.

The two natural images in part D at first seem to clash with the social life of the previous section, though ultimately they strengthen it. The tusked boar itself has no specific meaning or significance beyond itself. We are simply invited to hear him "grumble in his ivy-slick" (224). The imperative, exclamatory "Listen!" conveys the excitement and emotional intensity of that moment's privilege, as if the experience itself is better known than described. The boar's grumble is followed by silence, interrupted by the call of the jay, "sudden as conscience," like the "thrill of the taste of—on the tongue—brass." Though the jay and boar are part of the natural harmony, they are also sources of dissonance. The boar is an omnivore, the jay a scavenger; they exist in a Darwinian environment of natural competition. They are elements of mortality and time, like the crow and the snow soon to fall on the hanging corpses in "The Dream He Never Knew the End Of." The jay's call is like the "taste of brass"—bitter, unexpected, false. It violates, perhaps, the harmony of Audubon's vision, which, wholly a product of imagination, nature cannot sustain. Part E returns to Audubon's joy in nature, tempering it with his (or the poet's) apparent frustration at being unable to communicate that joy in words. Such an expression would effectively penetrate the membrane, accomplishing the merger Audubon seeks. The inability of human language, of any medium, to convey this joy is a measure of nature's otherness, its separateness from the individual. Nature will not bear interpretation or discovery, instead calling attention to itself through such untranslatable phenomena as the boar and the jay:

> The world declares itself. That voice
> Is vaulted in—oh, arch on arch—redundancy of joy, its end
> Is its beginning, necessity
> Blooms like a rose.

> (224)

These lines are among the richest in the poem. They are a mystic apprehension of the natural process, of reproduction and evolution, that sustains the life force. The "world declares itself" with a "voice" characterized in the architectural metaphor of a Gothic cathedral, a place of worship. Yet Warren speaks of the natural cycles of reproduction and death in the wilderness where all things occur according to ubiquitous natural laws. "Redundancy of joy" suggests the reproductive cycles, with each generation of life a new cause for joy. The "end" is death, yet from the detritus of mortality new life grows. All happens as it should and must: "necessity / Blooms like a rose." This is religious exaltation, not of God but of nature and of natural processes. The truth found in nature cannot be described in words; it "can only be enacted, and that in dream, / Or in the dream become, as though unconsciously, action." Only in the woods can Audubon "know" or "enact" truth, and even then he can do so only in pursuit of an unattainable dream of harmony and merger which motivates his life of isolation and art, a life enacted, after all, according to the principles it seeks to embody, a life of action. Audubon's life thus becomes, for himself and in the poem as a whole, an expression of joy.

The fourth poem ends by stressing Audubon's profound aloneness in the world of men. Again we are reminded of his self-containment and happiness: "He walked in the world. He was sometimes seen to stand / In perfect stillness, when no leaf stirred." This pose is enigmatic. Is Audubon listening for the call of the bird he is tracking? Is he seeking imaginative fusion with the wild? The concluding appeal ("Tell us, dear God") implies that he awaits, like the rest of us, "the sign / Whereby we may know the time has come" (225). Is this Audubon's appeal, or Warren's? And what sign, and what time? The sign by which Audubon will know he has fulfilled his destiny? The moment of his death? The contrasts between the social and wilderness selves suggest he may await some sign that he can abandon his search, surrender, and return to society, which will be, for his life in the woods, death. As the opening lines of "The Sign Whereby He Knew" imply, this was the inevitable end of his life, which was "not what / He had known he ought to be," but was still the best he could manage. More likely, he awaits the moment when he will find his prey, his destiny, the moment which can never come, but in anticipation of which he must live his life.

In the three parts of "The Sound of That Wind," the fifth poem of the cycle, Warren intensifies his obsession, first attempting to convey an objectively historical image of Audubon, then appearing to abandon it entirely, returning to the perspective of the present time. This poem makes clear that it is not the historical Audubon who interests Warren so much as the figure which has come to exist in his imagination. The first section is the most clearly biographical section of the seven poems, reviewing Audubon's life from boyhood to death through brief anecdotes and journal citations. This factual Audubon at points contrasts with the figure in Warren's imagination. In fact, the documentary nature of this part of the poem seems the poet's overt effort to reconcile the imagined image with the actual man. The journal excerpts provide glimpses of Audubon's ambition and pride, but the central vision of the man never fades. The poem thus seems engaged in the same struggle between ideal and compromise that plagued the naturalist in his own life. Audubon himself ultimately succumbs to that struggle and enters "On honor" into the world of men ("into his earned house, / And slept in a bed, and with Lucy" [227]). The poet, through his poem, stubbornly resists.

The historical Audubon's failure seems only to strengthen the poet's belief in the Audubon of imagination. The journal excerpts reflect the poet's admiration for the historical man, whom his imagination continues to transform. Some of the entries concern Audubon's achievements as a naturalist; for example, "He proved that the buzzard does not scent its repast, but sights it. / He looked in the eye of the wounded white-headed eagle." Others reflect his respect for Audubon's resistance to the lures of domesticity, affluence, and power: Daniel Webster, one entry proudly notes, "would give me a fat place was I willing to have one; but I love indepenn and piece more than humbug and money" (227). Warren also makes clear Audubon's concern for the future of the wilderness: "The bellowing of buffalo" which is "like distant ocean" is contrasted with, superseded by, bones which "whiten the plain in the hot daylight." In the American Indian, Audubon "felt the splendor of God . . . for there I see the Man Naked from his / Hand and yet free from acquired sorrow." Both the buffalo and the Indian were threatened with extinction as the wilderness diminished. Warren associated the Rosseauistic optimism of this man who could so praise the Indian (oblivious to the miserable Indian of the second poem) with the fate of the wilderness in general, with an American dream that vanished with the wilderness. Though such biographical details allow Warren to understand the events of Audubon's life and character, they do not supplant the figure in his imagination. He finally abandons such details entirely. Ultimately, Audubon "enters in" and succumbs to the domestic pleasures and financial temptations he had so long resisted. But even in his submission Warren finds something to admire. Peddling his prints for *The Birds of North America:*

> Far, over the ocean, in the silken salons,
> With hair worn long like a hunter's, eyes shining,
> He whistled the bird-calls of his distant forest.
>
> Wrote: ". . . in my sleep I continually dream of birds."
>
> (227)

The purity of such vision is the purity which engenders art, yet the wildlife paintings, hardly mentioned throughout these poems, seem more the by-product of vision than its realization. Audubon's dream, his persistence in its pursuit, becomes the *lived* incarnation of art, whose strength and purity of purpose can affect those who come after it, those such as the poet. This is the second vision alluded to in the subtitle *A Vision:* the poem is as much concerned with the example of the man's life as with his view of the American wild (a view akin to that of Meriwether Lewis and Jefferson in *Brother to Dragons*).

This vision of the historical man carries us out of the years of Audubon into the present in part B and its emphasis on the natural forces of time and mortality, of universal infinitude, that inevitably limit human vision. "Night leaned," Warren writes, denoting time's passage, not merely the time of Audubon's mortal existence but also the time intervening between his day and our own. Night is death as well as darkness, that which separates the past from the present and which renders Audubon's vision unattainable. Time is an absolute, no part of our world, but possessing utter sway over it: "Grass does not bend beneath that enormous weight / That with no sound sweeps westward." In illustration, the poem evokes the "wreck of a great tree, left / By flood . . . the root-system and now-stubbed boughs / Lifting in darkness" (227). This is the metaphoric partner of the great tree from which the woman and her sons were hanged in the second poem. There the snow and the crow, agents of time, were soon to begin their work on the corpses. Here that work has been completed. Time has effaced the bodies and the tree and Audubon himself. The tree's up-turned roots are "white as bone" (the color of death and mortality, recalling the earlier image of the whitened buffalo bones). That whiteness is reflected in "dark water, and a star / Thereby." The transcendent image in the river extends the venue of time beyond the specific, the American continent and the poem itself, to the universal, the realm of the star. Yet the image works in reverse too, against transcendence. The whiteness of the roots is the same color of the star. The cosmic whiteness of fusing helium and hydrogen nuclei is the same whiteness of death. Death and time are principles not merely of the earth here below, but of the universe. In that sense, there is no transcendence. Death is the end of consciousness, otherwise merely one stage in an unending cycle. Audubon, the woman, the great tree, the star itself must ultimately pass away. Imaginatively the image evokes an Emersonian sense of unity and oneness. In meaning it is not Emersonian at all, but a coldly naturalistic image of apocalypse casting all into an immense void of cosmic forces where there is no meaning. Imagination must fashion meaning out of that void.

The next image reinforces the effect of the reflected star. The perspective is no longer that of the Mississippi but of a sheepherder's shack in the Bitterroot, "The candle is blown out. No other / Light is visible" (228). The perspective shifts again, and the snuffed candle's light is translated to the light of "The Northwest Orient plane, New York to Seattle . . . winking westward." The sense of isolation and aloneness is both spatial and temporal, the separation of death and life, of height, of distance, of time. The effect removes the reader from the immediate concern with Audubon's life and vision and from the more general concern with the continental wilderness to which he devoted himself. Four distinct perspectives are implied, that of Audubon (receding rapidly into the past), of the observer on the river bank, of the observer watching the light from the Bitterroot cabin and from the plane overhead, and, even, that of the passenger on the plane gazing down on the land beneath him (a perspective Warren used often, as in "Immortality Over the Dakotas" and "Caribou" from "Altitudes and Extensions" (1985), in the opening poem of "Homage to Emerson," in the final section of *Chief Joseph* and in *At Heaven's Gate*). The isolation which separates them becomes a unifying force. In the poet's mind the pattern of Audubon's life at the least establishes him as time's victim, at the most as an emblem of the American experience, its loneliness and its quest for assuaging identity. And as the concluding poem suggests, the poet feels himself time's victim, as much cut off from the age in which he writes as the now antiquated ideals of Audubon.

The meaning of the final series of images in part B is enforced in the opening of part C, from *Ecclesiastes:* "For everything there is a season." Yet Warren, moving away from the real toward the imagined, immediately qualifies and expands, "But there is the dream / Of a season past all seasons" (228), returning his attention again to Audubon's quest for his wilderness ideal. The ideal is epitomized a final time in the oxymoronic image of "the wild-grape cluster" which "High-hung, exposed in the gold light, / Unripening, ripens." A waiting lip moistens with anticipation of the grapes; it is "stained" because it has already eaten of the grapes once and awaits another taste. This then is an image of the impossible dream attained. Yet in the real world such a dream can exist only in imagination, and into that realm the poem has moved in section C. The final image, which does not directly concern Audubon at all, is probably the persona's memory of a loved woman: an image of timelessness in which the lip is "undrying" even in the "bright wind." That wind cannot be heard because it is the wind of time, which alters and levels all things, except in the imagination, where it has no force, where the ideal is immortal. In "American Portrait: Old Style," Warren calls imagination "The lie we must learn to live by, if ever / We mean to live at all" (*NSP,* 138). In "Delusion? — No!," it is the source of truth:

> Yes, stretch forth your arms like wings, and from your high stance,
> Hawk-eyed, ride forth upon the emptiness of air, survey
> Each regal contortion
> And tortuous imagination of rock, wind, water, and know
> Your own the power creating all.
>
> Delusion — No! For Truth has many moments.
>
> (*NSP,* 79)

In *Audubon,* imagination is the one force against which all else is powerless.

Section C seems almost digressive, with its personal allusiveness and the lover's "undrying" lips. Yet it expands and generalizes Audubon's dream. It is the dream every individual treasures, the dream which nurtures and sustains life and is the center of being. In rare instance, as in the case of the artist, it moves beyond the personal, as the sixth poem, "Love and Knowledge," illustrates.

The sixth poem returns briefly to Audubon, not to the man but his passion, which the poet shares. Warren makes clear that in his role as a painter of nature, Audubon became an authentic artist and symbol-maker, a shaper of national consciousness and imagination. The poem opens with a description of birds as Audubon perceives them in their ideal form. Like the heron in the first poem, they are presented as wholly nonhuman creatures completely at ease in nature:

> Their eyes are round, boldly convex, bright as a jewel,
> And merciless. They do not know
> Compassion, and if they did,
> We should not be worthy of it. They fly
> In air that glitters like fluent crystal
> And is hard as perfectly transparent iron, they cleave it
> With no effort.
>
> (229)

They exist in pure harmony with their environment. With their "merciless" eyes and lack of compassion, they embody nature. The ease with which they cleave the air is the state of being Audubon sought for himself. Yet their nonhumanity is what allows them the harmony Audubon covets. (They are like the channel catfish beneath the ice in *Brother to Dragons* or the "ungazing sheep" in "A Way to Love God.") They are oblivious to the painful exigencies of existence, of the iron-hard crystalline air. They are the Other, the Not-Me, even the Divine, the sublime Ideal which has been the object of Audubon's passion. They are another emblem of the "membrane" he never penetrates. Yet they do not exist at all. They are constructs of imagination, frozen and preserved, idealized beyond the real, transformed in Audubon's (and the poet's) imagining mind from a specific Particular into the Platonic thing itself. This is a précis of the process which occurs throughout the poem whereby Audubon the Historical Man is transformed into a symbol and icon not merely of an American obsession with the wild but of the very sustaining powers of Imagination itself.

It is Audubon's vision, his fidelity to vision, but, more, Warren's fidelity to the vision of the Audubon he has created for himself, that makes the painter so important to the poet. Unable to fashion his life after the vision of his imagination, he captured it in his study and paintings of birds, the private symbols of vision. He thus preserved the vision for those who came after him: "He put them where they are, and there we see them: / In our imagination." He helped define the American image of its relationship to nature and the wilderness. He also insured the enduring memory of his life, which stands today as a symbolic condensation of the American individual's idealized relationship with nature. Audubon's life in the wilderness, devoted to the study and painting of wildlife, stands in the national

consciousness as a symbolic remnant of the Edenic land that, in the imagined historical, national memory, greeted the early settlers. With that wild
land's disappearance, his life and work are reminders of the national failure
to honor the obligations which settling it once imposed.

That Audubon killed the birds he loved in order to study them may at
first seem surprising and paradoxical. Warren purposefully inserts this information after the description of the "merciless" birds to shock the reader
into recognizing the real nature of Audubon's love. His killing of the birds
is another means of rendering the specific into the universal. In his lifetime
hunting and killing wildlife bore no negative connotations. Hunting was a
means of securing food, of enjoying and appreciating the wilderness, certainly no threat to its survival (though it ultimately became a threat). Audubon's marksmanship ("He slew them, at surprising distances") is proof
of his hunting prowess. Yet the poem emphasizes that he slays the birds
to study them, to spread knowledge of them in the world. Killing is thus
a creative gesture, the knowledge thereby attained even providing for the
preservation of wilderness by heightening public awareness. For love of
the birds ("What is love?" Warren asks; "One name for it is knowledge"
[229]), he kills them in order to paint them accurately, to preserve them as
he imagines them, to "put them where they are, and there we see them: /
In our imagination." For Audubon, shooting the creatures to which he has
devoted his life is a means of fulfilling his destiny, a physical enactment of
the metaphor of the fourth poem, "lined up / Like sights, the self that was,
the self that is, and there, / Far off but in range, completing that alignment,
your fate" (223).

Audubon: A Vision thus presents Audubon not merely as one representation of the American experience with nature but as a paragon to be venerated
for his aspiration to a mode of belief and ideal so pure as to lie beyond
mortal human reach. The American distinctiveness of Audubon, according to Helen Vendler, extends as well to the contradictions he embodies:
"He is a hero peculiarly acceptable to the American mind. . . . Audubon,
who blended art and science, the natural and the cerebral, the tender and
the violent, without any consciousness of unease, appears irresistibly as
a model." [10] Partially because of these contradictions, Audubon is also a
symbol of crucial personal importance to Warren.

The concluding poem contrasts the promise of the past with the despair
and need of the present day. It implicitly presents Audubon's life as a model
worth emulation—a life well lived and the embodiment of a philosophi-

cal attitude which insures personal satisfaction and purpose. Warren here emerges clearly as the persona, ready to establish and define a particular attitude towards his subject, which the preceding poems have already implied. In fact, the final poem implies that Warren's persona has been active throughout the cycle. The poet finds his subject significant not merely for his attitudes towards the American wilderness or for the character of his life but for specifically personal reasons. Audubon is Warren's own token. Oddly, he is never mentioned in the final poem. Instead, Warren calls for a story of "great distances, and starlight," of "deep delight" (230), a reference to the life Audubon led, the implication being that whatever its failures, it was a life of significance and purpose, dedicated to worthy ideals, a life of real importance to "this century, and moment, of mania."

Why must Warren look for such a story in "this moment"? Perhaps certain current events of the 1960s have disheartened him, convinced him that his own time can offer no source of wonder to provoke and enlarge the imagination.[11] The publication date of 1969 has specific pertinence, for 1968 was among the most tumultuous years in American history. Civil rights and anti-war demonstrations, some of them violent, were proliferating. Two national leaders were assassinated. A political convention was disrupted by riotous police and demonstrators. An unpopular war on the other side of the world caused grave discord at home. The very fabric of the nation seemed ready to tear. Perhaps more than ever before, the nation seemed to have despaired of its founding ideals. Or perhaps the despair in this poem belongs merely to the poet. Warren expressed similar feelings in other poems. The "Internal Injuries" poems of *Incarnations* (1968) indict the urban America of the 1960s, while "Interjection # 4: Bad Year, Bad War: A New Year's Card, 1969" (in *Or Else*) despairs over the Vietnam war, though Warren views it as no worse than any other war, ironically praying "To be restored to that purity of heart / That sanctifies the shedding of blood" (*SP,* 43). Clearly, the optimism for the nation's future expressed in such earlier works as *Who Speaks for the Negro?* has been notably tempered. The poem thus may serve as an invocation to the past, a calling up of meaning and significance, a reminder of a time when the validity of belief and ideals was never questioned.

To rise above the turmoil of the present day, the poet returns in the first section of the seventh poem to his own youth. He recalls standing in the Kentucky twilight by a dirt road and being moved by the honking of geese migrating north overhead. The contrast with the image of the plane "winking westward" in the fifth poem, along with the fact he is recollecting a childhood memory, emphasizes the gap between past and present and the nature of something that has been lost, inherent in the difference between invisible geese honking in the night sky and the distant winking lights of a transcontinental jet. The geese provoke inchoate longing: "I did not know what was happening in my heart." In this sense the boy stands parallel to Audubon, who was also moved by the flight of birds and who spent much of his life trying to understand what they signified. The boy's idealistic yearnings are like Audubon's, like the nation's in the first half of the nineteenth century, when Audubon lived.

Especially within the context of the preceding six poems, "Tell Me a Story" suggests the disillusionment of the persona and, more generally, of the nation. But there are ways to combat disillusionment and the cynicism which may follow it. Audubon's life has been presented as an example of disillusionment successfully parried. Thus, in part B the poet calls for a story "of deep delight" so as to imply his need for the meaning and inspiration which the present day denies him. The childhood refrain "Tell me a story" expresses his desire to regain the innocence and ideals of boyhood, the wonder with which he once looked forward to the adventure of the life before him.

The most abstruse and disturbing lines of the seventh poem concern the nature of the story the poet asks be told him: "The name of the story will be Time, / But you must not pronounce its name" (230). Presumably, the story's "name" is "Time" because it is rooted in the past, to which the poet cannot return except imaginatively and through the legacies of those who lived in the past. The story's value lies in its pastness, in its embodiment of meanings and values unavailable to the present. Yet it is a story of Time, whose name cannot be pronounced. Audubon's life in the seventh poem becomes a representation of the ideal, which Audubon pursued in his life and to which Warren turns for meaning and inspiration. In seeking to recover that life, the poet longs for that which is beyond reach. The past thus becomes the ideal, to which those in the present can turn for meaning, inspiration, and the roots of identity. Why must Time's name not be pronounced? The ideal of the past, of the envisioned Audubon, exists in a timeless realm. To pronounce Time's name is to make it real, to submit it to the forces of logic and the world, to demystify and overthrow it, yet at the same time to recognize it as insuperable. Time itself is an unbridgeable gap of years and mortality between past and present, while in fact what the poem proposes is an utter continuity between past and present, especially through the poet's appropriation of the example of Audubon for his own life and time. To pronounce Time's name would be to create a barrier which even imaginative vision could not surmount. Warren's main focus throughout these poems has been Audubon and his life, not the abstract forces to which that life finally succumbed. Warren wishes to remind us, to remind himself, that it is Audubon's vision of nature which bears importance, not the physical life itself, which Time extinguished. In that pure intensity of vision the poet wants to participate, vicariously, by the listening to and the telling of the story, not merely for relief from modern angst but as a means of celebrating and invoking the poetic and artistic processes in Audubon's life and career, which in various ways he finds parallel with his own.[12]

The third poem in *Audubon: A Vision,* "We Are Only Ourselves" introduces a notion similar to the Wordsworthian concept of preexistence: knowledge once possessed in innocence but lost in the process of growth and maturation, to be regained through meditation and closeness to nature. At points in the second poem, Audubon seemed on the verge of a recognition and remembering through which he could bridge his separateness from nature and the human world. In the larger context of American history the poem as a whole concerns the gap between past and present, innocence and experience, ideal and compromise. Through Audubon's desire to regain that harmonious relation to nature which Wordsworth says the individual loses as he grows away from childhood, Warren expresses his own desire for a restoration of the idealism, principles, and innocence which he associates with the early days of the Republic. Just as Audubon seeks in the woods to regain the lost harmony of preexistence and, failing that, to portray it in his work, so does Warren treat these same matters in his poem which mourns the loss of ideals, the failure of vision and wilderness stewardship, and which preserves those qualities in the artist whose life it extols.

From a Freudian perspective this wish to regain innocence and ideals is a desire for return to the primal womb. From a Christian perspective it is a desire for Eden. From the historical perspective it signifies a desire to regain the wilderness in its pristine state. In the first seventy years of the nation's existence, the American frontier receded from the western edges of New York and Georgia to California. Even early in the nineteenth century, when he began his wanderings, Audubon must have realized what this expansion portended (the buffalo bones which "whiten the plain in the hot daylight" suggest as much). Why did this expansion occur? Economic, demographic, and political explanations aside, the nation's westward movement reflected a desire by settlers and frontiersmen to escape civilization and lose themselves in the New Eden, a desire doomed from its very conception, for they spoiled Eden by their very arrival, as the old woman of the second poem so vividly shows. In fact, the second poem can effectively be seen as a parable of the wilderness's doom. (She willingly exploits all comers to her cabin, the new arrivals to the wilderness like Audubon as well as the men who lived there to begin with, like the wounded Indian. She embodies human amorality and rapacity and is thus a symbolic representative of the white settlers who invade the American wilderness and slowly, inexorably destroy it.) This knowledge of what has transpired in America since Audubon's death, of wilderness desecration, must have been a central stimulus to the poet's imaginative appreciation of Audubon, as it was with his treatment of Meriwether Lewis in *Brother to Dragons,* as it would be later in his poetic tribute to Chief Joseph of the Nez Perce.

In "Homage to Emerson," written a few years earlier than *Audubon: A Vision,* Warren can hardly muster even begrudging esteem for America's most famous idealist.[13] The seven poems of this cycle are narrated from the perspective of an airliner 38,000 feet above the earth, where "Emerson / Is dead right" (*SP,* 153). Only in this position of spatial estrangement from solid earth can Warren for a moment admire Emerson, and even then admiration is tinged with contempt. Against what Warren regards as Emerson's facile optimism loom images of a corrupt and hollow modern America, of human fear and blindness. A city passing beneath the plane resembles the still burning lights of a Christmas tree flattened by a steam roller. From the end of a Coney Island pier "The empty darkness howled like a dog . . . The sea secretly sucking the piles of the pier with a sound like / An old woman sucking her teeth in the dark before she sleeps" (157). All of America is emptiness:

> The wind comes off the Sound, smelling
> Of ice. It smells
> Of fish and burned gasoline. A sheet
> Of newspaper drives in the wind across
> The great distance of cement that bleeds
> Off into blackness beyond the red flares.
>
> (157)

More disturbing than this external emptiness is the emptiness of the human soul. Images of emptiness occur throughout the poem. The poet's heart "Is as abstract as an empty / Coca-Cola bottle" (153). God is not a spider but "a funnel, and you / The clear liquid being poured down it, forever. / . . . You do not know what is beyond the little end of the funnel" (154–55). A crying baby and a ringing telephone become nightmarish tokens of meaninglessness. When the plane dips perceptibly, a man sitting next to the poet intones not a prayer but multiplication tables. Emerson's nineteenth-century hopes for the great American nation, his faith in human virtue and potential, seem wholly fatuous in this context. Only in the final poem, "Does the Wild Rose?," can Warren struggle towards some sense of hope, some affirmation of the old Emersonian ebullience, but his questions ("*Does the wild rose know your secret / As the summer silence breathes?* . . . Do you think you could tell me / What constitutes the human bond?" [158]) go unanswered, his struggle unrewarded.

Why should Audubon earn such admiration from Warren, and Emerson such scorn? Part of the answer may lie in the fact that Audubon was a practitioner, an artist and scientist who went out into the wilderness in pursuit of his ideals. He founded his optimism in a knowledge of nature to which he gave eloquent expression in his art. He also did not entreat others to follow him. Emerson was a theorist and exhorter, a leader of the Higher Law movement whose dangers Warren laments throughout his career, from *John Brown: The Making of a Martyr* to *The Legacy of the Civil War*. Audubon led no one, sought isolation, and fits exactly Warren's conception of the artist/hero.

In the final poem of *Audubon: A Vision* the poet wishes for "a story of deep delight" as consolation for "this century, and this moment, of mania." *Incarnations,* published one year earlier, explores in detail the contemporary urban life which to the poet seems a fundamental sign (and symptom) of what has gone wrong in America since Audubon's time.[14] The book consists of three related groups of poems. The first and third are set in Europe, the second in America. Its title, "Internal Injuries," signifies the poet's attitude towards contemporary America. These are very much poems of the late 1960s. They express deep concern with the social injustices and inequities which were the object of that decade's activism. They focus as well on two citizens especially victimized by these conditions. Both have been displaced. One is a rural poor white. The other is a Southern black woman. They are given to us here as citizens of the modern world, the un-sheltered victims of contemporary life. In this sense they are representative modern individuals. Dehumanization and depersonalization, key words in Warren's lexicon, are the symptoms of contemporary life illustrated here, along with the gnawing sense of doom evident in the opening poem, "Keep That Morphine Moving, Cap," about a prisoner dying of cancer. The domi-nant images throughout are drawn from the contemporary, technological world: highways, automobiles, construction workers, and airplanes which "prowl" the sky above the city.

The "Internal Injuries" poems are frenetic and intense, often emotionally searing. Their language is earthy and vernacular, sometimes sensational-istic, couched often in the slang of the people they describe. In tone they verge on melodrama. "Keep That Morphine Moving, Cap" exploits the tra-ditional folk-song motif of a condemned man awaiting execution. The final stanza establishes the man, whose name is Jake, as an archetypal figure whose fate approximates the ultimate destiny of us all:

> Listen to that
> Small sound, and let us, too, keep pulling
> For him, like we all ought to, who,
> When truth at last is true, must try,
> Like him, to tough it through.
>
> (32)

What Jake must "tough through" is the death he is condemned to by the cancerous mortality within him ("deep inside, / Inside his gut, inside his gut, / The pumpkin grows and grows"). There is little consolation for him. He simply must endure his lot, which he accepts stoically enough: "Just keep that morphine moving, Cap," he promises. "And me, I'll tough it through" (31). In the penitentiary, denied the basic decency of privacy, he sits on the toilet in the only position which can relieve his pain:

> and only
> In such a posture humped, can he
> Hold tight his gut, and half believe,
> Like you or me, like you or me,
> That the truth will not be true.
>
> (32)

The dripping of his sweat to the floor ("each drop, on the gray cement / Explodes like a star") is the passage of time, ticking away as he waits to die. Morphine serves him not merely as a painkiller but as a shield against reality, a substitute for the religion or the community of friends and family which in an earlier day might have given him solace and support. Warren thus sees contemporary existence as reduced to the ultimate fate, pain and death: oblivion.

The modern world's true character comes clear when the poet moves beyond the penitentiary in "Night: In the Motel Down the Road from the Pen" and "Where They Come to Wait for the Body: A Ghost Story." Outside the pen we briefly encounter the longed-for components of nature so important in *Audubon:* the night, the stars, and the river flowing near the hotel. But these offer no relief for Jake's suffering. Instead nature is here a polluted and soiled victim of the modern age:

> the dead catfish slides
> All night glimmering down the river
> That is black and glossy as
> Old oil bleeding soundlessly
> From the crank-case.
>
> (36)

The motel is a symbol of mobile, transient American society. Jake appears there again, this time as the dead prisoner's ghost, waiting to be taken home. But the place he called home no longer exists:

> his eyes stare moody
> Down a road all different from the last time he passed,
> And the new slab whirls at him white now and steady,
>
> And what he might recognize snaps by so fast
> That hill and stream and field all blur
> To a misty glitter . . .
>
> (38)

As a ghost of the past, Jake contrasts with the frenetic rootlessness of the present. He represents a time when "home" had specific geographical meaning and was associated with a set of values now lost. Through Jake the poet is reminded of his own separation from the past and his uncertain place in the contemporary world:

> And me, I'm gone too, as I flog the U-Drive-It
> Toward Nashville, where faces of friends, some dead, gleam,
> And where, when the time comes, you grab the jet.
>
> (38)

In no literal sense can one flog a rented truck, nor "grab" a jet, yet these are the catch phrases of contemporary life, distorted echoes of an earlier way of life and transportation. Only rarely do we glimpse that former world, beyond the confines of the Southern city with its expressways and penitentiaries, its "Old orange peel and condoms and / That dead catfish, belly white" (42). There is this brief image: "Far off, a red tractor is crossing the black field. / Iron crushes the last dawn-tangle of ground mist." But the joy of this image is quickly subsumed by the pain of the woman in "The Event."

"The Event" and the seven subsequent poems form the thematic center of *Incarnations*. In them Warren provides his final tableau of modern urban existence. An old black woman has been run over by a truck and lies apparently dying in the street. She is thus like Jake, facing death. Bad luck, her own identity, and the city where she lives have condemned her to a lonely, painful death. Her death in fact is not a death at all. It is merely an "event." Yet it holds the key to all things. These eight poems form a disjunctive, disconnected, unified sequence of perspectives, each focused on a slightly different aspect of her situation, gradually moving towards an epiphanal realization which the persona (hidden behind a taxi window nearby) seeks to avoid. A slowly mounting tension builds towards hysteria. The injured woman is the unluckiest of the unlucky: she is black, old, female, and alone ("your daughter off in / Detroit, in three years no letter, your son / Upriver, at least now you know / Where he is, and no friends" [43]). Moreover, she has just been fired from her job. It is, as the poet addresses the woman, "enough to be / Yourself . . .":

> enough to be
>
>> Merely to be—Jesus,
>> Wouldn't just *being* be enough without
>> Having to have the pee (quite
>> Literally) knocked out of
>> You by a 1957 yellow Cadillac driven by
>> A spic, and him
>> From New Jersey?
>
>>>> (43–44)

Like Jake, she faces death without family or community. She is the ultimate social outcast, the prime urban *misérable*. She belongs to and possesses nothing. She is by the modern world, by displacement from family and home and ultimately from life, wholly dehumanized.

Her scream is the prime expression of modern horror. It is "as regular as a metronome" (45). The poet, sitting in the taxi, attempts studied indifference towards her. He can cope with what she signifies only by ignoring her, pretending she isn't there. He attempts quite literally to make her a dehumanized *thing* which he need not pity:

> there
> Must be some sort of clockwork
> Inside you to account for such
> Perfection, perhaps you have always
> And altogether been clockwork, but
> Not realizing its perfection, I
> Had thought you merely human.
>
> (45)

The noise of her suffering melds with the horrific uproar of the city. In this way she is blotted out completely:

> Pneumatic hammers
> Are at work somewhere. In the period
> Of non-scream, they seem merely a part of the silence.

Her suffering is just another street scene, to be marveled at like a bulldozer at a construction site. The poet observes the sidewalk superintendents who "stare" at the woman and then includes himself among them, "with my / Own face pressed directly to the / Window of your pain to peer / Deep in your inward darkness" (46). The city becomes then a predatory beast, the woman's hat "right under a truck wheel" and the "jet prowling the sky" (47). Her suffering envelops the city, becomes its emblem in this Magritte-like image:

> The scream floats up, and up, like a
> Soap bubble, it is enormous, it glitters
> Above the city, it is as big as the city,
> And on its bottom side all the city is
> Accurately reflected, making allowance
> For curvature, upside-down, iridescent as
> A dream, oh pale!
>
> (48)

These are Baudelairean poems of city as nightmare, filled with predatory machines and indifferent, vaguely human forms, a place of annihilation which reduces the human essence to a statistic in the city bureau of records, "a piece of white paper filed for eternity on the sharp point of a filing spindle" (50). The woman is virtually stripped of identity, of any human context. Only the oxymoronic image of "The orange-colored helmets of the construction workers," which "bloom brilliant as zinnias," reminds us of her origins:

> When you were a child in Georgia, a lard-can of zinnias
> bloomed by the little cabin door.
> Your mother had planted them in the lard-can. People
> call zinnias nigger-flowers.
>
> (50)

But this brief identifying image is negated once more by the "white paper filed in the dark on the point of a black-enameled spindle forever" (50). And above this horror, the jet continues to prowl "the edge of distance like the raw edge of experience." The jet has replaced the vulture. It is a carrion bird, and the poet knows that "It must be hunting for something." It is a mechanical, soulless substitute for the hawk which presides elsewhere in Warren's vision of nature, as in "Evening Hawk" and "Red-Tail Hawk and Pyre of Youth." It is a source of menace and alienation, of the scene's removal from anything remotely familiar and human. The poet's rural Southern origins make him doubly aware of the old woman's displacement in the city and of his own displacement as well.

All of this brings the poet to recognize that "The world / Is a parable and we are / The meaning," yet he fears that "Nothing is real, for only / Nothingness is real and is / A sea of light" (52). Finally, he wonders whether the construction workers standing over the woman

> know the message, know the secret names and all the
> slithery functions of
>
> All those fat slick slimy things that
> Are so like a tub full of those things you
> Would find in a vat in the back room of a butcher shop, but
> wouldn't eat.
>
> (53–54)

He is reduced then to the possibility that, if the meaning of life resides in the human being, and the human being is nothing but a tub of guts, life simply has no meaning. "Driver," he asks the man at his taxi's wheel, "there's an awful glitter in the air. What is the weather forecast?" (54). This concluding question is both hideously inhumane to the woman now (who can be ignored, since she is no longer in view) and apocalyptically appropriate. For this scene may prefigure the world's end, the collapse of civilization, the ultimate loss of community and dehumanization, the final extinction of the human species as a cultural entity. This is Warren's despairing view of urban America in the late 1960s. The great momentum of life and history runs out in this apocalypse on a city street, the final reductio ad absurdum of the human self, a tub of guts smeared across the asphalt.

In *Audubon: A Vision* Warren averts his eyes to the past and its mythic figures. In *Incarnations* the uplifting humanism of Jefferson, Audubon's visionary exaltation of the wilds, Emerson's hope for the common man and the new democracy   all of these have come to naught. The bloody and inhumane spectacle of the Northern city street is too much to bear. The present day offers no hope or inspiration. Although for the rest of his career Warren continues to address the present—in *Democracy and Poetry* and *A Place to Come To* and numerous poems—the events which provoke and move him belong increasingly to the past: his own private past or that of the American nation. His final great long poem *Chief Joseph of the Nez Perce* and the poetry of *Or Else, Now and Then, Being Here, Rumor Verified,* and "Altitudes and Extensions" (in the final *Selected Poems*) are fortunate products of this preoccupation.

CHAPTER 4

Recovering the Past:

Chief Joseph of the

Nez Perce

In the poem "Going West," from *Rumor Verified,* Warren describes a drive towards the American West. As he moves from the prairie into the dry range country, the details of the land he is passing through grow increasingly less distinct: "Blur of burnt goldness / Past eye-edge on each / Side back-whirling, you arrow / Into the heart of hypnosis." He adds, a third of the way through the poem, "This is one way to write the history of America." What does he mean? The farther west he moves, the less real, the more illusory the world seems. The land becomes an abstract, mystical vision, and ultimately he expects it to offer up not mountains but prophecy:

> Now do I see the first blue shadow of foothills?
> Or is that a cloud-line?
> When will snow, like a vision, lift there?
>
> *(NSP,* 93)

Travel west is movement towards unreality. It is in this sense the pursuit of a dream, an unattainable ideal. It is thus a metaphor for American history, as it was for Willie Proudfit in *Night Rider,* Jack Burden in *All the King's Men,* Jeremiah Beaumont in *World Enough and Time,* and Meriwether Lewis in *Brother to Dragons.* As these works show, the dream can be blinding and dangerous. This is indeed the case in "Going West," where the metaphor becomes more than a mere pattern of action when the car strikes a pheasant:

The bloody explosion, right in my face,
On the windshield, the sun and
The whole land forward, forever,
All washed in blood, in feathers, in gut-scrawl.

(93)

Later, the windshield cleaned off with "Clumps of old grass, old newspaper, dry dirt" (94) and water from a gas station, the car again moves
westward, but the encounter has transformed the landscape, "red sunset
now reddening to blood streaks." Finally the poet gives us to know that
the experience recounted is a memory of some long-ago experience still
lingering in his mind, "Even now, long afterwards, the dream." The final
three lines explain the dream's persistence:

I have seen blood explode, blotting out sun, blotting
Out land, white ribbon of road, the imagined
Vision of snowcaps, white in their purity.

(94)

It is the dream of the American West this poem is about, and the idealistic
zeal it fostered in the nineteenth-century imagination. It is a dream which
lulls one into narcosis and moral carelessness, a dream which illuminates the
stark contrasts between the ideals and the realities which propelled American history. "It's the bloody story of the West," Warren said of the poem in
a 1984 interview. "The poem is really about the bloody history of the conquest of the West. It's not a charming romance. One of the most murderous
stories we can think of." [1] That is, the ideals and dreams which motivated
the opening of the West were so powerful that they blinded frontiersmen
and settlers to the brutal treatment suffered by the American Indian, to
"blood" and "feathers" and "gut-scrawl."

The encounter with the pheasant becomes for Warren an inescapable
image of American westering. He attempts to efface it from memory by
washing the blood from his windshield. Yet even then he cannot forget it: it
has the power of a dream, of nightmare. So he must confront it, accept it as
part of his being and reality by preserving it in a poem. In a broader, more
encompassing sense, that of a national rather than merely personal perspective, he engages in the same process in *Chief Joseph of the Nez Perce*,
his last great narrative poem. Warren in fact noted this similarity himself.[2]
Though he mourned the devastation of American wildlife and wilderness in
such works as *Night Rider* and *Brother to Dragons, Chief Joseph* provides

his most eloquent and scornful account of the settlement of the West. The fate of the Indian, like slavery, belies the egalitarian vision of the Declaration, and in the experience of the Nez Perce tribe during the summer of 1877 and later, Warren identifies that vision's most profound betrayal.

Throughout his career, Warren assumed the traditional though nonetheless sound attitude that knowledge of history, of the past, provides a crucial way of understanding the present and preparing for the future. In his view, however, the American popular memory and imagination often distort and trivialize the substance, thus the truth, of historical events. This happens, he argued, because Americans wish to think themselves a virtuous, even anointed people, free from blemish. He told journalist Bill Moyers in 1976,

> We've got to quit lying to ourselves all the time. Now, the Civil War was the biggest lie any nation ever told itself. It freed the slaves. Then what did it do with them? And the big lie was told, and also, we're full of virtue, we did it, we freed the slaves and it came home to roost a hundred years later. But we lie to ourselves all the time. The lying about Vietnam was appalling. . . . Now, there's the lying about our dealing with Mexico from the very start.[3]

The result is a peculiar blindness to the American capacity for corruption. It prevents not only a proper understanding of the past but fosters as well the potential for serious blunders in the present. Just such a blindness, Warren shows in *Brother to Dragons, The Legacy of the Civil War, Who Speaks for the Negro?*, and *Democracy and Poetry,* led to the nation's abandonment of the freed slaves in 1877, the victimization of the American Indian, and a number of other iniquities as well.

Though the Indian plays a minor role in a number of Warren's works, in the long narrative poem *Chief Joseph of the Nez Perce* (1983) he becomes the central subject: a victim and symbol of the nation's expansion westward. *Chief Joseph* is an eloquent poem of considerable importance to Warren's lifelong concern with American history. Only in *Audubon: A Vision* did he more artfully link the disparate elements of nineteenth-century America—the frontier, the opening of the West, the gradual corruption of the ideals of the founders—to the present state of affairs and the modern individual's need to discover and be reconciled to the national past. It is in this sense that James Justus calls the poem a "quietly understated epic" incorporating "the poet's historical re-imagination in the service of a national conscience."[4] *Chief Joseph* can thus be seen as part of the new historicist movement in American literary criticism and history, which early in the 1970s began to focus on writers and events previously unattended to by traditional scholarship. In fact, in *American Literature: The Makers and the Making,* the massive anthology he coedited with Cleanth Brooks and R. W. B. Lewis, Warren had already moved in this direction by including significant selections of literature by American blacks and Indians. While the new American historicism is primarily radical in ideology, Warren's orientation is traditional and conservative, but he arrives in the poem at many of the same conclusions.

Chief Joseph centers on the Nez Perce War in the summer of 1877. The conflict began when the federal government, violating several of its own treaties, ordered a band of less than one hundred Nez Perce, led by Chief Joseph, to move from their native grounds in Wallowa, in northwestern Oregon, to a reservation in Idaho. Attempting to obey, the Indians were attacked by federal soldiers, who wrongly believed them responsible for an attack on nearby settlers.[5] (The violence was committed by a few young Indians from another Nez Perce band, against the orders of their chiefs. Some twenty whites were murdered, a number of women raped, and several farms burned.[6]) For the next three months, the Nez Perce successfully engaged government troops in numerous skirmishes. But their defeat was inevitable. In the prefatory note to the poem, Warren describes the end: "On September 5, 1877, Joseph surrendered to Colonel [Nelson H.] Miles, in eastern Montana. The terms given by Miles were generous, but these were murderously broken by [William Tecumseh] Sherman, now Commanding General of the U.S. Army. Chief Joseph's life now became a constant struggle for the observation of the terms of Miles, but only after many years and many deaths were his people returned to the high country of the Northwest—though not to Wallowa" (xii). The Nez Perce were interned at Fort Leavenworth, where twenty-one of them died from malaria and other diseases by July of the next summer, when they were moved to a reservation in Kansas. By October 1878, forty-seven more were dead, including all six of Joseph's children. One observer commented that the choice of Leavenworth as an internment camp seemed to be "for the express purpose of putting an end to Chief Joseph and his band."[7] Most accounts agree that the Nez Perce war was among the bleakest of episodes in the American government's long and unhappy relationship with the Indian.

As a historical commentary on this event, *Chief Joseph* serves a threefold purpose: it places the Nez Perce war in the larger context of post–Civil War materialism, corrects the historical record (and adjusts the American self-image accordingly), and suggests that the forces which led to the war remain evident in America today. As poetry, *Chief Joseph* is Warren's sustained meditation on time and mortality, the inevitability of history, and the value of human integrity in the face of overwhelming odds.

The poem's opening epigraphs reflect the conflicting perspectives of idealism and pragmatism which order Warren's vision of American history. Thomas Jefferson's hope that white Americans would "live with [the Indians] as one people, and . . . cherish their interests as our own" (ix) seems naive in light of what transpired in the nineteenth century. In contrast to General Sherman's observation that "the more [Indians] we can kill this year, the less will have to be killed the next year, for the more I see of these Indians, the more convinced I am that they will all have to be killed or be maintained as a species of paupers" (ix), it seems even foolish. A fundamental theme in Warren's treatment of American history is the annihilation of Jeffersonian idealism by the greed of those more concerned with economic gain than the forging of a democratic nation. The Jeffersonian ideal underlies the poem as a pledge of harmony and good will, broken by Sherman and his subordinates in their pursuit of the Nez Perce people. (Though as president Jefferson himself was not blameless: he took steps to initiate the relocation of the Indians in the Southeast, and his purchase of the Louisiana Territory set the stage for conflict with the Indians of the West.) By extension, Warren represents through the Nez Perce the federal government's mistreatment of the Indian in general and its failure to honor the ideals of the founders. He means there to be no coincidence in the fact that the Nez Perce war occurred in the same year as the Hayes-Tilden Compromise, another betrayal by the federal government which effectively ended Reconstruction and erased most of the gains made by American blacks since the end of the Civil War.

Chief Joseph explores and seeks to preserve a significant dimension of American history and tradition. Underlying the poem is the premise that the Indian heritage is slipping quickly from our national memory, primarily because it does not belong to the white Anglo-Saxon ancestry traditionally perceived as the central component of the nation's ethnic heritage. Warren seeks to remind his mostly white, Anglo-Saxon readers that such a reason does not justify committing to oblivion an essential and representative episode of American history. Indeed, that memory's preservation becomes all the more important. It concerns, in general, the matter of the American Indian; in specific, the matter of Chief Joseph and his tribe. The third introductory epigraph to the poem, spoken by a Duwamish chief, announces the Indian's unseen presence in the American tradition:

> When the last Red Man shall have perished, and the memory of my tribe shall have become a myth among the white men, these shores will swarm with the invisible dead of my tribe, and when your children's children think themselves alone in the field, the store, the shop, upon the highway, or in the silence of the pathless woods, they will not be alone . . . At night when the streets of your cities are silent and you think them deserted, they will throng with the returning hosts that [once] filled them and still love this beautiful land. The White Man will never be alone. (ix)

Warren turns to the Nez Perce not as their defender, nor as an apologist for the white Americans. He does not condemn the expansion which drove the Indians from their lands—"There is only / Process," states the poem, "which is one name for history" (63). Such expansionism in his view is an inescapable consequence of history; at least it has been so for several thousand years. Economic cannibalism, militaristic imperialism, and cultural racism are only a few of the guises under which it has occurred. These are other names for history, morally opprobrious names to which the Nez Perce fall victim. Though Warren does not mention these names, he nonetheless means to illustrate them. What the poem attacks, then, is one aspect of American expansionism in the West: the inhumane treatment of the Indian in the name of progress and manifest destiny. Warren has elsewhere discussed, in *The Legacy of the Civil War, Homage to Theodore Dreiser, Democracy and Poetry,* and *Jefferson Davis Gets His Citizenship Back,* the corruption of American ideals in the nineteenth century. That corruption was evident enough during the westward expansion. For the second generation of settlers, those who followed the pioneers and began in earnest the exploitation of the frontier, he offers these harsh words:

> Frontiersmen, land-grabbers, gold-panners were dead.
> Veterans of the long chase skull-grinned in darkness.
> A more soft-handed ilk now swayed the West. They founded
> Dynasties, universities, libraries, shuffled
> Stocks, and occasionally milked

The Treasury of the United States,
Not to mention each other. They slick-fucked a land.

(54)

The events of *Chief Joseph* are presented as a direct consequence of the gilded age in which they occurred. But post–Civil War corruption is of secondary importance to the main subject: Chief Joseph himself, the last of Warren's representative American figures.

At moments *Chief Joseph* suggests another poem, the beautiful and little-known "Sanctuary," by Donald Davidson, which implores the people of an invaded land to retreat to the wilderness and preserve their way of life and heritage, even fade into obscurity and myth, rather than give in to their conquerors and be assimilated:

> Do not wait until
> You see *his* great dust rising in the valley.
> Then it will be too late.
> Go when you hear that he has crossed Will's Ford.
> Others will know and pass the word to you—
> A tap on the blinds, a hoot-owl's cry at dusk.
>
> Do not look back. You can see your roof afire
> When you reach high ground. Yet do not look.
> Do not turn. Do not look back.
> Go further on. Go high. Go deep.[8]

Davidson's specific referent is the Old South, whose existence the Civil War brought to an end. Warren's concern in *Chief Joseph* is not the Old South, though Southern culture provides an analogue to the Nez Perce. Warren's concern lies more generally with Western tradition and civilization, whose existence he regards as imperiled by the dehumanizing forces of technology and war. Through the voice of the Indian Joseph (sold like his biblical predecessor into bondage), Warren implores his readers to acknowledge the memory of a culture and a way of life whose symbolism lies at the heart of the nation's genesis, the symbolism of the American Eden. This fact helps account for the poem's romantic surface and tone, its apparent willingness to invoke many aspects of the white man's romanticized memory of the American Indian, a vision often far removed from the historical reality. At times this romanticism threatens the poem's realism, verging not only on myth but on sentimentality as well. Usually, however, the predominant mood is one of nostalgia for the remembered ideal which Joseph represents.

If the opening epigraphs prefigure the general concerns of the poem, the brief prose introduction clearly establishes the focus, matter-of-factly describing the tribe and recounting details of the three-month Nez Perce conflict. It emphasizes the peaceful lifestyle of the Indians in harmony with the elements: "They moved about with the offerings of the seasons, digging camas root, taking salmon at the time of their run, and making long hunts, across the Bitterroot Mountains into what is now Montana, for buffalo. . . . The Nez Perce, however, were not nomadic in the sense of the Plains Indians and were, for the most part, devoted to their homelands" (xi). They are depicted metaphorically as original inhabitants of an American Eden. They prided themselves on peaceful relations with the white settlers and observed the covenant to which they felt their existence on the land obliged them, a covenant the white settlers failed to respect almost from the beginning. Their ordeal can thus be seen as a symbolic despoiling of the American wilderness, which white Americans and Indians view in distinctly different ways. The Indians consider it god-given:

> The land of the Winding Waters, Wallowa,
> The land of the Nimipu,
> Land sacred to the band of old Joseph,
> Their land, the land in the far ages given
> By the Chief-in-the-Sky.
>
> (3)

To the Americans the wilderness is simply a geographical area, marked for conquest. At the distant edges of American white consciousness lies the mythic memory of this land, for what the Indians sought and found in their wilderness home—that knowledge of self and identity, of primal origins— is what the white man, the modern American in general (black, white, or otherwise), seeks as well. The poem begins by evoking the play of Indian boys riding their ponies, swimming in the water, and lying in the sun, clear images of a vigorous life force intensely associated with the Indians throughout the poem:

> Each year
> They go where from seaward salmon, infatuate,
> Unfailing at falls-leap, leap great stones. They leap
> The foaming rigor of current—seeking, seeking,
> In blind compulsion, like fate, the spawn-
> Pool that blood remembers. What does our blood,

In arteries deep, heaving with pulse-thrust
In its eternal midnight, remember?
We stir in sleep. We, too, belong
To the world, and it is spread for our eyes.

(3)

Like the world of Genesis (echoed here), the unmarked American wilderness greets the settlers as a new Eden, brimming with life and natural energy. Yet their civilized sensibilities have perhaps grown too dull to value it fully or to prevent them from abusing it.

The victimization of the Indian is part of the nation's "original sin," like slavery a part of the corruption of the American Dream which began almost at the same moment as the Dream's birth. Warren seeks to recover that sin's memory here and the profit it offers. In this sense the poem functions similarly to the Nez Perce concept of immortality, described in the prefatory note: "The lands where the fathers were buried were sacred, and, in their version of immortality, the fathers kept watch on sons to be sure that truth was spoken, and that each showed himself a man" (xi). That is, the poem seeks to inform modern Americans of their ancestral complicity in the Nez Perce betrayal and of their responsibility to acknowledge that betrayal as a genuine part of their history. (Warren reflected this corrective and prescriptive purpose in the epigraph he chose for *Democracy and Poetry,* from St.-John Perse: "And it is enough for the poet / to be the guilty conscience of his time" [ii].) It also seeks to prevent the legend of Chief Joseph, generated primarily by white newspapermen and historians, from camouflaging the unpleasant facts of the Nez Perce war. Warren notes how white Americans venerated Joseph after the war's end:

> Artists came to commemorate for the future
> That noble head. In bronze it was cast:
>
> .   .   .   .
>
> Great honor came, for it came to pass
> That to praise the red man was the way
> Best adapted to expunge all, all, in the mist
> Of bloodless myth.
>
> (54–55)

This honor included the travesty of having Joseph ride alongside Buffalo Bill Cody in the "procession to dedicate Grant's Tomb" (55). Cody, of course, was venerated by white America for his exploits as an Indian killer, a man who, Warren notes, "once sent his wife a yet-warm scalp, / He himself had sliced from the pate / Of a red man who'd missed him" (55). Warren wonders whether Joseph knew who Cody was, whether he understood that the man whose tomb he was commemorating had once promised to allow the Nez Perce to live on their land forever (Grant was president during the Nez Perce war), a promise broken when "some western politico, or such, / Jerked him by the nose, like a bull with a brass / Ring there for control" (56). Such veneration reduces Joseph to the most harmless of adversaries, the defeated, impotent enemy, respected for his valor in defeat, pitied for what he has lost (though no depth of pity could ever restore it to him). He is forced to remember his loss by portraying the chief he once was before the tomb of the leader ultimately responsible for his tribe's destruction. Grant, of course, was the vanquisher of another culture, that of the antebellum South, a fact which suggests that Warren is reflecting in this poem a general concern with conquered and disappearing cultures.

Chief Joseph elevates history to the level of ritual—ritual as poetry, ritual as Joseph's rhythmic, mantric narrative of his people's suffering, ritual as the poet's personal experience. Nothing stands unresolved at the poem's beginning.[9] The events of the Nez Perce war have already occurred and lie in the distant past. The narrative exists inherently and explicitly in the past tense (except for the final section), and the details of events are not so important as the manner in which events are recounted, the narrative style, its effect on the poet-chanter, Warren-Joseph, and on the reader. The language of presentation is crucial. The poem shifts among the voices of the poet, of Chief Joseph, and of the men (most of them U.S. military officers) involved in the Nez Perce conflict. Warren serves overtly as philosopher-historian until the final section, where he emerges as an active participant in the narrative. Joseph's persona dominates, though much of the narrative is not given in his voice. His is the voice of the defeated, abused, and outraged chief, of the Other, a culture and consciousness now extinct, violated and destroyed by the culture and consciousness of the white men whose own dry, counterfeit voices periodically interrupt it. The juxtaposition of these voices imbues the poem with the dramatic tension (though any sense of drama is necessarily illusory) of a conflict between white men and Indians, a collision of two modes of consciousness, a dialectic between past and present. Dramatic portrayals of history are not at all foreign to

Warren's method, as the dramatic versions of *All the King's Men* (originally conceived as a play entitled "Proud Flesh") and *Brother to Dragons* attest. As in other poetic works by Warren, the poet's own willed merger with his subject in the concluding section in effect resolves these contrasting forces, or intentionally leaves them in suspension.

The epigrammatic quotations which punctuate the narrative invest the poem with a historical identity. The Nez Perce war becomes a metaphoric vehicle through which Warren examines the development of the American nation. He does not alter historical events to suit his perspective (though he does exercise some selectivity of detail). The facts he presents are for the most part beyond dispute. Their interpretation by various speakers, especially Joseph and Gen. Oliver O. Howard, commander of the American forces, *can* be disputed, and their viewpoints are meant to clash. The Nez Perce war was the conflict of two cultures inherently at odds, one bound to prevail over the other, the superior forces of the whites leaving little doubt as to the final outcome. Warren makes this clear in his conclusion: "There is only / Process, which is one name for history" (63). Yet history as process is a cold and abstract notion. Warren humanizes it through the voices of the various individuals involved in the Nez Perce episode.

In the clash of these American voices (both white and Indian), Warren uncovers several disturbing elements in the nation's sense of history and identity. First, American historical memory is biased towards the viewpoint of the predominantly white, European settlers (most American historians, of course, are their descendants). Second, because of that bias, the "official" account of the Nez Perce war portrays the Indians as renegades whom American soldiers acted courageously to put down. The Indians are the villains in this view, incapable of nobility or heroism. Finally, the Nez Perce war is a "necessary moment" in American history. Herein lies the painful historical irony the poem illuminates. Although nineteenth-century Americans spoke of manifest destiny and a glorious national future, they seemed largely unmoved, or unaware, that these must come at the cost of another people's homeland and heritage. Conventional histories have not often emphasized this cost. The prevailing historical view is thus delusive, dehumanizing, and immoral (as the poem's final section suggests), not only for the injustice it does the Nez Perce but for the false sense of moral smugness it allows the white victors. This view is similar to the Northern Treasury of Virtue in *The Legacy of the Civil War,* where Warren argues that Northerners felt that because the Civil War had emancipated the slaves they could view the war in hindsight as a moral crusade, divinely ordained. Its victorious outcome excused them from responsibility for its consequences, ultimately permitting what Warren terms the Big Sell-Out of 1877, in which Northern Republicans offered to end Reconstruction if Southern Democrats would allow Rutherford B. Hayes accession to the presidency (*Legacy*, 59–66).

One of the most interesting of the poem's humanizing epigraphs is spoken by General Sherman, whose wartime success Warren wryly attributes in *The Legacy of the Civil War* to a fusion of philosophical pragmatism with military strategy. ("War was hell, and Sherman sought to make it so, but once the logical end was accomplished he could write that the suffering of the South was 'beyond comprehension'"—another conciliatory comment about a defeated enemy [*Davis*, 66–67].) As the epigraph demonstrates, Sherman found ample praise for Joseph once the war was over: "The Indians throughout displayed a courage and skill that elicited universal praise; they abstained from scalping; let captive women go free; and did not commit indiscriminate murder of peaceful families. . . . They fought with almost scientific skill" (54).[10] Such praise would normally suggest that the victor's intentions towards his defeated enemy were benevolent. In a statement missing from the poem, however, Sherman added that "indiscriminate murders" are the "usual" habit of the Indians. The Nez Perce "would not settle down on lands set apart for them, ample for their maintenance; and, when commanded by proper authority, they began resistance by murdering persons in no manner connected with their alleged grievances. . . . They should never be allowed to return to Oregon or to Lapwai [their homeland]." Before the war ended, Sherman ordered that the Nez Perce be offered no terms for surrender and that when captured they were to be treated with "extreme severity" and their leaders executed.[11] (The poem does not note this fact either, but it makes clear Sherman's intentions: by sending the defeated Indians to drink the "slime-green waters of Leavenworth," he "gave more death than ever his subordinate generals" [54].) His praise rings hollow, and like most of the soldiers in the war he could offer qualified sympathy only with the Indians defeated and under his control. His concern is with the sins of his enemy, and he is unwilling to concede American atrocities, presumably unaware, for instance, that although the Nez Perce never took scalps, American military scouts at one point dug up Nez Perce graves and scalped the corpses. Sherman reflects the prevailing government view that the Indians possessed no rights and held no claim to their land (a point Joseph readily admitted, arguing that no one could own the land, whites included). Of course, such an attitude makes feeling guiltless easy. As the poem shows, few representatives of the American government felt the Nez Perce had suffered an injustice. Only Col. Nelson Miles proved a consistent though ineffective defender. In an epigram, Warren cites a brief report from the Portland *Oregonian* as evidence of the typical white attitude towards the Indians in the Northwest region: "A party of miners returned to Owyhee from a raid on Indians with twenty scalps and plunder. The miners are well" (49). Back East, however, the Indian was a more distant and romantic figure. Readers enthusiastically followed newspaper accounts of Nez Perce victories in the war, a fact which largely accounts for the fame accorded Joseph after the surrender.

In the poem's final section, set in the present time, Warren recounts his visit to the site of the final battle of the Nez Perce war. As in *Brother to Dragons,* the poet's visit to a scene of past history brings about a sort of reconciliation between past and present, not in fact but in metaphor, and more directly in the poet's mind, for it is the poet, or his persona, who undergoes the transformation the poem seeks to bring about.[12] (It seems unnecessary to distinguish here between poet and persona; this poem is about the poet as well as Joseph.) Yet the reconciliation achieved is singularly unimpressive. It reveals nothing of substance, only a series of emotions felt by the poet. He cannot even be sure that the scene remains as it was in 1877:

> If you climb the slope, say a mile and a half,
> Or two, to the point where Miles must first
> Have debouched from the Bear Paws, and look north,
> You see what he saw—or what erosion has done.
>
> (61)

There is merely a sense of remoteness, of the past's separation from the present, the isolation in time of its inhabitants and events. Warren can make out only faint traces of the battle, obscured by the official government markers ("The large bronze plate on granite propped / By the Republic to honor the name / Of every trooper who, in glory, had died here" [60]). He observes the steel pipe which marks the location of Joseph's tepee and other steel pipes noting "where each man died— / If he was white or of consequence" (61). Yet he finds it difficult to connect these signs of past people and events with what they signify: the link is tenuous, evident primarily in the emotions aroused by the scene and the events which occurred there:

> Alone on that last spot I stood, my friends
> Now prowling and far on the high land. No snow
> Now on brown grass or red leaf
> Or black buffalo robe ceremonially swept
> To its blackness. All
> Now only a picture there in my head.
>
> (62)

The poet imagines the chief standing before him, "the old weapon / Outthrust, firm in a hand that does not / Tremble. I see lips move, but / No sound hear" (62). Joseph addresses him in this image, speaks to him directly, though the poet hears nothing. What does Joseph say? His words are lost and with them whatever historical reality they convey. But Warren seizes on the dimension of the man most important to him, his duty to tradition and knowledge of the inevitability of history. As chief of the Nez Perce, Joseph bore willingly the burden of tribal tradition and identity:

> he, eyes fixed on what strange stars, knew
> That eyes were fixed on him, eyes of
> Those fathers that incessantly . . . rifled
> Through all, through darkness, distance, Time,
> To know if he had proved a man, and being
> A man, would make all those
> Who now there slept know
> Their own manhood.
>
> (62)

To know one's manhood implies several meanings. Pertinent among them is simply the knowledge of self, of identity. In this sense Joseph, the dead and defeated Indian chief, stands parallel to Warren, the aging poet of the present day. The chief's awareness of his responsibility to tradition is what most moves the poet. Both men, by circumstance as much as choice, have the "eyes of the fathers," of tradition, fixed "incessantly" on them. Joseph (like the poet) "could see afar, beyond all night— / Those ancient eyes, in which love and judgment / Hold equal glitter, and, with no blink, / Strove always toward him" (63). Joseph's great significance is that

He strove to think of things outside
Of Time, in some
Great whirling sphere, like truth unnamable. Thus—
Standing there, he might well,
Already in such midnight, have foreknown
The end.

(63)

"The end" which Joseph foreknew was his own obsolescence as an individual and a Nez Perce. Because Joseph understood his own destiny, and
that of his people, "there is no ultimate / Irony. There is only / Process,
which is one name for history" (63). Process is also a name for change and
evolution, both of which, as Warren shows repeatedly in his writings, are
inescapable. Why then, sensing certain failure, did Joseph not abandon the
quest to lead his tribe to safety in Canada? For Warren, the answer is simply
that Joseph had to be true to his identity as a Nez Perce, true to the eyes of
the fathers who stare in judgment at him ("You must never sell the bones
of your fathers—," his father implores from his death bed, "For selling
that, you sell your Heart-Being" [10]). The answer must also be Joseph's
acquiescence to historical process, his acceptance of the tribal and racial
destiny he knew to be inevitable.

Does the poem grow then from Warren's own sense of impending obsolescence, from his fear that the civilization to which he belongs is rapidly
hurtling towards extinction? Mortality and time are surely significant aspects of his attitude, the mortality not only of individual human beings but
of entire cultures. Whatever his fears, he evinces no great sense of kinship
with his own world. The poem's final section conveys primarily cultural estrangement and alienation. What are his culture's icons? A ticket stub (*"La
Guardia to O'Hare, American Airlines, October 9, 1981, Ticket 704 982
1454 4, Chicago. By Northwest to Great Falls"* [58]), the steel markers and
historical plaque of the battlefield, the mayor of Spokane ("whoever the
hell he may have been" [63]), the traffic lights, and the "squirming throng"
(64), the "squirming myriads far at / My back" of the American public
(63). Burning here is an intense sense of the diminished present marked
by no sign of Joseph's character and will: in the present day, awareness of
tradition is a sign of weakness. Modern America is a nation of will-less
conformity, unconscious motion, "faceless to facelessness" (64). Certainly
the poem's account of the Nez Perce betrayal gives one explanation for why

the conquering American culture would necessarily doom itself to diminishment. Indifferent to the traditions and values of less powerful peoples, how could Americans sufficiently value their own traditions to want to preserve them, especially when many of their ancestors came to the new world to escape the past to begin with?

Warren presents Joseph as the embodiment of several basic precepts. He demonstrates the value of remaining true to one's self, despite the self's inevitable obliteration by whatever forces—time or a stronger culture's invasion. He exemplifies Warren's conviction—belonging not only to agrarianism but to modernism as well—that knowledge of tradition is essential to knowledge of one's self, to the retention of a meaningful identity. Modern America is "faceless" precisely because of its loss of the past. Finally, he provides hope for a meaningless present. He cannot lend coherence to modern American culture, but for the individual, the memory of Joseph's life, of the legend he became, which insures his immortality, can provide a source of moral strength and sustenance. Warren wonders

> if when the traffic light
> Rings green, some stranger may pause and thus miss
> His own mob's rush to go where the light
> Says go, and pausing, may look,
> Not into a deepening shade of canyon,
> Nor, head now up, toward ice peak in moonlight white,
> But, standing paralyzed in his momentary eternity, into
> His own heart look while he asks
> From what undefinable distance, years, and direction,
> Eyes of fathers are suddenly fixed on him. To know.
>
> (64)

This sudden, epiphanic awareness means recognition not merely of the white fathers who founded the nation but of the others too, those pushed aside by the nation's growth yet still a part of its heritage, the Indians, whose ghosts, as the Duwamish chief predicted in the initial epigraph, would "still love this beautiful land" and always keep the white man company, whether he remembered them or not.

Warren thus elevates Joseph to the status of a Theodore Dreiser, Thomas Jefferson, or John James Audubon, honored elsewhere in his work as representative figures of American history. Joseph personifies those values

Warren associates with the elusive American ideal: a valued tradition, communal responsibility, love of the land, fidelity to one's people and culture. Ironically, fidelity to cultural values placed Joseph at odds with the expanding American nation. A similar fidelity placed Warren, America's first poet laureate, in an equivalent relation to the modern age. Joseph and his tribe provide an emblem of the American nation's failure to honor its own dream, which the Nez Perce in their own way shared. They and others like them fell victim to the materialist greed and ambition which consumed, in Warren's vision of American history, the self-evident truths of the original Declaration.

CHAPTER 5

Warren and the Crisis

in Civil Rights: "The

Burden of Our Time"

The appearance of *Segregation* in 1956, followed by *The Legacy of the Civil War* in 1961, marked the formal beginning of a new phase in Warren's career, that of national and cultural diagnostician. In those two books, and in *Who Speaks for the Negro?* (1965), *Democracy and Poetry* (1975), and *Jefferson Davis Gets His Citizenship Back* (1980), Warren offered incisive, informed, and perceptive commentary on the state of affairs in contemporary America and their origins in history. Inevitably these works ply two essential aims: to demonstrate links between current conditions and their genesis in past events and to argue for the moral duty of the individual to confront responsibly the problems of the modern day—problems ranging from the civil rights crises of the 1950s and 1960s to the threat of nuclear war and consequent cultural and national obliteration.

Warren's work often reveals a streak of the moralistic diagnostician. Even in his first book, *John Brown: The Making of a Martyr,* he seems to suggest that the American tendency to become obsessed with abstractions is fundamentally self-destructive, a notion developed more fully in *Legacy,* though it was also important in such novels as *World Enough and Time* and *Band of Angels,* and in *Brother to Dragons.* In the early essay "The Briar Patch" he admonished Southern white farmers to respect the work and produce of Southern blacks. At the Fugitives' Reunion in 1956, he even went so far as to disagree with the New Critical notion that poetry ought not to be diagnostic (to a speaker who criticized a poem for being diagnostic, Warren countered, *"The Waste Land* as a diagnostic poem is as much a creation to me as, well, say, a poem like, what? *Lycidas?"*).[1] Later, in *Democracy and Poetry,* he suggested that art can have "therapeutic" value: Art "is the process by which, in imagining itself and the relation of individuals to one another and to it, a society comes to understand itself, and by understanding, discover its possibilities of growth" (76). To enhance his society's capacity for self-understanding and growth—these are primary aims of his nonfiction writings about American society and history.

There is no reason to believe that Warren did not compose his nonfiction essays with the same care and commitment that produced his poems and novels.[2] That is, there is no reason why the nonfiction should not be accorded status as art, if art of a lesser level than *Audubon: A Vision* or *World Enough and Time.* It is clear that Warren regarded these essays as serious excursions into central issues of the age. It is clear too that he sought through the nonfiction to benefit his nation and culture—to diagnose national ills and prescribe therapeutic cures, with the ultimate goal of strengthening the land and investing it with moral and historical awareness. But these essays also serve Warren as a personal therapy, a means of discovering his own feelings on particular matters, such as the civil rights movement, and of reaffirming his link to a personal and cultural past, as in *Jefferson Davis Gets His Citizenship Back.* This personal element is always present in the great poems and novels.

Written during periods when Warren was busily involved with other creative projects, the nonfiction essays are closely linked to the fiction and poetry. *Wilderness* and *Legacy* (both published in 1961, both about the Civil War and related philosophical issues) are companion pieces, as are *Democracy and Poetry* and *A Place to Come To* (both concerned with the problem of identity in the modern, technological world). They demonstrate a breadth and depth of knowledge about literary, political, historical, economic, and cultural affairs which few men or women can claim, and they offer an assessment of American society by an established artist that ought not to be ignored. If Warren sets himself up in these works as a kind of cultural shaman, he is doing nothing more than what any artist does in poetry or fiction, where the veil of fabrication protects the artist from being criticized for stepping out of bounds.

In many ways the least regarded among Warren's nonfiction social writings, *Who Speaks for the Negro?* concerned a particular moment in American history, the American civil rights movement in 1964–65. Very much a topical, even journalistic work, it compares favorably with other examples of the New Journalism which had begun to appear during the mid-1960s. Yet in many ways it now seems outdated.[3] Even the key word in its title, "Negro," once a respectful and enlightened way for whites to refer to blacks, is now regarded as patronizing derogation by the blacks to whom it is addressed. Such key figures in the 1960s civil rights movement as Martin Luther King, Jr., Roy Wilkins, James Baldwin, and Malcolm X are dead, and leadership has passed in the 1980s to a generation of individuals largely unmentioned in the book. The movement's very nature has changed, and there is good reason to argue that the term movement—in the sense of an organized effort to bring social change—no longer applies.

Warren researched *Who Speaks for the Negro?* mainly in 1964, the year of the Mississippi Summer Project, a time when the civil rights movement was still predominantly biracial, though whites were playing an increasingly secondary role. It was thus written several years before "black power" and Afro-American nationalism became prominent forces (though these are already important concerns to many of the speakers in the book, especially the younger ones, whom Warren interviews). In 1964 American blacks stood for the most part on the verge of the entrenched white society, prepared and determined to join, though in what form at the time was unclear. Now a quarter-century later, though many racial problems remain, blacks in large numbers have long since assumed the rights and privileges which were among the goals of their struggles in the 1960s.

In many ways the questions which *Who Speaks for the Negro?* seeks to answer have thus been answered, and many of Warren's concerns in the book—so pertinent in 1965—now seem either moot or irrelevant. Nonetheless, this compilation of interviews, narrative, and social commentary is an important work. It is informed by Warren's characteristic vision of American history in process and occupies a unique place in his writing. It is also, in its own way, a vivid account of the era, an oral history told to a significant extent through the words of leaders and participants in the movement.

Who Speaks for the Negro? is one of the only works by a major white American author to deal directly and in detail with the American civil rights movement. It is one of the only works by an American writer to confront that movement not merely in its political context but in a cultural and humanistic one as well. It is also an attempt by Warren to discover and explore in the matrix of contemporary human affairs the important themes and patterns of his poetry and fiction. It is an excursion into the process of history still being made. In typical Warren fashion it views the American civil rights movement not merely as a contemporary event but as the dramatic and dynamic consequence of history and as the source of history still to come. It regards the movement also as a human phenomenon, inspired by the leadership of Great Men, sustained by the hard work and suffering of American men and women who wish to translate their vision of justice and opportunity to reality. James Justus observes that *"Who Speaks for the Negro?* is personal in its exploration of freedom and fate, motive and act, the contingency of event and the exertion of will, the paradoxes of history, identities both private and public, the pragmatic uses of an idea, the psychology of the reformers: in brief, the subjects and themes which account for the aesthetic integration of Warren's work as a whole."[4]

Perhaps in terms of the works he had already written, *Who Speaks for the Negro?* might seem a book of contradictions. The 1930 essay "The Briar Patch," despite its defense of respect and fair treatment for Southern blacks, still advocated a segregated society. *Who Speaks for the Negro?* advocates the opposite. One of the major arguments of *The Legacy of the Civil War* (1961) is that the extremism of the nineteenth-century Northern abolitionists, who heeded Higher Law over United States civil law, helped make the Civil War inevitable. Yet in this 1965 book Warren sympathizes with the advocates of nonviolent civil disobedience used by the civil rights movement during the 1950s and 1960s, that form of protest which seeks to change laws by breaking them, on the assumption that what is morally right is more important than what the law judges to be right. Yet this is not a contradiction after all. Warren views nonviolence as an effective means by which the oppressed can change unjust laws, sway their oppressors, and at the same time protect and even strengthen the nation's stability. Civil disobedience is, as the book emphasizes (sometimes skeptically), a tactic based on the Judeo-Christian ethic of "loving your enemy as yourself," an ethic devoted in this case to the ideal of promoting a racially harmonious society.

More importantly, Warren views the civil rights movement as an effort to recover the American Dream. A young black woman states the theme for him during an interview:

LUCY THORNTON: If the black man does indeed achieve his goals, he is actually strengthening the theories on which the nation's founded— also it might strengthen white people, those who are talking in terms of a lost theology or lost ideals, lost goals; in fact, it might even help to reiterate what we once said is the nation's basis for existence. (370)

Warren appears not so much to believe that black Americans will alone effect such a regeneration, rather that their movement for equality may force Americans to reassess the patterns of national history and to recognize their failure to live up to the values and ideals in which they profess belief. It was, after all, the American government's failure after the Civil War to address effectively the problems of the freed slaves that made the civil rights movement necessary a hundred years later, and that failure, as Warren illustrates in a number of places, was one among many symptoms of the American Dream's failure at the end of the nineteenth century.

Warren repeatedly expressed his notion of history as drama. "The inwardness of the story of those characters from the Civil War gives the attraction of drama," he wrote in *Legacy* (89). He praised *An American Tragedy* for its "drama of self-definition" and viewed Theodore Dreiser's life in those same terms (*Homage,* 131). For Warren, life in its essence is drama, a constant shifting tension between the ideal and the actual, the struggle of the individual self to adjust to the demands of the actual and by force of will to mold the future, to direct and shape events. It is thus no surprise that he chose the interview as the underlying structure of this book. Among the movers and shapers of the civil rights movement, at virtually every level, he discovers a drama of self-definition extending from the individual black or white volunteer to the awakening conscience of the nation as a whole. Everyone involved, even tangentially, is a participant in the drama. The Southerner will be compelled to assess the meaning of his history: "Discovering his past, the Southerner might find himself, and the courage to be himself; he might free himself from a stereotype which does violence to some of his own most deeply cherished values and to the complexity of his history" (428). For the Northerner, Warren suggests, the movement will force a similar self-recognition: "The worst shock for the Yankee is to discover what he, himself, really feels. He has to find out if he really wants a Negro family next door. If he really wants to take orders from a Negro department head. . . . He is, in fact, not only going to find out what he really wants. He is going to find out what he himself really is" (430). Of course, the movement is a fundamental process of self-definition for American blacks. Paradoxically, or perhaps not so at all, Warren tells Wyatt T. Walker of the Southern Christian Leadership Conference that he is involved in "this project" because he "wanted to find out about things, including my own feelings" (232). So for Warren too the movement, and his urge to write about it, compels a personal drama of self-definition.[5]

In fact, Warren knew his "own feelings" clearly enough ten years earlier to express them in a *Life* magazine essay entitled *Segregation: The Inner Conflict in the South,* lengthened and published as a book in 1956. In contrast to *Who Speaks for the Negro?,* where he sought to remain relatively objective and anonymous, Warren figures prominently in *Segregation* as a narrator and a character, seeking to dramatize his own moral struggle, and the South's, in the early days of the civil rights movement. The central themes of *Segregation* are history as dramatic process and the discovery of identity through confrontation with history. The essay seems always aware of the dynamic change brewing in the South. Yet other themes explored more fully in other Warren works are also touched on, especially the individual's obligation to history. Moreover, Warren makes vitally clear his concept of American culture as an assembly of numerous different individuals and beliefs. Above all else, *Segregation* imparts a vivid sense of history in process, especially from the retrospective vantage point from which we now read it. As Warren interviews proponents and opponents of the incipient struggle for racial equality, it is clear that he believes he is talking to men and women who are about to make history, who bear on their shoulders responsibility for the nation's future, and who, sometimes at least, are quite conscious of the burden.

Yet *Segregation* also rests on the premise that the history about to be made is the result of events which occurred long before in the nation's past. Warren reminds one white segregationist that "whatever the constitutional rights and wrongs of the Civil War were, we got a new Constitution out of it" (46), a document more open to interpretation and change, more responsive to the shifting needs of the people for whom it was designed. (One suspects, however, from all his emphasis on stable government and the Law, that Warren would have preferred a less malleable document.) Throughout the essay he evokes the growing dynamic tension between past and present, the desire to preserve the heritage and tradition of the past weighed against the moral imperative of the need for change and justice in the present.

This dynamic tension is apparent early in the essay. Warren sits in a plane just departed from the Memphis airport and looks out the window at the Southern landscape below. (The entire essay can be seen as occurring within Warren's mind, a sustained meditation as he gazes out the window.) He recalls driving along a rural north Mississippi road only a week before, observing signs of progress as he passes them, the electric wires and lights, remarking as well the "rows of tenant shacks, Negro shacks set in the infinite cotton fields. . . . When I caught a glimpse in the dusk, of the interior of a lighted shack, I usually saw the coal-oil lamp" (4). The lamps assure him that though progress might have come to the Mississippi farmlands, some things haven't changed, such as the poverty and subsistence-level existence of the people in the tenant shacks. He remarks a black family walking along the road, the man with the croker sack, the woman with the small child at her bosom, the other children trailing behind. "Yes, they are still here," he muses. He is tempted to believe that nothing has changed since the first time, thirty years before, he drove through these farmlands. But change has come, as he well knows from the vantage point of his airborne window, and its impact is the focus of this essay. Warren always views events such as the Civil War and the civil rights movement in the larger historical context. The civil rights struggle is in this sense a collision of past and future, of the desire to maintain a stable identity and lifestyle rooted in past traditions conflicting with the responsibility to change in order to rectify injustices rooted in that tradition.

In ways *Segregation* is far more exciting and dramatic than *Who Speaks for the Negro?* It is a product of the early public days of the civil rights movement, of a time when many white Southerners, and white Americans in general, were just awakening to what was happening. The essay's dramatic structure, which contrasts the views of white segregationists with those of the integrationists, and of the blacks themselves, evokes the tension and anticipation of that day. As usual, Warren is well aware of the stereotypes and clichés which erupt from such historical situations, and he is quick to deflate them or to illuminate the reality they convey. He describes the defenselessness of a black woman whose husband was murdered by a white man, her desire to escape the murderer whom she is sure will be acquitted and will come looking for her: "He get 'quitted, that man, and maybe I die, but I die goin" (9). Warren observes, "It is the cliché of fear. It is the cliché come fresh and alive" (9). Soon after he describes another cliché, that of a fifteen-year-old boy visiting a replica of Fort Nashborough in Nashville. The boy expresses awe at the historic setting, but when asked about the racial situation in Atlanta, he answers almost involuntarily: " 'Niggers' . . . I hate them bastards," he says, with a shuddering, automatic violence, and averts his face and spits through his teeth, a quick, viperish, cut-off expectoration" (10–11). His emotions are, Warren reports, "automatic": "The cliché had come true: the cliché of hate. And somehow the hallowedness of the ground he stood on has vindicated, as it were, that hate" (11). That is, hallowed traditions justify hatred of those things which seem to threaten them. Clichés though they be, these automatic emotions determined to a great extent the thoughts and behavior of many Southerners confronted in the 1950s with the dilemmas of the civil rights movement. Both reflect an awareness of history. History has taught the black woman to fear the white man's vengeful power. The boy sees the history he reveres as somehow threatened by the demand of blacks for equal rights and perhaps too by his own unarticulated recognition of the justice of their demand. That recognition simply quickens his bitterness.

Warren is interested in the reasons underlying the clichés, as he implies in his reference to the hallowed grounds of Fort Nashborough which vindicate the boy's hatred. Those reasons have as much to do with loyalty to a region and its values as with blind, fearful resistance to an overwhelming wave of abstract change. Warren cites an unidentified black scholar's observation that many Southerners "just don't like change. It's not merely desegregation they're against so much, it's just the fact of any change. They feel some emotional tie to the way things are" (32). A white college student observes: "It's just that people don't like to feel like they're spitting on their grandfather's grave. They feel some connection they don't want to break. Something would bother them if they broke it. . . . And sometimes something bothers them if they don't break it" (32). Warren suggests, without irony, that both scholar and student are talking about something called "piety." By this he means deeply felt loyalty to a region, its tradition, and its way of life. This is the idea of *patria* expressed by Jed Tewksbury in *A Place to Come To,* "The things that made you what you are and that must be lived by you because you are you" (232). It is modernity Warren sees the segregationists as resisting, the age of uncertainty and displacement, of individual helplessness and insignificance. They fear loss of identity, a fear Warren perhaps shares. Not a little of the purpose of *Segregation* would seem to be to make non-Southerners understand something of what Southerners were feeling in the 1950s, why some resisted as stolidly and viciously as they did.

At the heart of this anomalous work lies the divided Southerner, mainly the divided white Southerner, to a lesser extent the divided black Southerner. The division is complex, but it boils down finally to what Warren identifies as a conflict between recognition of the moral justice of integration and one's fidelity to tradition, one's regional heritage and home. Warren suggests that many white Southerners instinctively sensed what was morally right, but they could not bring themselves to stand up for justice if they had to feel that they were turning against their region or supporting its enemies. The consequence for them was internal anguish and uncertainty: "There are almost an infinite number of permutations and combinations, but they all amount to the same thing, a deep intellectual rub, a moral rub, anger at the irremediable self-division, a deep exacerbation at some failure to find identity. That is the reality" (54). Warren observes that some Southern integrationists sided with the segregationists simply because they disliked the federal government's intrusion into regional matters. Yet ultimately he finds this reasoning to be nothing more than rationalization, a moral evasion. The segregationists

> are caught in a paradox; in seeking to preserve individualism by taking refuge in the vision of a South redeemed in unity and antique virtue, they are fleeing from the burden of their own individuality—the intellectual rub, the moral rub. . . . By using the argument of mere social continuity and the justification by mere mores, they think of a world in which circumstances and values are frozen; but the essence of individuality is the willingness to accept the rub which the flux of things provokes, to accept one's fate in time. (55)

In the final interview, a self-interview, he comments, "We have to deal with the problem our historical moment proposes, the burden of our time" (65). Clearly, whatever else it might have been said to be, resistance to integration finally amounts to cowardly retreat from that burden, a shirking of basic moral and human responsibility, a denial of regional and personal identity.

Although Warren remains objective and uninvolved, asking questions, offering commentary, synthesizing and analyzing, his belief in the just cause of civil rights is clear from a fairly early moment in the essay. Also clear—ironically so in a writer for whom the foibles of human nature are a basic theme—is his apparent faith in human goodness. He argues that a deeply ingrained *moral sense,* itself the product of regional values, will ultimately respond to the challenge of the crisis. He describes a white woman who, in a room full of segregationists, suddenly expresses, almost involuntarily, her sympathy for a black man who had been berated for coming to a white man's front door instead of the back: "Maybe he did take a lot on himself, coming to the front door. But I can't stand it. He's human" (59). Another woman complains, "I can't feel the same way about a Negro as a white person. It's born in me. But I pray I'll change" (59). And the white school superintendent who explains, "A man can hate an idea but know it's right, and it takes a lot of thinking and praying to bring yourself around. You just have to uncover the unrecognized sympathy in the white man for the Negro humiliation" (58). (In *Who Speaks for the Negro?,* Warren is considerably less sanguine about the willingness of Southerners to change their racial views. Events intervening between the publications of his two civil rights books revealed just how deeply entrenched the resistance was among some white Southerners.)

Warren is the obvious persona and protagonist of *Segregation.* He is the quintessential divided white Southerner, questing for a resolution to the dilemma, and from this perspective he addresses readers in the South and throughout the nation in an often openly didactic manner. In the concluding self-interview, he calls for responsible action: "If the South is really able to face up to itself and its situation, it may achieve identity, moral identity. Then in a country where moral identity is hard to come by, the South, because it has had to deal concretely with a moral problem, may offer some leadership" to the nation as a whole (65–66). In 1956 such a hope might have seemed idealistic in the extreme. Even today, though blacks have attained many rights in the South and the rest of the nation, the minds and attitudes of many people remain unswayed. Still, one might argue that the South did precisely what Warren hoped: led the nation in the integration of public services, facilities, and schools and offered in such cities as Atlanta and Birmingham models of racial cooperation and amity. Having done so, it has left even further behind, more deeply divided and bereft of identity in place and time, those who cling to the hatreds of the past.

Who Speaks for the Negro? expands and modifies the narrative perspective of *Segregation*. Warren continues as a subjective participant as well as an objective observer of the civil rights movement. Yet if in *Segregation*, written early in the movement's development, Warren was in some sense testing the waters, making known to himself his own views, his sense that what was happening in the South was not only inevitable but morally *right*, he was also establishing his independence as a Southerner from the sort of regional loyalties which can blind one to moral realities and enable the writing of such a statement as the "Briar Patch" essay, which, even in 1930, as he explains in the first chapter of *Who Speaks for the Negro?*, had given him "some vague discomfort, like the discomfort you feel when your poem doesn't quite come off, when you've had to fake, or twist, or pad it, when you haven't really explored the impulse" (11). Such independence does not require the rejection of his Southern identity (whatever that identity might mean). Instead it means that he was affirming, for himself and for others, that one may remain true to a region and its values while eschewing certain beliefs (white supremacy, racism) and practices (segregation) which that region for so long mutely accepted as inescapable aspects of its being. In fact, in both his civil rights books Warren strongly suggests that one *must* reject those beliefs and practices to remain true to the essential values the agrarian South has traditionally embodied: individualism, community, moral integrity, human compassion.

In *Who Speaks for the Negro?* Warren retains his Southern identity only in the sense that he does not abandon it. That identity is not an active presence (as it was in *Segregation*), though it is apparent in the questions he tends to ask (some of which would simply not occur to non-Southerners) and through the values and principles which underlie his treatment of the movement. (Some may find it ironic that the values and principles which compel his support of civil rights were Southern and agrarian by nature.) His perspective throughout can be defined only with great difficulty, if at all. (The failure of categories as an accurate means of defining character and the individuality of human experience is a subordinate theme.) It is clear from the beginning (as in *Segregation*) that his sympathies lie with the civil rights movement. He seems to admire the use of nonviolent tactics as a way of winning victories and concessions and of gaining respect from adversaries. And he is clearly concerned about the possible introduction of violent tactics into the movement. He pointedly condemns the racist, at times murderous behavior of certain opponents of civil rights, especially the July 1964 murders of three young civil rights workers in Philadelphia, Mississippi. He does not hesitate to criticize, where criticism is warranted, black leaders and workers in the movement and seems especially wary of such individuals as Malcolm X, of such groups as the Black Muslims, and of all advocates of violence and divisiveness. He finds in the movement's lack of a generally recognized leader the danger of a demagogue rising to take over. He criticizes white Northern liberals for hypocrisy and white Southern liberals for a lack of timely humanity. Acknowledging the artistic achievement of James Baldwin, he faults the writer's egotism and his willingness to make his life the archetype of all black experience: "The Voice of Hope does not ask the Negro, or the Revolution, or us to do so and so; it asks *me*—asks James Baldwin, or rather, asks the Elder Brother, who is 'the brightest boy in the house'—to create a new nation. . . . This 'interior' life of James Baldwin and the exterior fate of the country are, for dramatic purposes, merged, identified. . . . It is *me*—the drama of James Baldwin, again" (281). One of the greatest virtues of *Who Speaks for the Negro?* is its probing objectivity, its at times studied skepticism, its refusal to accept the labels, stereotypes, and shallow platitudes which social movements tend to generate. Out of this skepticism rises a concrete portrait of the civil rights movement, its leaders, and the issues which confront it at a critical point in its history.[6]

In *Segregation* Warren wrote as a Southerner seeking to discover what changes and moral obligations the civil rights movement would impose on the South. In *Who Speaks for the Negro?* his perspective is less regional and more broadly humanistic. He centers on humanitarian rather than regional issues, though because the South is the focus of the movement's attention, it naturally plays an important role. As much as possible, Warren assumes a transparent, objective perspective, one overtly neither Southern nor Northern, though he might argue that the values he espouses in the book have persisted longer in the South than the North. He rarely pronounces his opinions openly; even in the concluding chapter he tends mainly to analyze and describe, at times to predict, the significance of what he has discovered. Throughout he allows the "characters" of the civil rights movement to speak for themselves. He describes their appearance and mannerisms, at points attempts to draw some connection between physical demeanor and inward motivation, but typically does not judge them as right or wrong, good or bad. Consider his description of Martin Luther King, Jr.:

I have mentioned the physical compactness, the sense of complete-
ness, that Dr. King gives. This is related to something else, something
more significant, that appears as soon as you put a question to him.
Even if it is a question that you know he has heard a hundred times
before, there is a withdrawing inward, a slight veiling of the face as it
were. There is the impression that . . . he must look inward to find a
real answer, not just the answer he gave yesterday, which today may
no longer be meaningful to him. It is a remarkable trait—if my reading
is correct: the need to go inward to test the truth that has already been
tested, perhaps over and over again, in the world outside. (210)

Warren seems to admire and even stand in awe of the man, but he never
flatly expresses his opinions, though he later implies that King's importance derived more from his role as an "image" and a "symbol" than as an
engineer of the movement.

For a clearer understanding of King, Warren questions others in the
movement and allows their responses to contrast or coincide as they will.
Certain opinions held by more than a few of the respondents do emerge:
King's importance as a model to black youth, for instance; his inability to
speak effectively to the youth of Harlem and other Northern ghettos; the
difficulties in his philosophy of loving the oppressor. What emerges here is
a portrait of King as he was viewed by others in the movement. We can
barely sense Warren's own view, almost as if he is withholding judgment
until he has compiled sufficient evidence and had time to sift through and
consider it, when at last his admiration becomes apparent. (In "A Dearth
of Heroes," Warren cited King as the only man since World War II with "a
serious claim" to the status of American hero: "The theme was high, the
occasion noble, the stage open to the world's eye, the courage clear and
against odds. And martyrdom came to purge all dross away. King seems
made for the folk consciousness, and the folk consciousness is the Val-
halla of the true hero."[7] Warren's discomfort with King is thinly veiled
here. Although he never expressed any open reservations about the man, he
seemed consistently to withhold judgment, to allow the judgment of others
to stand in his place. The reasons for this discomfort are unclear. But the
emphasis here, as elsewhere, falls on the "folk consciousness," for whom
King became both symbol and hero of the struggle for racial equality in
America.)

We do find lapses, flaws in the veil of impartiality behind which Warren hides. He *is* a writer of a particular time, race, and region; the marks of his individuality and his heritage become evident, despite his attempts to transcend or at least ignore them. Certain issues appear more important to him than others, and they frequently are ones which were prominently mentioned in conversations about civil rights among white Southerners in the 1950s and 1960s. He asks several interviewers whether integration will mean a diminishment in the blood-identity of the Negro race, revealing a concern with "race-mixing," or miscegenation (fear of which was a prime white-racist argument against integration). His repeated efforts to pin down his subjects on the future of public schools, busing, the importance of "the land" to Southern blacks and whites, and Gunnar Myrdal's belief that slaveholders ought to have been compensated for their emancipated slaves suggest that he did not come to his subject without preconceptions. But a remarkable aspect of this book is the objective impartiality its author achieves, his willingness to embrace his subjects on their own terms, in the context of their own struggle, and not in the terminology and context which he might have wished to impose.[8] Furthermore, his refusal to limit the study to the South, his interest in civil rights as a national phenomenon, as much an issue in Detroit and New York as Jackson and Montgomery, invests the book with an American identity that places the struggle in the context of the American past and future, which views it not only as an effort to insure rights and privileges for a particular minority but as an essential redefinition of what America can and should mean.

The form and organization of this book reflect both Warren's view of the civil rights movement as dramatic history in the making and his envisioning of it as a particularly American phenomenon. The interview, a narrative device in *Segregation,* is important throughout *Who Speaks for the Negro?* In "The Big Brass," the chapter devoted to leaders of the movement, interviews are transcribed word for word, with an apparent minimum of editing. Warren seems to abdicate his authorial role, to reduce himself to a mere participant in the conversation, a voice equal in authority to the voices of those he interviews. On occasion his subjects disagree with and even rebuke him, and he presents these instances candidly with no attempt at self-justification. On the one hand he uses the interview to create the illusion of objectivity, to avoid subjective judgment of the speakers. Their own words certify or invalidate their integrity (though Warren does maintain control through selection and placement of the interviews, and in the tone of the passages introducing and explaining them). In other chapters he abandons transcripts and instead summarizes interviews in more traditional narrative form, but his emphasis remains throughout on the words of the people interviewed, not on the reactions of the interviewer. Whether presented as transcript or summary, the interviews evoke the dramatic tension which Warren finds penetrating the whole of the civil rights movement.

The chapters of *Who Speaks for the Negro?* likewise reflect Warren's sense of the scope of the civil rights movement, which he shows as embracing all social and racial strata in the nation. Each chapter focuses on a different category of people. The first surveys the views and experiences of individuals working in Louisiana; the second concerns workers in the Mississippi Summer Project of 1964; the third presents a series of interviews with various black leaders of the movement; the fourth regards various examples of successful blacks in American society: two writers, a banker, a judge; the fifth examines the role of the young in the movement and their potential influence on its future, while the sixth, "A Conversation Piece," offers Warren's own views and conclusions.

The structure of the first chapter, "The Cleft Stick," portends the structure of the book as a whole: different voices placed in contrast with one another, refracting like a prism varying views and dimensions of the movement. The chapter begins with a long oral narrative by a black minister named Joe Carter who describes his attempt to register as the first black voter in West Feliciana Parish, twenty-five miles north of New Orleans, Louisiana. Carter's is the voice of the uneducated, unsophisticated common man, not a leader or organizer of the movement but an individual who has lived and breathed in the most primary form the oppression the movement seeks to relieve: "Well, I met the CORE—Ruby Livermore, that's his name. And Ronnie Moore. And I met them on a Thursday in August. They explained to me concernen the red-ishen and I told them that I had tried and that I couldn't get none of my neighbors to go with me" (3). In the stolid, mute figures of the registrar and sheriff who oppose him, Carter dramatizes all the forces of racist stasis that he and the movement seek to abolish. The second section of the chapter focuses on the president of Southern University, Dr. Felton Clark, who had recently bowed to the command of the Louisiana State Board of Education to expel student demonstrators. Clark speaks articulately of the demands created by the movement for civil rights and admits, concerning the expelled students, that "If I had things to do over, I would do them a little differently" (16). Though he was responsible for the expulsion of black students who were demonstrating for their civil rights, including the right to vote, he speaks fervently about the necessity of taking part in the democratic process. Warren then remarks the irony of the contrast between a college president who can speak abstractly of the vote's importance and an uneducated black minister who risks all to assert his right to vote:

> I think of Reverend Joe Carter, all alone, going to register in West Feliciana Parish. There is some irony in this juxtaposition in my recollection—Dr. Clark in his office with me, Reverend Joe Carter standing naked in his jail cell. . . . Would it have been self-indulgent heroics for Dr. Clark to defy his Board? Should Dr. Clark have supported the demonstrators and had the University closed down? What obligation did he owe his students to keep their education in process? Or how neatly did self-indulgence coincide with an obligation to keep the University open? (26–27)

In these questions Warren finds the "cleft stick of history . . . the tragic dilemma of opposing goods, and opposing evils. And only Dr. Clark—and God—can assess the purity of his heart" (27). For Clark the implications and consequences of the civil rights movement are abstract and convoluted. For Carter they are concrete and simple: he wants the right to vote. Other voices are more articulate and grammatical, but Reverend Carter epitomizes in an immediate and deeply lived sense the significance of the civil rights struggle.

Contrast is a major structural device in the book, an important means of evoking the drama of the movement. In his chapter about black leadership, Warren contrasts various figures on the basis of their personal motives and principles, political views, their advocacy of nonviolent versus violent protest, and their view of the role of the Black Revolution in American democracy. He begins with Harlem congressman Adam Clayton Powell, whose own words reveal his ambition for power and publicity and his detachment from many of the movement's goals. Powell's self-interest is made sharply clear by the portrait which follows of Roy Wilkins, whose altruistic vision of the movement's outcome is "To live together in mutual respect" (157), and by the treatment of the practical Whitney Young, who "does not flinch from facing the unpleasant fact of the Negro's condition" (170). Discussions of Martin Luther King, Jr., Wyatt T. Walker, and Bayard Rustin, all of whom seek in one form or another a racially harmonious and unified America, contrast markedly with the portrait of Malcolm X, advocate of violent confrontation and black separatism.[9] A similar contrast frames the fourth chapter, "Leadership From the Periphery," in the portraits of James Baldwin (whom Warren regards as driven by his extremist obsession with apocalyptic solutions to America's racial problems) and Ralph Ellison (whose pragmatic humanism accords more with Warren's own thinking). Inevitably, Warren sides with those speakers who envision an America strengthened by the movement and brought closer to the ideals of the Declaration.[10]

It is no coincidence that *Who Speaks for the Negro?* appeared in the centennial year of the Civil War's end. The Civil War and the civil rights movement were two closely related episodes in a historical process which formally began with the Declaration of Independence in 1776, which in fact commenced with the importation of slaves to the American colonies in 1619. As he attests in his repeated questions about the federal government's failure during Reconstruction to solve problems which a hundred years later would still remain, Warren sees the civil rights movement as an inevitable consequence of past events: of the importation of slaves to America, their emancipation, their being granted and then denied the full rights of citizenship, their betrayal via the Hayes-Tilden Compromise in 1877 by the same political party which in 1866 had promised them redemption.[11] *Who Speaks for the Negro?* thus views the civil rights movement as historically determined, a product of events which preceded it, an essential stage in America's history and in the will of the nation to survive.

Warren's explanation of why Americans should study the Civil War thus applies equally well to the movement for racial equality: "We shall not be able to anatomize this portentous richness, but we feel that we must try. We must try because it is a way of understanding our own deeper selves, and that need to understand ourselves is what takes us, always, to the deeper contemplations of art, literature, religion, and history" (*Legacy*, 81). Understanding the Civil War and the civil rights movement is a process of understanding the individual and the national self, of discovering one's identity in relation to other selves, to the community, the nation, and history. What Warren lacked in 1965 was the one-hundred-year perspective which in *Legacy* allowed him to view the phenomenon of the Civil War as the deeply philosophical and human event it was. He composed that book as a legatee of the war. He compensates for the absence of that perspective in *Who Speaks for the Negro?* with a wealth of human detail that evokes the drama of the civil rights movement up close, from the perspective of one who is, if not a participant, an immediate observer and sympathizer. If the 1965 book lacks the deeply meditative, syncretic quality of *The Legacy of the Civil War,* its tone of tense and expectant immediacy at least conveys something of the ambience of the year it chronicles.

No matter how separate he tried to remain, the process of preparing this book constituted for Warren a "way of understanding" his own deeper self and his attitudes towards the civil rights movement and of testing his willingness to commit to its goals. The book's preparation became, we can suppose (based on ample evidence in the text), a way of uncovering deeper layers of his own identity, which perhaps accounts for the apparent energy with which he pursued it. It is clear too that identity is a primary theme, not merely for Warren, who remains mostly in the background, but especially for participants in the movement. Responding to Felton Clark's description of the Negro Revolution as "part of a world movement for freedom, for a sense of identity," Warren muses: "I seize the word *identity*. It is a key word. You hear it over and over again. On this word will focus, around this word will coagulate, a dozen issues, shifting, shading into each other. Alienated from the world to which he is born and from the country of which he is a citizen, yet surrounded by the successful values of that world, and country, how can the Negro define himself?" (17). This is a central question in the book and one of the crucial issues of Warren's career. In a world often hostile and indifferent, in an environment which minimizes individual human worth, how can the black American, how can *any* individual, define himself?

When Warren prepared and wrote this book, primarily during 1964, blacks had yet to define the roles they would assume in American society. They had yet, as it were, to declare their roles as citizens, and as the book shows, they had become clearly aware that the power to make such a declaration lay within their own hands rather than in those of the whites. Warren is much concerned with what their declaration will be. He sees complete separation from the white world as one possibility: the assumption of equal rights and opportunities but the maintenance of a separate identity and culture. Complete assimilation into the white world is another alternative, including even the extreme of biological assimilation. Warren returns often to W. E. B. Du Bois's theory of the psychic split in the Negro, "the tension between the impulse to Negro-ness, the mystique noire, and the impulse to be absorbed into the white West European–American culture—and perhaps bloodstream" (97). But he clearly hopes for some middle ground between separation and assimilation which will enable blacks to develop a distinctive cultural identity within the larger context of the American community. As an answer to his question about whether "the Negro Movement of our time invokes a discovery of identity," Warren allows Ralph Ellison's statement to stand as his own:

> ELLISON: I don't think it's a discovery of identity. I think rather that it is an affirmation and *assertion* of identification. And it's an assertion of a pluralistic identity. The assertion, in political terms, is that of the old American tradition. In terms of group identity and the current agitation it's revealing the real identity of a people who have been here for a hell of a long time. Negroes were American even before there was a United States, and if we're going to talk at all about what we are, this historical and cultural fact has to be recognized. And if we're going to accept this as true, then the identity of Negroes is bound up intricately, irrevocably, with the identities of white Americans, and especially is this true in the South. (346–47)

Ellison implies, and Warren concurs, that mutual dependence between the races can benefit whites as well as blacks and that whites ought to heed and profit from the fact. The ideal of a communal America, unified and strengthened by racial harmony, is a motivating vision of the book, and the participants in the movement who share it are clearly the figures whom Warren favors.

This desire for communality suggests a prescriptive and cautionary dimension of *Who Speaks for the Negro?* concerning the response of the American white power structure to black demands for equality. (In 1965, as today, how much the power structure was willing to accommodate those demands was unclear.) Throughout the book Warren evinces his concern over the future of the civil rights movement: what it will demand, whether it will employ violence and drift towards separatism. He expresses much of this concern in the main structural theme: the search for a black leader, which prompts him to interview figure after figure in the movement, looking for a consensus about that leader and not finding one. Conditions are ripe, he fears, for the rise of a demagogue, but he observes that so far one has not arisen. Instead, he finds, "merely, a number of Negroes who happen to occupy positions of leadership" (405) and who have served their cause responsibly. Even ambition, he says, "grisly as it appears in certain lights, can mate, if uneasily, with love of justice and dedicated selflessness. . . . And one should not, in fact, be too ready to risk an *argumentum ad hominem* in dealing with, even, the most ambition-bit demagogue. . . . On any particular issue, they may be right, after all" (406).[12] This seems a reaction to the tendency of the media in the 1960s to emphasize rivalries among different factions of the movement and the tendency to pay special attention to such controversial figures as Adam Clayton Powell or Malcolm X. (The concern with black responsibility and with fairness to the black leadership, minor but pervasive themes, is a benign manifestation of the faint paternalism which underlies the book.) Generally, Warren argues, white Americans should concern themselves not with the internal struggles of the movement but with their own reactions to what the movement seeks to achieve. He thus accedes to the black desire for independence from white manipulation and control—conceding that there is no reason for whites to try to influence the movement, that prudent decisions will ultimately be made and right causes served. How white Americans respond to the movement will in large part determine what direction the movement takes, whether towards violence or constructive participation in the American system: "In general, the Negro leadership has given the public little reason to be appalled, for in a situation as complicated as this it would not be easy to imagine a higher level of idealism, dedication, and realistic intelligence. If leadership of that quality is supplanted by other, less savory types that are already lurking in the wings, and that certainly do not have any vision of a reconciled society, the white man has only himself to blame" (406). In this sense the book seeks to uncover and invalidate false white assumptions about the black race, an effort already undertaken in such novels as *Band of Angels, Wilderness, Flood,* and even the early *At Heaven's Gate*. Such assumptions degrade or sentimentalize the black man and impede the white man's understanding and acceptance of him.

In the book's final chapter, "A Conversation Piece," Warren argues that American blacks can play, are playing, a redemptive role by pointing out the failures of white civilization associated with the "crisis of culture" written about by "Pound and Hemingway and Eliot and Auden and a hundred others" (440–41):

> The white man must grant, of course, that Western civilization, white culture, has "failed." We—the white race—have failed to respect the worth of the individual soul and person, to respect the rights of man, to achieve a common liberty, to realize justice, to practice Christian

charity. But how do we know that we have failed? We know it only by applying to actuality those very standards which are the central fact of Western civilization. Those standards are, paradoxically enough, the major creation of that civilization which stands condemned by them. (441)

The precise nature of this crisis Warren explained earlier in his analysis of Whitney Young, who "is up to more than an attack on segregation and poverty, up to more than a program for integrating the Negro into American society. He is attacking, instinctively perhaps, the great dehumanizing force of our society: the fragmentation of the individual" (171). These ideas later prove central to the essays of *Democracy and Poetry*. They were important to the impulses out of which he had earlier written *The Legacy of the Civil War*. He also sees them as central to Ellison's novel *The Invisible Man*, "the most powerful artistic representation we have of the Negro under these dehumanizing conditions; and, at the same time, . . . a statement of the human triumph over those conditions" (354). Dehumanization lies at the center of Warren's criticism of contemporary America and modern life: the dehumanization of the individual, the devaluation of existence. In the black man's alienation and disenfranchisement, he discovers an analogue to his own modern estrangement. Yet the black man occupies a position from which he can, or may, redeem this condition, make the white American aware of it. But he can do so only in an American context, as an American aware of certain grave flaws in the national fabric:

> If he is to redeem America, he will do so as a creative inheritor of the Judeo-Christian and American tradition. . . . He will point out . . .
> that the white man is to be indicted by his own self-professed, and self-created, standards. For the Negro is the Negro American, and is "more American than the Americans." He is, shall we say, the "existentialist" American. He is a fundamentalist of Western culture. His role is to dramatize the most inward revelation of that culture. (442)

Characteristically, Warren now qualifies himself, suggesting that the white man may learn from the black man's response to "our spiritual bankruptcy" and may thus come to redeem himself by "confronting honestly our own standards. For, in the end, everybody has to redeem himself" (442).

Who Speaks for the Negro? examines a specific aspect of modern America's failure to live up to the demands of its own ideals. In ways the book is, now more than twenty-five years later, an anachronism, especially in light of the move in the mid-1960s towards Afro-American nationalism, the assassination of Martin Luther King, Jr., in 1968, and other events Warren could not have foreseen. Perhaps the book was an anachronism when it was written: in it a sixty-year-old white Southerner, a former agrarian segregationist, tries to "find out about things, including my own feelings." High time in 1965, some might say. But Warren had struggled with his conscience and these issues for years, in his essay *Segregation,* in the murder of the slave in *Brother to Dragons,* even in "The Briar Patch." In his own way he came more quickly and directly to grips with the issue of civil rights than any other white Southern writer of the time, including Faulkner, who willingly involved himself in more abstract considerations of the crisis but who never confronted it in the direct, inward, and relentless way exemplified by *Who Speaks for the Negro?, Segregation,* and *Brother to Dragons.* Warren recognized the centrality of the civil rights movement to the American experience and saw the black struggle for equality and citizenship as a quest not only essentially American in character but as capable, perhaps, of reinvesting the nation with the original revolutionary ardor and idealism. He also saw it as a struggle for individual and human rights, for the survival of the individual in the Western world.

From the beginning of his career Warren portrayed American blacks in a fairly consistent manner. For the most part he avoided racist stereotypes. Yet he also did not portray blacks so as to arouse sympathy or concern for their condition. In contrast to William Faulkner, who in such novels as *Light in August* and *Absalom, Absalom!* directly addressed racial themes, with few exceptions Warren kept blacks in the background of his writing before 1953. In the 1950s and 1960s, however, the cultural and social oppression of blacks became for him an overt issue. On several occasions he alluded to their plight as a symptom of the American Dream's failure. In *Brother to Dragons* (1953) the murder of the slave John symbolizes the moral hideousness of slavery and the inherent contradictions between the ideals of the American founders and the reality of the world in which they lived. In *Band of Angels* (1954) and *Wilderness* (1961), black characters play prominent roles, and both novels address clearly racial themes. And in the "Internal Injuries" poems of *Incarnations,* the fate of an urban black woman, run over by a truck, stands not only for modern racism but for the general endangerment of the individual in the modern world.

Even when black characters do illustrate a racial theme, Warren still seems more interested in them as human beings than as symbols of oppression. Through Amantha Starr's discovery of her blackness in *Band of Angels* he explores the mystery of self-knowledge and identity; the racial issues which grow out of her discovery seem of only secondary importance. In *Flood* Mortimer Sparlin, the "Jingle Bells" gas attendant at the Seven Dwarfs Motel, comes South from Chicago to experience "what it felt like to be a Negro in the South," and he learns that "It felt like being himself" (366). In *A Place to Come To* the Indian swami and drug salesman, Rozelle Hardcastle's third husband, occasionally must eat a meal of "sowbelly, chittlings, collards, corn meal, and sorghum" (366) so he can remember that he is really a black man from Alabama. For these black characters, as for all of Warren's characters, the fundamental concern is always identity.

The black figures who occasionally appear in the poetry usually serve the same themes as the white characters, especially the theme of identity. Race is an aspect of identity in these poems but rarely the central issue, though in some of the later poems it becomes a barrier which the poet must transcend in order to achieve human understanding. "Pondy Woods," a poem from the 1920s, explores the theme of human mortality in the figure of "a big black buck" named Big Jim Todd. Cast in the style of a folk ballad, replete with a philosophical buzzard which speaks about mortality and the afterlife, "Pondy Woods" is not wholly successful. Big Jim's crime is unclear, apparently some act committed in town the previous Saturday afternoon and for which the sheriff's posse is hunting him. Jim's blackness is not an issue, except as it defines the social helplessness of his position, but it does allow Warren to portray him as an extreme example of the hopelessly fated man: doomed by the society he lives in for the crime he committed.[13] There is no escape for him, just as there is no escape for any human individual. All must die. Jim is Everyman in this sense, and through him Warren drives home the poem's almost sardonically pessimistic theme.[14]

Analogous to Jim in this poem is Bogan Murdock's servant Anse in *At Heaven's Gate*. Anse is working his way through a local college, hoping ultimately to enroll at Columbia University. When Murdock's daughter is murdered, however, he is wrongly jailed for the crime, primarily because his race makes him the most likely suspect. He is ultimately threatened with lynching. Obviously his own race and the society in which he lives have a major bearing on the plight he finds himself in. Yet through him Warren illustrates the role of chance in human affairs and the destructive effects of a corrupt society. Anse has committed no crime, unlike Big Jim in "Pondy Woods," but in his society a black man does not have to commit a crime to be adjudged guilty.

"The Ballad of Mister Dutcher and the Last Lynching in Gupton" does have a racial theme, but the concern is not so much the injustice of lynchings as the psychology of the lyncher, a quiet unassuming man who, after his wife and son's deaths, becomes one afternoon the motivating violent force in the lynching of a black man wanted for robbery and murder. For Warren the mystery lies in the meaning of the link between that quiet grey man and a particular skill he possesses:

> It
> was the small gray-faced man who, to
> general astonishment though
> in a low, gray voice, said: "Gimme
> that rope." Quick as a wink, six turns
> around the leader, the end snubbed,
> and there was that neat cylinder
> of rope the noose line could slide through
> easy as a greased piston or
> the dose of salts through the widow-
> woman, and that was what Mister
> Dutcher, all the days, weeks, and years,
> had known, and nobody'd known that he knew.
>
> (*SP*, 37)

The poet considers returning to Gupton to find Dutcher's tombstone and even to "try to locate / where that black man got buried, though / that would, of course, be somewhat difficult" (39). Dutcher is a type relatively alien to the modern world, a man out of place even in his own time. The poet's desire to locate his tombstone is a desire to understand the inner life and passions suddenly inflamed when the crime of a black man against a white comes to light, as if to understand the man would in some way allow an understanding of racism itself.

"News Photo," a related poem which, like "Mr. Dutcher," appeared in *Or Else* (but not in the 1975 or 1985 *Selected Poems*), explores the psychology of the lyncher in more depth. As the epigraph announces, the poem is prompted by a news photograph of a man just acquitted of the murder of an Episcopal minister "Reported to Be Working Up the Niggers." Warren depicts the acquitted man as plagued by guilt and inexplicable unhappiness, despite his conviction that he did the right thing and that the "nigger-loving bastards" were

> coming at him, and they
> was disguised like preachers but they
> was Comminists, and if they was preachers, they
> was not Baptists nor even Methodist
> preachers, and sure-God not no
> Church of Christ preachers.
>
> *(Or Else,* 69)

Later, the man admonishes his college-bound son not to "*listen to a single word none of them perfessers is gonna say against your raising, and not even open any durn book that says different*" (71). The poem's final section, which occurs after the man's death, expresses his consternation that "nothing is what he had expected," that his deed of honor and patriotism was ignored: the governor did not attend his funeral, there were no honor guards, and the corpse of Robert E. Lee, who *did* attend, "is laughing fit to kill, or would be / if he weren't dead already" (73). The acquitted murderer exemplifies the quality of piety discussed in *Segregation:* that fidelity to traditions and cultural values. At the same time he has failed to achieve the moral identity which Warren in that essay called for the South to muster. Instead of helping his region to change so that its virtues might endure, he unwittingly acts to bring about their extinction. He is the sort of man Warren had in mind when he suggested in *Who Speaks for the Negro?* that "the obscene caricatures of humanity who have made Philadelphia, Mississippi, newsworthy are scarcely the finest flower of Southern chivalry or the most judicious arbiters of the Southern tradition" (428). Yet at the same time he is a man whom Warren pities, and whom the poem compels the reader to pity through an understanding of the forces which created him.

In "Last Meeting" Warren recalls with regret and guilt his final encounter with a black woman who tended him as a child. He resolves to find her grave, to bring some zinnias there: "It's nigh half a lifetime I haven't managed, / But there must be enough time left for that" (*NSP*, 52). (The finding of an ancestor's grave often signifies for Warren a primal confrontation with one's origins, the past, thus one's identity. Consider the graves of Amantha Starr's real mother in *Band of Angels,* Israel Goldfarb in *Flood,* Jed Tewksbury's father in *A Place to Come To*.) Warren's guilt in "Last Meeting" results not from some sense that he mistreated her because of her blackness, but rather that he never adequately appreciated the genuineness of her love for him, perhaps even that, on their last meeting, it somewhat embarrassed him. The poem emanates from his own recognition of her humanity, and from the fact that for the first time as an old man himself he comes to appreciate her declaration:

> "Chile, yore Ma's dead, yore Pappy ole,
>
> "But I'm hangen on fer what I'm wuth."
>
> (*NSP,* 52)

The recognition, years after the fact, of a shared humanity is also the theme of one of Warren's finest poems of the 1970s: "Old Nigger on One-Mule Cart Encountered Late at Night When Driving Home from Party in the Back Country." The poem concerns the failure and subsequent recovery of human perception and imagination. It concerns as well memory and the contemplation of personal mortality. It is a poem of contrasts, of age versus youth, white versus black, heat versus cold, flesh versus spirit, North versus South, winter versus summer, blindness versus vision. The first half of the poem presents the poet's memory of driving home from a late-night party one summer night in Louisiana and nearly colliding with a black man on a mule-drawn cart full of junk. The man first appears to him as the stereotypical Southern black:

> the fool-nigger—ass-hole wrong side of
> The road, naturally
>
> .   .   .   .
>
> Man-eyes, not blazing, white-bulging
> In black face, in black night, and man-mouth
> Wide open, the shape of an *O,* for the scream
> That does not come.
>
> (*NSP,* 171)

The image is one the poet cannot let go. He awakens later that night to find "floating in darkness above the bed the / Black face, eyes white-bulging, mouth shaped like an *O.*" He decides that the image is the source of a poem, but the formal sonnet he tries to write, only one couplet of which he can remember ("One of those who gather junk and wire to use / For purposes that we cannot peruse" [172]), he rejects with rancor.[15]

Only years later does the significance of this encounter come clear. In "Another / Land, another love, and in such latitude" the poet rises in the cold winter night, a direct contrast to the hot Louisiana summer night of years before. Gazing at the "star-crackling sky," imagining what it would be like to lose himself in the cold whiteness of the mountains, he wonders, with some bitterness, over the forces that make life what it is:

> In the lyrical logic and nightmare astuteness that
> Is God's name, by what magnet, I demand,
> Are the iron and out-flung filings of our lives, on
> A sheet of paper, blind-blank as Time, snapped
> Into a polarized pattern.
>
> (*NSP*, 172–73)

Suddenly the black man's image is there in his mind: "his face / Is lifted into starlight, calm as prayer." He who once was merely a "death-trap" and "fool nigger" is now "Brother, Rebuker, my Philosopher past all / Casuistry" (173). Warren suddenly recognizes his humanity and, in the self-contained simplicity of what he imagines to have been the man's existence, accepts a rebuke to the deceptions and pretensions of the complex life he himself has lived. More, the black man becomes for him a philosopher whose appreciation of darkness, the star-lit sky, defeats all other modes of understanding. There is only awe. He has become for Warren a symbol of personal identity, a fellow human being who has come to terms with himself and his life, his "own cart of junk," but who possesses as well "A hard-won something that may, while Time / Backward unblooms out of time toward peace, utter / Its small, sober, and inestimable / Glow, trophy of truth."

The unnamed and unknown black man is the catalyst and symbol of Warren's own adjustment to the world and of his transformation from indifferent irritation to enlightenment, from bitter contemplation of the void to wonder at the heavens. He is a bringer of reconciliation and redemption, but only because his presence in subconscious and then conscious memory goads the poet into recognition of his own mortality in the world. He is proof as well, suggests Aldon Lynn Nielsen, of how racist stereotypes can "impede the progress of human happiness." [16]

Those stereotypes often dissolve before Warren's eyes in *Segregation* and *Who Speaks for the Negro?* A similar phenomenon is occasionally evident in the later fiction, in the figure of Rau-Ru of *Band of Angels,* Mortimer Sparlin of *Flood,* and the Indian swami of *A Place to Come To.* But the most prominent instance is Mose Talbutt in *Wilderness.* In him we see the fictional manifestation of impulses which helped shape the nonfiction works of the same period. Protagonist Adam Rosenzweig comes to America to fight for the North in the Civil War, which he regards as a struggle for freedom and the emancipation of the slaves. Black Americans in particular he idolizes not only as victims of oppression but as symbols of a noble revolutionary cause. Yet when he arrives in America, he finds a nation, a war, and a people quite different from his expectations. The Northern states are torn with dissension over how the war is being fought, even over the fact that it is being fought at all. On his first day in New York he comes across a murdered black man hanging from a lamp post, a victim of the conscription riots then in progress. At first Adam believes the man to have been killed by invading Confederates. Only gradually does he realize that New Yorkers committed the deed. All that he can discern is that what happened to the black man was wrong and unjust, precisely the sort of injustice—the Bavarian pogroms and restrictions against Jews—he had hoped to escape by coming to America. In the image of the lynched black man, whom at first he does not even recognize as black (he has never seen a black man), he comes face to face with the American equivalent of himself, with the utter negation of the ideals that brought him across the Atlantic: "He stared up into the face, and in the sympathy of blood beating in his head and the stoppage of his own breath, he felt the agony that had popped those eyes and darkened that face" (44).

The riots, an enraged response to the Federal Conscription Act of 1863, provide ironic proof that the ideals for which Adam has come to fight are linked only tenuously to reality. According to some accounts, fifteen hundred people died in the riots, though more likely the figure was closer to three or four hundred victims, most of them blacks. The killing was done mostly by mobs of Irish New Yorkers, immigrants themselves or the offspring of immigrants, fearful that blacks would take their jobs and contribute to the overthrow of Tammany Hall. But mainly they blamed blacks for the war, which they were being conscripted to fight. It was one of the worst race riots in American history and one of the most severe outbreaks of civilian violence during the Civil War.[17] The Irish rioters came to America in search of a better life, to escape harsh economic conditions and British oppression.

And they fail to see the irony, the contradiction, inherent in their violence against another group of immigrants, themselves brought involuntarily to the continent and enslaved. The viciousness of the fat woman who screams "Shag that nigger" at one of the mob's intended victims vividly illuminates the utter absence of the ideals Adam expected to find. For him the dream of American freedom holds redemptive value. He expects to be transfigured by it. For the rioters, there is nothing redemptive at all in the dream. It is a material dream, the hope of a better life. They riot to deny it to those whom they fear will deny it to them.

The Conscription Act itself provides additional evidence of the absence of Adam's ideals. The unwillingness of Northerners to volunteer in sufficient numbers to "fight for freedom" made the act necessary. Aaron Blaustein, an old friend of Adam's family, comments that "the war will be lost if there is not conscription. You see . . . when the heroes are dead, you have to fill the ranks some way. Even with ordinary mortals. Who much prefer to stay at home and make money and sleep with their wives" (70). The irony is intensified by the fact that the act allowed a man with three hundred dollars to buy his way out of having to serve. Volunteers were enticed to join with similar payments. Another bounty was paid the recruiters of "substitutes," most of them foreign immigrants, to serve in place of citizens who wished to avoid service. Adam secured passage to America by agreeing to become such a substitute. Thus the rich could buy their way out of the war. The poor could not. This is why Aaron Blaustein can muse sardonically that "it is rather refreshing to be attacked by the mob merely for being rich. Not for being a rich Jew. It makes all the trouble of coming to America seem worth while" (73).

Wilderness was published in the same year as *The Legacy of the Civil War,* at the beginning of the Civil War centennial. It appeared when the American civil rights movement was making its power clearly known, when segregation in the South and elsewhere in the nation at last seemed doomed. *Wilderness* and *Legacy* offer two different sorts of commentary on the civil rights movement by demonstrating that responsibility for racism lies in the North as well as the South. The danger of the Northern Treasury of Virtue, *Legacy* argues, is that it can deceive Northerners into believing they are exempt from such responsibility. The racism of such Northerners in *Wilderness* as Simms Purdew, who pays black men to bob for apples so he can watch and laugh, the paternalism of Aaron Blaustein, who speaks to Adam about "your Negro," and the bigotry of various Federal soldiers (one is outraged that Mose, a black man, is allowed to watch the whipping of a white prostitute's "bare doup") illuminate the historical facts well enough.

Adam Rosenzweig's idealism and his intense moral outrage over slavery also pertain to the civil rights movement. When Adam arrives in New York, he has never met a black person. Blacks to him are only victims: abstract symbols of the oppression he believes the Civil War is being fought to eradicate. By idealizing blacks, he defines them as more than human, thus implicitly dehumanizing them in his own mind. He consequently misjudges the black men he meets, especially Mose Talbutt, and simultaneously misjudges himself. Adam bases his friendship with Mose on the misconception that because Mose is black, the victim of white oppression, he must necessarily be morally superior to his oppressors. That Mose rescued him from drowning in a New York cellar, intentionally flooded by the rioters, further assures him in this delusion. In Mose, Adam believes he has found a kindred spirit: Mose the black man who has suffered in America as Adam the Jew suffered in Bavaria. Adam thus imposes on Mose a set of impossible expectations which neither man can ultimately live up to. When Mose begins to disappoint them, Adam finds resenting him all too easy.

Mose at first knows nothing of Adam Rosenzweig's ideals and hesitates to accept friendship with him. Finally he comes to trust and rely on him. His dependence, an implicit admission of need and thus weakness, nurtures Adam's resentment. A series of admissions from Mose, intentional or not, that he is human, not a paragon of perfection, complicates the situation. Mose's sexual jokes about white women particularly offend Adam. But when Adam learns that Mose Talbutt is really Mose Crawfurd, a deserter from a black Federal army regiment instead of an escaped slave, and that Mose saved him from drowning only to be sure of saving himself, his disillusionment is complete. The racism he has sublimated since he saw the lynched black man in New York at last breaks out. He calls Mose a black son of a bitch (to Mose, the worst of insults) and in so doing falls victim to the age-old conflict of white and black, master and slave—the very injustice he came to America to fight.

Adam immediately recognizes and regrets this betrayal, but he continues to deny Mose his humanity. Falling to sleep that night with Mose on the other side of the tent moaning in grief over the insult, Adam thinks, "*I have done what I have done. I must live with what I have done. Until he forgives me*" (223)—forgiveness he does not ask for, which he apparently believes will be automatically forthcoming: "Mose Crawfurd. Let him sleep. He needed no forgiveness, not for anything. He had done nothing. History needed forgiveness. . . . Yes, tomorrow Mose Talbutt—Mose Crawfurd— would again be himself and his secret knowledge, beyond blame or pity because totally himself. Mose Crawfurd had, somehow, conquered History. He had escaped from History. He was outside History. . . . Adam Rosenzweig thought: *When he wakes, he will forgive me*" (225–26).

The next morning Mose is gone. Unable to conceive that Mose has deserted him, Adam at first believes he has committed suicide. He then discovers their partner, Jed Hawksworth, whom Mose hated, dead, his throat cut and his money belt missing. This is how Mose Talbutt, "beyond blame or pity," conquered History. Adam never considers that Mose really does need blame and pity. For a moment he refuses to believe that Mose would act so as to violate his own vision of the man. Refusing to acknowledge Mose Talbutt as a human being, Adam forced him to certify his humanity by committing two of the most fundamentally human crimes, robbery and murder.

Adam Rosenzweig's discovery of Mose Talbutt's humanity is only one of a number of revelations he experiences in the course of *Wilderness*. In the context of the movement for civil rights, which it to some extent addresses, the novel clearly illustrates the need for human understanding. By investing the naive yet fervent Adam Rosenzweig with some of the more extreme traits of the Northern Treasury of Virtue, by using the Civil War as a setting and focusing on the friendship of a black and white man caught up in the conflict, Warren links the Civil War to the consequence it spawned nearly a hundred years later, the crusade for civil rights. The result is a parable whose message is that the abstract desire to slay injustice and redeem the oppressed must be accompanied by a recognition of common humanity and a subsequent humble acceptance of its meaning and obligations. The message might be specifically addressed to young and idealistic whites like Adam Rosenzweig, who fervently believed in the moral righteousness of the movement without fully understanding or appreciating the humanness of the people it primarily involved. What Adam learns at the end of *Wilderness* is the meaning of his own humanity. That gained, he can at last understand and accept Mose Talbutt, and himself. Warren thus implicitly urges his readers to regard the movement for civil rights as a human movement rather than a moral or political one, a movement for the reconciliation and redemption of both sides, a movement whose participants must act with wisdom and realism so as to avoid the damaging consequences spawned by the Civil War a century before.

In fiction and poetry, Warren's black characters confirm his fundamental valuation of human beings as individuals with a variety of strengths and weaknesses and idiosyncracies. They reflect as well his resistance to preexistent racial, sexual, or social stereotypes. Even Big Jim in "Pondy Woods" serves this purpose. The poet's recognition of Jim's humanity, his oneness with all other human beings as he faces death, cuts through the racist stereotype of the fugitive black criminal and invests the poem with its uncomfortable power. Beyond the issue of their humanness, black Americans signify for Warren the social and moral paradox of slavery, that institution so totally at odds with the egalitarian ideals of the American genesis. Only through a bloody civil war did slavery come to an end. Its aftermath—poverty, second-class citizenship, injustice—was nearly as bad. In Warren's American vision, blacks, racism, and the legacy of slavery constitute a continuing challenge to the nation's concept of its heritage and identity, its basic values, and the meaning of democracy.

Though it is clear in *Who Speaks for the Negro?* that Warren viewed the civil rights movement as both a political and economic phenomenon, it is clear too, as in *Segregation* and in the fiction and poetry, that he preferred to view it as a human one, the struggle of people to understand one another, to understand themselves. This humanistic vision is prefigured in the epigraph to the book, from Joseph Conrad's novel *Under Western Eyes* (whose title itself is significant to this subject): "I believe that the future will be merciful to us all. Revolutionist and reactionary, victim and executioner, betrayer and betrayed, they shall all be pitied when the light breaks." The epigraph implies a larger perspective than that of economic or political theory, a perspective encompassing the humanity of all involved and embracing the goals of personal, racial, and national redemption towards which Warren envisioned the movement for civil rights to be striving.

CHAPTER 6

Civil War, Nuclear War,

and the American Future

The central document in Robert Penn Warren's treatment of American history is his 1961 essay *The Legacy of the Civil War*. Published at the beginning of the Civil War centennial, the essay explored the importance of the "irrepressible conflict" to the contemporary American's sense of identity and allegiance to a particular national heritage. "The Civil War is," Warren begins, "for the American imagination, the greatest single event of our history. Without too much wrenching, it may, in fact, be said to *be* American history" (3). Warren regards the Civil War as having shaped, more than any other factor, the essential American character, that fusion of idealism and pragmatism, of self-righteous zeal and naked acquisitiveness, of technological self-confidence and moral self-deception. Most of all, he regards it as the beginning of the modern technological age. *The Legacy of the Civil War* expresses a vision of American history which Warren explores at length in his poetry, fiction, and essays. Yet many of the observations he offers in *Legacy* are not his alone. He frequently acknowledges the wide range of historical sources which provide part of the essay's foundation. He does not pretend to offer fresh explanations for the war and its causes. Instead, he approaches the war as a learned observer who seeks to explain its importance for modern Americans.

Warren's conviction that the Civil War gave America an identity and a "history" merits attention. He finds the nation of the present significantly removed from the vision of the founders, though not completely dissociated from it. The Civil War stands as the central cause of that division.

If it did not directly generate many of the nation's problems, it at least catalyzed their development and the genesis of the conditions and ways of thinking which Warren finds characteristically "modern": pragmatism, the technology of mass-production and modern warfare, a strong central government, a national code of values founded on financial success rather than the egalitarian ideals of the Declaration of Independence and the practicality of the Constitution.

Warren also measures the cost of the Civil War in more intangible terms, especially in its psychological effects. He explains, for instance, that defeat gave the South the opportunity to present a united front to the North and the rest of the world. Until that defeat, Southerners disagreed on numerous issues, including slavery and secession. But when the war ended, "the Confederacy became a City of the Soul. . . . In defeat the Solid South was born —not only the witless automatism of fidelity to the Democratic Party but the mystique of prideful 'difference,' identity, and defensiveness" (14). Defeat thus entrapped the South in a cultural stasis from which it has struggled for escape ever since. As he makes clear, however, victory created equally devastating problems for the North.

The Civil War also marked a profound change in how Americans regarded the concept of a democratic union. Related to this change was the rise of pragmatism as a predominant way of thinking, defined by Warren as "the state of mind that saw history not in terms of abstract, fixed principles but as a wavering flow of shifting values and contingencies, each to be confronted on the terms of its context" (*Davis,* 62). In both *The Legacy of the Civil War* and *Democracy and Poetry* Warren cites Oliver Wendell Holmes as the representative pragmatist of his time (though he remarks as well the pragmatism of such figures as Lincoln, Cooper, and Melville):

> Justice Holmes held that the locus of the law is not in the stars or in the statute book, but on the lips of the judge making the particular ruling; that the "life of law is not logic but experience," that is, "the felt necessities of the time"; that law is "predictive" of the way the force of society will act against those who would violate custom or those who would obstruct demanded change; that the document, say the Constitution (which he said is "an experiment as all life is an experiment"), cannot envisage the future contexts of applicability; that the process of seeking truth through the free collision, coil, and jar of ideas is more important than any particular "truth" found, for truth must be under-

stood in the ever-unfolding context of needs and the *I-can't-help* of believing. (*Legacy,* 19)

The failure of the ideals of the Declaration, the disappointment of the vision of the founders, necessitated a fundamental change in attitude towards the republic itself: "The old religious devotion to democracy is undercut, and Jefferson and Whitman seem strangely callow, along with Lincoln, to whom . . . the Union, that embodiment of democracy, had risen to the sublimity of religious mysticism" (*Democracy,* 11). And it is pragmatic thinking, the skill of learning from experience, which Warren credits as a major reason for the North's victory in the Civil War.

The rise of American pragmatism did not mean the immediate appearance of ruthless demagogues who, appealing to the base desires of the Jacksonian masses, gained sway over the land. This was to come primarily in the next century. For the time being, pragmatists such as Lincoln and Grant —whatever their personal faults and virtues—were devoted to the cause of democracy and union, and they worked to preserve it. But Warren does see a clear link between pragmatism and the financial adventurism of the Gilded Age which followed the Civil War. The Gilded Age was the expression of profound changes occurring in American economy and industry, primarily mass industrialization (initially encouraged by the Northern army's need for armaments during the Civil War) and the rise of what we commonly refer to as Big Business, wherein profit and national welfare were (mis)taken as synonymous. The Civil War, Warren writes, "catapulted America from what had been . . . an agrarian, handicraft society into the society of Big Technology and Big Business" (*Legacy,* 8). Similar changes took place in government, with its instinctive compulsion to order and organize: "The old sprawling, loosely knit country disappeared into the nation of Big Organization" (9). The Civil War thus created a new nation which defined its goals in material as well as democratic terms, a nation sublimely convinced of its own irresistible and faultless purpose.

As a poet and novelist who often wrote about history, Warren was always quick to recognize links and parallels between past and present. In *Legacy* these links are far more important to him than any regional or antiquarian interests he might have. For Warren, history in the guise of the Civil War affords the modern American not only a source of identity but also an exemplum, a guide for coping with the problems of contemporary life. The analogical level is thus one of the most interesting dimensions of *Legacy*. Warren regards the Civil War as "the prototype of all war" (83), as an event in history, the consequence of certain forces, causes, and effects; the source of other forces, causes, and effects as well. The lessons Warren sees to be learned from the Civil War pertain especially to the contemporary world situation—that is, the world situation in 1961 and in 1983, when *Legacy* was reprinted by the Harvard University Press. In fact, it is tempting to view the reprinting as a fortuitous response to the general national apprehension of the early 1980s, occasionally verging on hysteria, about the tense relations between the United States and the Soviet Union. More than a commentary on the most important of American wars, *The Legacy of the Civil War* is a prophetic admonition to the nation, to the Western world at large, concerning individual and national responsibility for the future.

Warren centers his admonition in the question of the war's evitability, which ultimately leads him to the issue of humankind's control over history. "Historians," he explains, "are bound to pick the scab of our fate. They are bound to turn to the question underlying the assessment of all experience: To what extent is man always—or sometimes—trapped in the great texture of causality, of nature and history?" (100). Was the Civil War truly inevitable, as some historians argue, or could it have been avoided? The answer is of specific relevance to the modern age: if the Civil War was unavoidable, can the same be said of nuclear confrontation between the United States and the Soviet Union?

The analogy between Civil War and nuclear war thus concerns the responsibility which individuals and nations are willing to assume for their actions and their desire to evade that responsibility. In fact, as William C. Havard has argued, *Legacy* directly concerns "the refuges available to those who refuse to confront the moral difficulties of existence and the consequences which flow from evasion of responsibility."[1] The assumption of responsibility matters not merely in the consideration of events and individuals which propelled the nation towards battle but also in how Northern and Southern states viewed the war once it was over. Warren notes a number of groups and individuals in both North and South who contributed to the momentum. Radical abolitionists viewed their struggle against slavery as a sacred quest ordained by God, immune to the considerations of human law and reason. They engendered an extremism which Warren finds dangerous: "The man who is privy to God's will cannot long brook argument, and when one declines the arbitrament of reason, even because one seems to have all the reason and virtue on one's side, one is making ready for the arbitrament of blood. So we have the saddening spectacle of men courageously dedicated to a worthy cause letting their nobility grow so distempered by impatience that sometimes it is difficult to distinguish love of liberty from lust for blood" (20). Abolitionist James Redpath, for example, announced that "if all the slaves in the United States . . . were to fall on the field or become the victims of vengeance . . . if only one man survived to enjoy the freedom they had won, the liberty of that solitary negro . . . would be cheaply purchased" (20–21). Such fervor converts opposition to slavery from a moral, social, and political issue—capable of resolution in a manner fitting to democracy, reason, and justice—to one which commands its proponents in emotional and religious terms so intense that considerations of reason and humanity become irrelevant. Put simply, fanatical abolitionists believed they took their orders from God and that nothing else mattered. Refusing compromise, negotiation, or the possibility of more gradual change, they contributed enthusiastically to an inexorable momentum towards apocalyptic battle between the forces of good and evil, momentum founded on John Brown's favorite biblical verse: "Without the shedding of blood there is no remission of sins" (22).

Most abolitionists were not so fanatical, but those who were (some of the most outspoken and influential leaders of the movement) strengthened the likelihood of national conflict. But abolitionists were not the only group at fault. Warren suggests that before the war Southerners were so firm in their defense of slavery that they could not admit the possibility of change in any form. After the war, they resorted to what he calls the Great Alibi to avoid confronting their problems, which they blamed on the war and the victorious North. Northerners, through victory having liberated the slaves and preserved the Union, felt free to proceed with the task of strengthening and enriching a restored nation. The South had caused its own problems, they reasoned. Let the South deal with them. With this attitude, which Warren calls the Treasury of Virtue, the North excused itself of any obligation to contend with the damaging consequences of the Civil War, especially those concerning racism and the freed slaves. The North felt "redeemed by history, automatically redeemed" (59). Because the North won the war, its Treasury of Virtue came to belong to the nation as a whole and influenced its attitudes towards a wide range of concerns, including foreign policy. American political speeches throughout the modern era have frequently addressed, in theological and moral terms, our national "mission" to defend freedom, individualism, and world peace. Such talk, and the attitudes which produce it, directly reflects our national self-image of virtue and righteousness and our perception of nations with which we are at odds, especially non-democratic, non-Christian nations.

The Treasury of Virtue is an expression of the same forces which converge in the argument for the Civil War's inevitability. To argue that it was inevitable, Warren suggests, is to argue that humankind exerts no control over history and thus cannot be held accountable for events which occur. He notes historian Arthur Schlesinger's belief that the Civil War was inevitable because the South, in Schlesinger's words, "closed in the defense of evil institutions thus create[d] moral differences far too profound to be solved by compromise" (94). Schlesinger characterizes the war as a clash between good and evil, a morally impelled conflict which *had* to be fought. The question of inevitability involves issues of free will and determinism, the extent to which individuals singly or communally can influence national and international events. It may be convenient to argue that the course of history stands beyond human control: one is thus relieved of the responsibility for what happens. So it is, Warren argues, that the Treasury of Virtue compelled the North to believe in the Civil War's inevitability: "the evil of the South made the Civil War *morally* inevitable, and the North was merely the bright surgical instrument in the hand of God, or History. There is one feature that most versions of the inevitability theory share—any of them may be invoked to demonstrate the blamelessness of the instrument in the hand of the surgeon" (98). It is not the war's inevitability that bothers Warren here: it is the illusion of blamelessness, the abdication of moral responsibility. "The man of righteousness," he observes, "tends to be so sure of his own motives that he does not need to inspect consequences" (74).

Warren refuses to accept the Civil War's inevitability. His reasons are quite simple: If we believe that events must occur as they will, that we cannot influence them, then events are likely to consume us. The result is surrender of will, a divorcing of the self from the lessons of the past and the possibilities of the future. It is moral self-annihilation. Turning a second time to Schlesinger's argument, Warren observes:

> The present momentous crisis of our history, when our national existence may be at stake, makes us demand what we can learn—if, alas, anything—from that great crisis of our national past [the Civil War].

Does a society like the USSR, "closed in the defense of evil institutions," create "moral differences far too profound to be solved by compromise"? If so, when do we start shooting? Or to drop the moral concern, does the naked geo-political confrontation with Russia doom us to the struggle? . . . Can we, in fact, learn only that we are victims of nature and of history? Or can we learn that we can make, or at least have a hand in the making of, our future? (101–2)

In 1961, the national crisis to which Warren referred was the intensifying cold war between the United States and the Soviet Union. The erection of the Berlin Wall, the Bay of Pigs invasion, the shooting down of an American spy plane in Russia—these and other events had raised tensions to a dangerous level. Only a year later, with the successful resolution of the Cuban missile crisis, would they seem to lessen slightly. The republication of *Legacy* in 1983 came at a time when tensions seemed on a similar rise. In particular there was the specter of a presidential administration which, in often bellicose fashion, spoke of the conflict between the U.S. and the Soviet Union in moral rather than political or economic terms: of good versus evil, piety versus atheism. The Soviet Union was, according to the U.S. president, an "evil empire" bent on the conquest of the free world. In just such an atmosphere, *Legacy* begged us consider, where is room for negotiation, compromise, humanitarian common sense? Why *not* start shooting and determine the matter once and for all? Despite Glasnost and the relaxation of U.S.–Soviet tensions in the late 1980s, the question remains pertinent.

Warren's attitude towards whether we are the mere "victims of nature and heredity" wavered over the years. His early novels *Night Rider* and *World Enough and Time,* and the long poem "The Ballad of Billie Potts," portray individuals who attempt to take control of their lives, to change their world and history, and who are obliterated for their efforts. Even in the 1980 essay *Jefferson Davis Gets His Citizenship Back,* a reiterative companion-piece to *Legacy,* Warren recalls with gentle irony his grandfather's contention that the Civil War could have been avoided and had been "just worked up by fools." "Perhaps," Warren muses, "he merely expected history to be rational—that most irrational of expectations" (11). Yet in other instances Warren portrays the individual as capable of achieving some accommodation with environment and circumstance. Jack Burden, in *All the King's Men,* is one such individual, but we may recall as well Amantha Starr in

Band of Angels, Jediah Tewksbury in *A Place to Come To,* and John James Audubon, who despite the failure of his ideals does not allow the world to disillusion him. Throughout his work Warren vigorously opposes the philosophical stance of passive fatalism, of historicism, blind submission to the inertia of events. He advocates an existence consciously and purposefully *lived,* affording the individual identity and dignity. *The Legacy of the Civil War* endorses such an existence. Its final emphasis falls on the lessons which *might* be learned from the past: "History cannot give us a program for the future, but it can give us a fuller understanding of ourselves, and of our common humanity, so that we can better face the future" (100).

The future as shadowed forth in such issues as nuclear war, democracy's survival, and the individual's place in the modern world concerned Warren frequently during the last four decades of his life. He expressed his anxieties about nuclear war on a number of occasions. The long poem "New Dawn" dramatizes the moral and humanitarian implications of the bombing of Hiroshima, Japan, on August 7, 1945. The poem recounts in a clinically dispassionate voice the activities of the crew of the *Enola Gay* as they prepare to drop an atomic bomb on the Japanese city. Never does any member of the crew pause to consider the consequence of what he is about to do. Indeed, the crew seems incapable of such considerations. Theirs is merely a job, part of the war effort, and when they accomplish their mission, they congratulate themselves and return to

> The brotherly hug, the bear-embrace, the glory, and
> "We made it!"
>
> The music, then solemn
> Silence of the pinning of the medal,
> The mutual salute. At last,
> The gorging of the gorgeous feast
> To the point of vomit, the slosh
> Of expensive alcohol
> In bellies expensively swollen.
>
> Some men, no doubt, will, before sleep, consider
> One thought: I am alone. But some,
> In the mercy of God, or booze, do not
>
> Long stare at the ceiling.
>
> (*NSP,* 39–40)

These men epitomize not merely the complete abnegation of human and moral responsibility (by both individuals and their society) but the dangers of a morally blind technology which wields a vast and terrible power whose significance the poem's structure conveys: "New Dawn" is probably the only poem in the English language to contain not only an accurate technical description of an atomic bomb's innards—

> Like the dumb length of tree trunk, but literally
> A great rifle barrel packed with uranium,
> Two sections, forward one large, to rear one small, the two
> Divided by a "tamper" of neutron-resistant alloy.
> All harmless until, backed by vulgar explosive, the small will
> Crash through to
> The large mass
> To wake it from its timeless drowse. And that
> Will be that. Whatever
> *That* may be.
>
> (35)

—but also a checklist of instructions for arming it. The first section, "Explosion: Sequence and Simultaneity," specifies the time in various cities— Greenwich, New York, Chicago, San Francisco—at the instant of explosion in Hiroshima: 8:16 A.M., August 6, 1945. The few human moments in the poem—Colonel Tibbets's brief pause for introspection before the bomb is dropped, his strangely equivocal observation that the brilliance of the bomb's explosion over Hiroshima was "a taste like lead," and the final stanza—are for the most part drowned out by the portrayal of committed men enveloped in a trivia of technical detail, routine and regimen, and self-congratulation. The poem does suggest their lack of compunction, but more significantly it implies that they and their world lack the moral discernment to recognize the nature of what they are doing. This lack of humanity, bred of a world ruled by machine rather than reason and insight, bodes ill for the future of all: clouds obscuring the primary targets hide not Japanese cities but "the doomed world," and when the bomb, dropped, descends to the programmed altitude,

> There,
> The apocalyptic blaze of
> New dawn
>
> Bursts.

Temperature at heart of fireball:
50,000,000 degrees centigrade.

(38)

Hiroshima time, the poem explains, is 8:16, August 6, 1945, but the rest
of the world, as the opening section implies, marks from that moment the
commencement of the modern age.

Apprehension of that moment, of the power it has spawned, leads Yasha
Jones in Warren's 1964 novel *Flood* to resign his position as physicist at the
University of Chicago when he learns of the bombing of Hiroshima (264–
66). This is the same power which compels Warren to worry in *Democracy
and Poetry* that

> somebody may, really, drop the big bomb; the air may really get un-
> breatheable; industrial resources are finite and our demands increasing
> exponentially; the possibility of crossing the fatal threshold for heat
> emission seems to be sliding toward probability. We may, indeed, have
> become, as Erik Erikson describes us, "a species mortally dangerous
> to itself." Or we may be approaching an age of bloody troubles to be
> followed, perhaps, by a neo-primitivism in which time will die into the
> mere succession of the seasons and history will die into ritual.[2] (44–45)

His concern is with the terrible human suffering nuclear war would cause,
the survival of the individual, of the Western world and its civilization. It is
also with the general question of whether civilization is capable of preventing its own technology from consuming it, of whether it can act to insure
its own survival.

Warren's nonfiction critiques of American culture and society present
the ideas of a man who has passed much of his life reacting against the
tenor of modern American life, just as he and other essayists in the agrarian
manifesto *I'll Take My Stand* did in 1930. Those essays were, from one
perspective, reactionary, theocratic, racist, elitist, neo-Confederate, and
unrealistic. Though Warren abandoned the more limiting aspects of this perspective early in his career, he remained an agrarian Southerner all his life.
But his agrarianism progressively enlarged to a national and international
level, one he described as "parochially of the Western World" (*Democracy*,
xii) and which implicitly expresses a concern for the survival of all nations
and cultures which value the individual.

Warren's support for the civil rights movement, well documented in *Segregation* and *Who Speaks for the Negro?*, grew from his recognition that

the movement was morally just, that it was a struggle for individual rights, an opportunity for the South to confront its past without resorting to Great Alibis. His advocacy of civil rights and his anxiety over nuclear war are genuine expressions of agrarian concern for the quality of modern life. His conviction that history and the Civil War offer valuable lessons for the present may indeed be old-fashioned. But the essential meaning he reads in the Civil War is of undeniable importance. Pretend that nuclear war won't happen, and it will. Turn international relations into a moral confrontation of good and evil, and apocalypse will ensue. Reject responsibility for our place and time in history, and the consequences will be dire. Sensing in modern America many of the same forces which drove the nation a century ago towards civil war, he questions whether they must precipitate another, much worse conflict. He urges Americans to decide whether they will become only "victims of nature and of history" or whether they "can make . . . our future" (102) and take destiny firmly in hand.

Warren's apprehension over nuclear war is only one aspect of his general concern with the quality of modern life. In his essay "Poetry and Selfhood," in *Democracy and Poetry,* he bluntly argues that the industrialized, technocratic world of the twentieth century directly endangers the survival of the individual. Such a world deprives the individual of meaningful links with a community, thus of personal identity. Identity means selfhood, which Warren defines as, "in individuation, the felt principle of significant unity" (xii). Felt means *experienced; significant* means "continuity—the self as a development in time, with a past and a future; and responsibility—the self as a moral identity, recognizing itself as capable of action worthy of praise or blame" (xiii). Our technocratic society allows no room for such a self, nor does it easily provide for the existence of democracy as a viable form of government: "a mechanistic society cannot . . . accommodate what John Stuart Mill long ago took . . . to be the basis of liberty: a variety of character and the chance for human nature to expand in different and even contradictory directions. Nor, on the other hand, can such a society foster a community of individual selves bound together by common feelings, ideals, and conceptions of responsibility" (45).

America's history rendered it particularly susceptible to the disorientation and alienation of the modern mechanistic world which it had such a major role in creating. In its own founding it sought to nullify time and to create itself *ex nihilo:* "Space replaced time as the prime category for [the free] citizen; and man, moving ever westward, was redeemed from the past, was washed in the Blood of a new kind of Lamb" (54). Nineteenth-century Americans, with the Revolution and the War of 1812 successfully behind them, sought consciously to break with the past, its traditions and conventions, to develop a genuine sense of identity, a national self. The Declaration and the Constitution constituted a major break with past governments and philosophical systems. Their emphasis on the right and responsibility of individual citizens to control their destinies became the cornerstone of American democracy. Yet the post–Civil War Treasury of Virtue, the growing technological and scientific expertise of the Gilded Age and the early twentieth century, the stress laid on progress and the future—these gave Americans a sense of confidence and even hubris which eventually led them to abandon the past entirely. "History is bunk," Henry Ford's pithy aphorism, Warren cites as the representative American attitude (54). In this view, America has no past, a vacuum Warren finds most damning:

> A society with no sense of the past, with no sense of the human role as significant not merely in experiencing history but in creating it can have no sense of destiny. And what kind of society is it that has no sense of destiny and no sense of self? That has no need or will to measure itself by the record of human achievement and the range of the human endowment? . . . The effect of the abolition of the past on the conception of the self is by a negative [*sic*], by denying the individual the chance to see himself in the perspective of human nature and human accomplishment. (56)

America as well became a nation with a public but not a community: quoting Kierkegaard, Warren observes that the "public is a kind of gigantic something, an abstract and deserted void which is everything but nothing" (61). Moral responsibility is a true mark of genuine selfhood and the democratic spirit, yet that mark the "public" lacks. In such a circumstance, the individual has abdicated responsibility entirely, yielding it up to some higher authority, in whose will he trusts: "The individual fades into abstraction, . . . as Jung describes the matter, being the 'idea of the State as the principle of political reality.' Thus, the moral responsibility of the individual, a mark of his selfhood, is 'inevitably replaced by the policy of the State,' and the 'moral and mental differentiations of the individual' replaced by 'public welfare and the raising of the living standard' " (65).[3]

Warren is not without hope for modern society. While in *The Legacy of the Civil War* he argued for a national assumption of moral responsibility, and in *Segregation* and *Who Speaks for the Negro?* he suggested that social movements founded on the rights and value of the individual might restore purpose to American life, in *Democracy and Poetry* he offers up the elixir of poetry, the highest expression of human experience, the "dynamic affirmation of, as well as the image of, the concept of the self" (68). Poetry provides a counterbalance, an alternative body of knowledge and values to the prevailing tones of modernity. As technology increasingly liberates man from the necessity of work, poetry (by which Warren means the arts in general) may provide a significant outlet for his free time. Poetry might then serve as an "antidote, a sovereign antidote, for passivity. For the basic fact about poetry is that it demands participation, from the secret physical echo in muscle and nerve that identifies us with the medium, to the imaginative enactment that stirs the deepest recesses where life-will and values reside. Beyond that, it nourishes our life-will in the process of testing our values" (89–90). Society might thus be redeemed from technocratic depersonalization. Though he offers this hope as nothing more than a possibility, he is not even sure that art can survive to work its redemptive effect. If the technological world continues to diminish the commonly perceived value of art, then it is unlikely that "a world in which art does not find a place would ever long harbor men who find, in some degree, intrinsic significance in the process of life" (85). Without poetry and the dialectic with democracy it can provide, "life, as we know it and esteem it, will cease" (93).

Warren was not the first to exalt art as the redeemer of civilization. He may have been among the last. He was perhaps idealistic and even naive, though in the most admirable sense, to suggest that art can affect society at all. Certainly art is the artist's personal response to social, cultural, and environmental conditions. And surely if art represents the certification of "the concept of the self," of the individual in the world, then we can easily understand why the artist readily finds himself at odds with a society moving steadily towards the self's nullification. What can poetry do that in any way can sway the world and alter this momentum? Nothing. That day when poetry served as a vital social force stands hundreds if not thousands of years in the past. Those who believe that a thing must possess measurable value, quantifiable force, to be of importance dismiss poetry with a sneer or relegate it to the pariah category of "charity" or, even worse, "culture," where it now languishes. Yet perhaps Warren did not intend poetry to be a vital public force at all. Perhaps he meant quite simply that the individual can profit from exposure to artistic expression: "A man need not create art in order to participate, with varying degrees of consciousness, in the order of experience from which art flows" (85). A major component of that experience is exposure to the perspective of another self in opposition to the world. Participating in the validation of the artist's self through the art he has created, the individual undergoes a similar validation of his own identity. Through that validation he recognizes his importance as a human being. The vision and confidence gained thereby may enable him, in this view, to cope better with the problems of the world, giving him a degree of what is commonly known as wisdom.

However society might have valued poetry in the past, it holds a negligible place in contemporary America. Only for the individual, whom it may provide enjoyment and personal insight, can it play a significant role, and even then we must wonder exactly what claim we can make for it. Such United States presidents as Abraham Lincoln, Theodore Roosevelt, and Jimmy Carter were well read in literature, but others, Lyndon Baines Johnson and Ronald Reagan, for instance, were not. What proof is there that literature better prepared Roosevelt for the presidency than Johnson or Reagan? In a world which values an object for its material worth or its ability to enhance conditions of life in a material way, poetry, literature, and the other arts hold a tenuous position. That position alone was for Warren sufficient proof of the imperiled state of the Western world and its traditions.

Warren's concern with the Western world's survival is especially evident in his late fiction. His last three novels—*Flood, Meet Me in the Green Glen,* and *A Place to Come To*—all deal in one way or another with the possibility of its disappearance. The first two center on the metaphor of a Tennessee Valley Authority reservoir about to inundate communities more than a century old. *A Place to Come To* explores Jed Tewksbury's apprehension of mortality and the modern world's moral anarchy. These novels and a number of the later poems deal specifically with what Warren regards as the symptoms of modernity: alienation, loss of self, dehumanization, the threat of cultural obliteration (the nightmare city of *Incarnations,* for instance). But the novels in particular offer vivid images of a possible future. The America glimpsed in *Flood* stands in imminent danger of permanent submergence. It faces the prospects not merely of inundation, but of being sentimentalized and cheapened beyond recognition by corrupted art forms and commercialism. In the opening scene, the protagonist Brad Tolliver returns to his home town of Fiddlersburg for the first time in twenty years and happens upon the location of his boyhood fishing hole. In its place he finds the Seven Dwarfs Hotel, all-encompassing symbol of national self-decay and narcissism, where one can "Rest in Happy Dell" and where concrete statues parody and pervert the natural setting they have replaced:

> The big sycamore by the creek was gone. The willow tangle was gone. The little enclave of untrodden bluegrass was gone. The clump of dogwood on the little rise across the creek—now that, too, was gone.
> But the trouble was not so much what was not there. It was what was there. The creek was there, but it flowed decorously between two banks where stones were mortised into the earth; and on a boulder a cement frog, the size of a young calf and the color of Paris green . . . crouched. On another boulder a gnome, dwarf, brownie or some such improbability, with a cement beard painted snow-white, sat studiously fishing. The line with which the creature was fishing was a real line. . . . But the water lilies were definitely cement. (4)

Fiddlersburg itself still resists modern artificiality but at the risk of becoming a stagnant backwater. It remains a community with a specific tradition and values. The blind woman Leontine Purtle is completely at ease there. She knows the streets and houses of the town perfectly and needs no cane or guide dog to lead her around. Another character, Israel Goldfarb, chose to settle in Fiddlersburg because its values and tradition made him understand what it meant to be a Jew. Yet in these senses Fiddlersburg is what the modern world is not. It is an enclave from time, but the waters of the encroaching lake work inexorably to destroy it. The big clock in the town square has long been stopped at 8:35 (like the watches found in Hiroshima, fused to a stop at 8:16). It is a symbol of the promise which lingers faintly in the modern world and of the processes which are fast acting to wipe it out. When Fiddlersburg is submerged, Leontine Purtle will be lost, and Israel Goldfarb's grave, the novel's crucial symbol of personal identity, will have vanished forever.

The American founders consciously set out to *make* a nation, believing in the possibility of beginning anew, of erecting a "city on the hill" which might avoid the mistakes of the past and forge a new and hopeful future. History proved this hope hollow. Throughout the course of American literature the theme of national failure has surfaced repeatedly, in a way which after two centuries begins to seem almost narcissistic: the specter of a nation's writers picking its scabs, groveling in the ashes of its ruins for a few fragments of old hopes to gum. Many twentieth-century writers have abandoned the theme entirely, ignoring it or proving in various ways its irrelevance. They have turned inward to the personal self and experience. External structures of religion, nationalism, and culture have ceased to offer metaphysical or emotional supports. (When such a writer as Paul Theroux, in *The Mosquito Coast,* intentionally returns to some of the old themes, he seems almost an anachronism, though his concern is not so much America as modern technology.) In *The Waste Land* T. S. Eliot lamented the external world's collapse and the individual self's inability to be self-sustaining. *The Four Quartets* celebrates his discovery of the sustaining power of Anglican theology, yet in a context of withdrawal from the external world. In a sense the smug self-congratulatory tone of Eliot's later poems, on occasion almost a justification for ignoring the external world completely, further confirms, rather than assuages, the pain of discovery in *The Waste Land,* at least for those readers unconvinced by Eliotic theology.

Though in his early poetry he at times seemed content to mourn with Eliot, Warren ultimately accepted the modern world's collapse as one of the givens which one who does not wish to perish in the ruins must simply accept. Yet he remained, in a sense, a genuine anachronism among modern writers, continuing to search for the possibility of meaning in a world which assumes for the most part that meaning does not exist. "I am a creature of the modern world," he explained to Peter Stitt, "but I am also a yearner, I suppose. I would call this temperament rather than theology—I haven't got any gospel. That is, I feel an immanence of meaning in things, but I have no meaning to put there that is interesting or beautiful. . . . I am a man of temperament in the modern world who hasn't got any religion." [4] That temperament is apparent throughout his poems. But he rarely seeks to analyze or understand what Transcendent Thing, if any, might lie beyond the sense of reverence, the sublime so often evident in the late poems. More often, he is skeptical. Balanced against the "naturalistic considerations" of *Brother to Dragons* which characterize the natural world without illusion, there is the need to believe—in something. But Warren rarely suggests where belief should lie. Belief, he implies, necessitates the suspension of reason, the faculty of the conscious mind. Thus, in "A Way to Love God," we encounter this image:

> I watched the sheep huddling. Their eyes
> Stared into nothingness. In that mist-diffused light their eyes
> Were stupid and round like the eyes of fat fish in muddy water,
> Or of a scholar who has lost faith in his calling.
>
> Their jaws did not move. Shreds
> Of dry grass, gray in gray mist-light, hung
> From the side of a jaw, unmoving.
>
> You would think that nothing would ever happen again.
>
> That may be a way to love God.
>
> (NSP, 165–66)

The sheep, like the fish (like the blind catfish beneath the frozen Mississippi in *Brother to Dragons*), do not think about God or the transcendent. They merely exist, live. There is joy in such mindlessness. But to begin to think about that joy is to submit it to the laws of the physical world, to destroy it. Yet such thought is the inescapable nature of the human.

The non-existence of the America envisioned by Thomas Jefferson and the other founders is a fundamental element of Warren's thinking. That mythic nation lies forever beyond attainment. Yet Warren never wholly abandoned belief in it. Nor did he abandon his conviction, expressed implicitly in such poems as *Brother to Dragons, Audubon: A Vision,* and "Homage to Ralph Waldo Emerson," that the old Jeffersonian ideals may yet serve some redemptive purpose. The very pursuit of the unattainable can be redemptive. The abandonment of hope, the submission to despair, on an individual and national level, is the most dangerous event that can occur. This is what can seem archaic and contradictory about Warren, this persistent belief and disbelief in the ideal of the "city on the hill," this persistent consternation at its absence.

Warren's American writings clearly reveal the agrarian perspective from which he viewed the world throughout his life. Yet his agrarianism changed significantly in the years following *I'll Take My Stand* in 1930. Or conversely, he compels a redefinition of what agrarianism really meant. For

Donald Davidson it remained to the end of his life an intensely regional concern. One need only compare his anti-integration stand during the 1950s and 1960s with Warren's civil rights writings which, despite their advocacy of a movement which meant to change the South profoundly, spoke from a strongly agrarian perspective. For Davidson agrarianism signified the preservation of Southern values and identity. For Allen Tate agrarianism came finally to signify, by 1950, conversion to Catholicism, a return to religious orthodoxy (which he would doubtless contend includes orthodox Southern values). For Warren, who transcended regionalism and whose religion verges on agnosticism (despite his adherence to a Judeo-Christian morality and vocabulary), agrarianism meant an intense individualism fused with an emphasis on the human community and the individual's place within it.

Warren's agrarianism is national and international in scope. It reacts powerfully against those forces of modern dehumanization which, threatening the individual, threaten the nation and the Western world. It calls for the mustering of those forces which can save the individual's place in the world, for "whatever works to make democracy possible is 'really' democratic. And it would seem clear that 'poetry' is an essential one of the 'whatevers.' For poetry—the work of the 'makers'—is a dynamic affirmation of, as well as the image of, the concept of the self" (*Democracy*, 68). Warren's writing throughout his career sought to explore the meaning of American experience, to validate the promise and the dangers of American ideals, and to urge the nation to take stock of itself and to struggle for control of its fate in history. Repeatedly and obsessively, he struggled to understand the complex and contradictory convolutions of American identity. In poetry and fiction that make identity a major theme, which reflect the conviction that art *must* have a place in the modern world, Warren affirmed his own identity as one of the most significant of makers in American literature.

N O T E S

The following abbreviations are used frequently throughout the study:
 SP Robert Penn Warren, *Selected Poems, 1923–1975*. New York: Random House,
   1976.
NSP Robert Penn Warren, *New and Selected Poems, 1923–1985*. New York: Random House, 1985.

Chapter One. Robert Penn Warren's American Vision

1. For reasons explained in chapter two, unless otherwise noted all references to
   Brother to Dragons come from the revised 1979 version.
2. Floyd C. Watkins and John T. Hiers, Jr., *Robert Penn Warren Talking: Interviews 1950–1978* (New York: Random House, 1980), 251.
3. *Robert Penn Warren Talking,* 198–99.
4. Sears is in one way the twin brother of the Northern officer in the second poem
   of "Two Studies in Idealism: Short Survey of American, and Human, History,"
   first published in *You, Emperor and Others* (1960). See *Selected Poems,* 216.
5. In a somewhat different context, recently naturalized novelist Bharati Mukherjee, a native of India, has observed that new immigrants to the nation have
   "lived through centuries of history in a single lifetime—village-born, colo-
   nized, traditionally raised, educated. What they've assimilated in 30 years has
   taken the West 10 times that number of years to create" ("Immigrant Writing: Give Us Your Maximalists!" *New York Times Book Review,* 28 August
   1988, 28).
6. *Robert Penn Warren Talking,* 199.
7. Harold Bloom, review, *The New Republic,* 30 September 1978, 34.
8. Harold Bloom, review of *Brother to Dragons: A New Version, The New Republic,* 1 and 8 September 1979, 31 (reprinted in *Robert Penn Warren's "Brother to
   Dragons": A Discussion,* ed. James A. Grimshaw, Jr. [Baton Rouge: Louisiana
   State University Press, 1983]).
9. Letter to John Adams, 28 October 1813, in *Thomas Jefferson/Writings* (New
   York: Library of America, 1984), 1305–6.
10. Robert Penn Warren, *All the King's Men* (New York: Harcourt, Brace, and Co.,
   1946), 54.

11. John Burt, *Robert Penn Warren and American Idealism* (New Haven: Yale University Press, 1988), 37.

12. The single-minded intensity of Lincoln's devotion to saving the Union is apparent in this letter to Horace Greeley, who had criticized him for not making better use of Negro troops in the war effort: "My paramount object in this struggle is to save the Union, and is not either to save or destroy slavery. If I could save the Union without freeing any slave, I would do it; and if I could save it by freeing all the slaves, I would do it; and if I could do it by freeing some and letting others alone, I would also do that. What I do about Slavery and the colored race, I do because it helps to save the Union; and what I forebear, I forebear because I do not believe it would help to save the Union" (quoted in Howard Zinn, *A People's History of America* [New York: Harper & Row, 1980], 186).

13. "A Dearth of Heroes," *American Heritage* 23 (October 1972): 97.

14. "A Dearth of Heroes," 4.

15. Obsession may be a better word than interest: anyone who could read both *The "Genius"* and *The Stoic,* apparently more than once, would have to be obsessed.

16. "A Dearth of Heroes," 97.

17. "A Dearth of Heroes," 99.

18. William Bedford Clark, "Robert Penn Warren's Love Affair with America," *Southern Review* 22 (1986): 672.

19. James H. Justus aptly defines the novel's political center: "If clear-cut, abstract, and arbitrary principles are unable to respond adequately to complex actualities, how flexible should they become in order to benefit archaic or local ways of life threatened or ignored by more progressive ways? Can justice be expected to survive the administrative disposition of law?" (*The Achievement of Robert Penn Warren* [Baton Rouge: Louisiana State University Press, 1981], 231). Justus goes on to suggest that *World Enough and Time,* "Prime Leaf," and *All the King's Men* "reflect their author's considerable observation of and meditation on the goals and tactics of Franklin D. Roosevelt's New Deal."

20. Introduction to *All the King's Men* (New York: Harcourt Brace Jovanovich, 1981), xiv.

21. John Burt, in *Robert Penn Warren and American Idealism,* calls Warren's concept of Union an "idea of nationality . . . a body of unconscious or half-conscious agreements that North and South share, that shape their habits of argument and their understanding of experience, and that bind them together in ways their conflict [the Civil War] can obscure but must not be allowed to destroy" (52).

22. He was, as Louis Rubin has noted, the prototype of a character with whom Warren would later much concern himself: "What fascinated [Warren] about the old man was what would constitute the stuff of each of his first five novels: the relationship of private, subjective moral idealism to complex social fact, and

the corrupting psychological temptation of power" (*The Wary Fugitives: Four Poets and the South* [Baton Rouge: Louisiana State University Press, 1978], 337).

23. In a 1961 exchange of letters with Nicola Chiaromonte, Warren argued that if an individual "trusts his society, and state, he knows that if he disobeys he violates the concept of law which is the guarantee of his right to protest; he knows that if he disobeys he undercuts the basis of democratic society." He later called such disobedience "*a revolutionary act*" (Warren's emphasis) and "an attack on democracy" but in his second letter admitted "the shakiness of my own position" (*The Yale Review* 1 (1961): 474–80). Within three years he had decided that disobedience for the sake of correcting injustice and strengthening society was defensible.

24. *I'll Take My Stand: The South and the Agrarian Tradition, by Twelve Southerners* (New York: Harper & Brothers, 1930; Baton Rouge: Louisiana State University Press, 1980), 22.

25. See Davidson's letter to Allen Tate in *The Literary Correspondence of Donald Davidson and Allen Tate,* ed. John Tyree Fain and Thomas Daniel Young (Athens: University of Georgia Press, 1974), 329–32.

26. Louis Rubin speculates: "Warren would have been happier if his argument could have been made without reference to the tilling of soil; for the way for the black man to achieve the kind of self-sufficiency and self-respect that Warren saw as necessary, while remaining in a racially separate society, clearly led through such untraditional ways as vocational education, greater literacy, improvement of economic conditions, and (though Warren tried his best to keep from making the overt statement) political franchise. The truth is that the only way Warren could have logically fitted southern racial segregation into an Agrarian argument was to have produced a standard Thomas Nelson Page depiction of the black man as a happy, child-like peasant, and Warren knew better than that" (*The Wary Fugitives,* 216). Aldon Lynn Nielsen compares Warren's difficult stance here to that of the antebellum Southern intellectual described in *The Legacy of the Civil War* as expending all his intellectual energy in a defense of the indefensible: "It was a position which Warren was not capable of occupying for very long, one which his intellect soon forced him to abandon" (*Reading Race: White American Poets and the Racial Discourse in the Twentieth Century* [Athens: University of Georgia Press, 1988], 114). "The Briar Patch" was one in a collection of statements about agrarian life in the American South. Perhaps Warren realized as he neared the end of his essay that he had better tend to the perspective he was supposed to promote.

27. Query 19, *Notes on Virginia,* in *Thomas Jefferson/Writings,* 290.

28. Marshall Walker suggests that the essay "was, in 1930, for Warren, the most humane possible expression of practical sympathy for the Negro within the structure in which both he and the Negro had been raised" (*Robert Penn Warren: A Vision Earned* [New York: Barnes & Noble, 1979], 34–35).

29. *Robert Penn Warren Talking,* 97.

30. *Robert Penn Warren Talking,* 22–23.

31. *Robert Penn Warren Talking,* 196, 217.

32. *Robert Penn Warren Talking,* 237.

Chapter Two. *Brother to Dragons* and the Sins of the Fathers

1. Victor Strandberg, *The Poetic Vision of Robert Penn Warren* (Lexington: University Press of Kentucky, 1977), 170–71.

2. Dumas Malone comments that "We can only conjecture how soon Jefferson learned of this sensational episode and how much he knew of its aftermath. No doubt he was informed of the indictment and suicide of his nephew Lilburne, and of the flight of Isham, but he seems to have left no reference to these nephews, whose dark deeds contrasted so sharply with his luminous career" (*Jefferson and His Time: The Sage of Monticello* [Boston: Little-Brown and Co., 1981], 154).

3. Floyd C. Watkins, "A Dialogue With Robert Penn Warren on *Brother to Dragons,*" *Southern Review* 16 (1980): 15.

4. William Bedford Clark, " 'Canaan's Grander Counterfeit': Jefferson and America in *Brother to Dragons,*" in *Robert Penn Warren's "Brother to Dragons": A Discussion,* 146; (reprinted from *Renascence* 30 (1978): 171–78). Professor Clark's fine essay has in many ways influenced my reading of Jefferson's character and meaning in the poem.

5. *Robert Penn Warren Talking,* 40.

6. *Robert Penn Warren Talking,* 39–40.

7. Watkins, "A Dialogue With Robert Penn Warren on *Brother to Dragons,*" 1–3.

8. Obviously, I differ with Richard N. Chrisman, who favors the 1953 poem in "*Brother to Dragons* or *Brother to Dragons, A New Version?* A Case for the 1953 Edition," in *Robert Penn Warren's "Brother to Dragons": A Discussion,* 211–25. Two other essays in the same volume, Margaret Mills Harper's "Versions of History and *Brother to Dragons*" (226–43) and Lewis Simpson's "The Concept of the Historical Self in *Brother to Dragons*" (244–49), favor the 1979 version.

9. Margaret Mills Harper, "Versions of History and *Brother to Dragons,*" in *Robert Penn Warren's Brother to Dragons: A Discussion,* 237. Professor Harper's excellent essay examines in detail the character and significance of the differences between the two versions.

10. Victor Strandberg, "*Brother to Dragons* and the Craft of Revision," in *Robert Penn Warren's "Brother to Dragons": A Discussion,* 202.

11. Cleanth Brooks, "R. P. Warren: Experience Redeemed in Knowledge," in *The Hidden God: Studies in Hemingway, Faulkner, Yeats, Eliot, and Warren* (New

Haven: Yale University Press, 1963), 99 (reprinted in *Robert Penn Warren's "Brother to Dragons": A Discussion*, 14).

12. For a fuller discussion of Dedalus and the labyrinth in the poem, see George Palmer Garrett, "The Function of the Pasiphaë Myth in *Brother to Dragons*," *Modern Language Notes* 74 (April 1959): 311–13 (reprinted in *Robert Penn Warren's "Brother to Dragons": A Discussion*, 77–79).

13. William Bedford Clark suggests that although Jefferson recognizes in Lilburne the symptom of universal human evil, "he never really acts as if he partakes of that condition himself. In effect, he hates and blames Lilburn less for the agony he inflicts upon the slave than for the fact that 'The Death of that black boy was the death / Of all my hope'" ("'Canaan's Grander Counterfeit,'" 147–48).

14. Watkins, "A Dialogue With Robert Penn Warren on *Brother to Dragons*," 10. See also the foreword to the poem, xiii.

15. Sigmund Freud, *Civilization and Its Discontents*, tr. James Strachey (New York: W. W. Norton, 1962), 59.

16. Clark, "'Canaan's Grander Counterfeit,'" 150.

17. For example, Dennis M. Dooley, "The Persona R. P. W. in Warren's *Brother to Dragons*," in *Robert Penn Warren's "Brother to Dragons": A Discussion*, 102 (reprinted from *Mississippi Quarterly* 25 (Winter 1971): 19–30); and Strandberg, *The Poetic Vision of Robert Penn Warren*, 181.

18. "'Canaan's Grander Counterfeit,'" 150.

19. Query 8, *Notes on Virginia*, in *Thomas Jefferson/Writings*, 288.

20. Lewis P. Simpson, "The Ideology of Revolution," in *The History of Southern Literature*, ed. Louis D. Rubin, Jr., et al. (Baton Rouge: Louisiana State University Press, 1985), 64, 66.

21. In "'Canaan's Grander Counterfeit,'" William Bedford Clark argues that Jefferson's "total surrender of selfhood" to the notion of unlimited human potential "bears a clear resemblance to the egocentric absolutism of the 'higher law' men whose position Warren attacks in . . . *The Legacy of the Civil War*" (147).

22. *Robert Penn Warren Talking*, 23–24.

23. Aldon Lynn Nielsen suggests that these lines are "the nearest Warren comes to truly arriving at the reality of the humanity as it moves behind the signifiers of race propagated by the likes of Thomas Page in books like his *Old South* and accepted as true, and there certainly are no like moments to be found in the poetry of Warren's associate, Allen Tate" (*Reading Race*, 119). Nielsen's elegant study of race and racism among white American poets overemphasizes Warren's agrarian identity and does not fully recognize the racial enlightenment represented tentatively in *Brother to Dragons* and more firmly in *Segregation* and *Who Speaks for the Negro?*, the latter of which leaves no doubt as to Warren's support for the cause of the American black.

24. Brooks, "Experience Redeemed in Knowledge," 15.

25. In his autobiography Jefferson remembered the Maison Quareé as "being con-

sidered the most perfect model existing of what may be called Cubic architecture" and initially planned to model the Virginia state capitol building after it (*Thomas Jefferson/Writings*, 41).

26. Justus, *The Achievement of Robert Penn Warren*, 67.

27. *Robert Penn Warren Talking*, 79.

28. In *Then & Now: The Personal Past in the Poetry of Robert Penn Warren* (Lexington: University Press of Kentucky, 1982), Floyd Watkins offers a parallel reading: percoon "was a medicine, but it was also a ritualistic passing on of some kind of gift or heritage from father to son—a plant and a name known now only by a folk doctor" (128).

29. Richard G. Law, " 'Doom Is Always Domestic': Familial Betrayal in *Brother to Dragons*," in *Robert Penn Warren's "Brother to Dragons": A Discussion*, 254–55, 262.

30. Robert Penn Warren, *Portrait of a Father* (Lexington: University Press of Kentucky, 1988). Originally published in the *Southern Review* 23 (1987): 33–67.

31. *John Brown: The Making of a Martyr* (New York: Payson and Clarke, 1929), 136.

32. Bloom, review in *Robert Penn Warren's "Brother to Dragons": A Discussion*, 183; Calvin Bedient, *In The Heart's Last Kingdom: Robert Penn Warren's Major Poetry* (Cambridge: Harvard University Press, 1984), 84.

Chapter Three. *Audubon: A Vision* and the American Imagination

1. Warren's poetic Audubon differs significantly from the historical man. Warren's Audubon is more introspective, more single-minded in his devotion to the woods, and considerably less worldly. See Justus, *Achievement of Robert Penn Warren*, 87–96; and Allen Shepherd, "Warren's *Audubon*: 'Issues in Purer Form' and 'The Ground Rules of Fact,' " *Mississippi Quarterly* 24 (Winter 1970–71): 47–56; William Bedford Clark, "Warren's Audubon: The Artist as Hero," *South Atlantic Quarterly* 81 (1982): 387–98.

2. William Bedford Clark has also recognized this desire for merger in "Warren's Audubon: The Artist as Hero," 393.

3. Michael Harwood and Mary Durant, "In Search of the Real Mr. Audubon," *Audubon Magazine* 87 (May 1985): 95–97.

4. "Love and Separateness in Eudora Welty," *Selected Essays* (New York: Random House, 1958), 162. The essay was originally published in *The Kenyon Review* in 1944.

5. Bedient, *In the Heart's Last Kingdom*, 136.

6. In his discussion of Eudora Welty's "A Still Moment," Warren offered a similar assessment of Audubon's paintings, at least in the sense of their separateness from nature: "Having killed the bird [in order to study and paint it], he knows

that the best he can make of it now in a painting would be a dead thing" ("Love and Separateness in Eudora Welty," 162).

7. "Experience," from *Essays: Second Series,* in Ralph Waldo Emerson, *Essays and Lectures* (The Library of America, 1983), 487.

8. The differences between part two, "The Dream He Never Knew the End Of," and the source in Audubon's *Ornithological Biography* are considerable, as critics have noted. In the prose sketch "The Prairie" Audubon mainly wants to tell the story of his narrow escape. He does not speculate on the possible implications of his tale, nor does he reveal his emotions or thoughts, other than to state his fear over what the frontier woman may do to him and his relief at his timely rescue (so timely as to cast doubt on the truth of the tale). Clearly then, Warren is presenting his own vision of the man. His purposes are poetic, not historical. As far as we know, the "Prairie" incident (whether true or not) played no significant role in Audubon's life. Warren makes his version the center of the poem, dramatizing Audubon's discovery of his kinship with the corrupt humanity from which he sought escape in the woods, thus his education in the knowledge that merger with nature will remain always unattainable to him. See Justus, Shepherd, and Clark.

9. *In the Heart's Last Kingdom,* 136.

10. Helen Vendler, review, *New York Times Book Review,* 11 January 1970, 5.

11. *Audubon* was first published in 1969, though Warren had worked on a version of it as early as the 1940s. See *Robert Penn Warren Talking,* 234–35, 275–76, 279–80.

12. Among the critics who have commented on this connection are Max A. Webb ("*Audubon: A Vision:* Robert Penn Warren's Response to Eudora Welty's 'A Still Moment'," *Mississippi Quarterly* 34 [1981]: 445–55) and James Justus (*The Achievement of Robert Penn Warren,* 87–96).

13. "Homage to Emerson, On Night Flight to New York," in *Selected Poems: 1923–1975,* 153–58; omitted from *New and Selected Poems: 1923–1985.*

14. None of the poems from this middle section were retained in the 1985 *New and Selected Poems.*

Chapter Four. Recovering the Past:
Chief Joseph of the Nez Perce

1. Edwin Thomas Wood, "On Native Soil: A Talk with Robert Penn Warren," *Mississippi Quarterly* 37 (1984): 186.

2. Wood, "On Native Soil," 186.

3. *Robert Penn Warren Talking,* 207.

4. James Justus, "Warren's Later Poetry: Unverified Rumors of Wisdom," *Mississippi Quarterly* 37 (1984): 161. In the years since its initial appearance in the *Georgia Review* (36 [Summer 1982]: 269–313) and its publication a year

later in much revised form as a separate volume, *Chief Joseph* (New York: Random House, 1983) has provoked only slight critical response. Discussions of the poem include Marilyn Callander, "Robert Penn Warren's *Chief Joseph of the Nez Perce:* A Story of Deep Delight," *Southern Literary Journal* 16 (Fall 1983): 24–33; Nicolas Tredell, "Shaman and showmen," *Times Literary Supplement,* 27 April 1984, 454; Monroe K. Spears, "Robert Penn Warren: A Hardy American," *Sewanee Review* 91 (1983): 658–59; Bedient, *In the Heart's Last Kingdom,* 86–87. Reasons for this inattention may range from the poem's relative newness to the fact that critics have never known quite what to do with long narrative modern poems (especially American ones) to the infrequently expressed but pervasive prejudice that old poets have nothing of interest to say. Warren does not confirm the latter prejudice.

5. Merrill B. Beal, *"I Will Fight No More Forever": Chief Joseph and the Nez Perce War* (Seattle: University of Washington Press, 1963), 243.

6. Page Smith, *The Rise of Industrial America* (New York: McGraw-Hill, 1984), 74–78.

7. Alvin M. Josephy, Jr., *The Nez Perce Indians and the Opening of the Northwest* (New Haven: Yale University Press, 1965), 637. Marilyn Callander, in "Robert Penn Warren's *Chief Joseph of the Nez Perce:* A Story of Deep Delight," 35, suggests Warren used this book as a source for the poem.

8. "Sanctuary," in Donald Davidson, *Lee in the Mountains and other poems* (New York: Scribner's, 1938), 56.

9. The lack of suspense may account for Calvin Bedient's judgment (a wrong one, in my opinion) that *Chief Joseph* is "less excited and exciting" than *Brother to Dragons* and that in it "Warren is strangely subdued" (*In the Heart's Last Kingdom,* 86).

10. Sherman made this statement in his "Message to the President of the United States," A.G.O. 3464–77, printed in *United States Senate Executive Documents,* vol. 1. It is quoted in Beal, *"I Will Fight No More Forever": Chief Joseph and the Nez Perce War,* where Warren may have found it.

11. Josephy, *The Nez Perce Indians,* 336.

12. Warren told Edwin Thomas Wood that he brought the poem up to the present day at this point "to give the poem its visceral reality, but at the same time to certify its literal reality" ("On Native Soil," 186).

Chapter Five. Warren and the Crisis in Civil Rights: "The Burden of Our Time"

1. *Robert Penn Warren Talking,* 10.

2. The prodigious research and numerous interviews he conducted for this project attest to the importance Warren apparently placed on it. Book reviews reveal that he had steeped himself deeply in contemporary writing about American

race relations ("Race," *The New York Times Book Review,* 8 October 1964, 7–9; "Who Shall Overcome," *The New York Times Book Review,* 22 October 1964, 8, 10; "The Negro Movement in Upheaval," *The New York Review of Books,* 18 August 1966, 22–25). Moreover, the introductory sections, which manuscript evidence summarized in James A. Grimshaw's bibliography allow us to surmise he wrote for *American Literature: The Makers and the Making,* reveal that he had studied many of the most prominent black American writers, including Booker T. Washington, Paul Laurence Dunbar, W. E. B. Du Bois, James Weldon Johnson, Langston Hughes, Jean Toomer, and Richard Wright, as well as the Harlem Renaissance (*Robert Penn Warren: A Descriptive Bibliography, 1917–1978.* Charlottesville: University of Virginia Press, 1981, p. 438). *Who Speaks for the Negro?* itself is full of references to works by black authors and scholars. Clearly, Warren prepared carefully for this book.

3. Warren's "journalism" often resembles the work of John Hersey, author of *Hiroshima* and *The Algiers Hotel Incident,* to whom Warren dedicated his poem "New Dawn," about the bombing of Hiroshima.

4. Justus, *The Achievement of Robert Penn Warren,* 150.

5. Walker responds to this confession with a retort—"It is very courageous of you"—whose irony and condescension Warren recognizes. At first he experiences a "cold flash of rage" but later writes in his notebook: "*The Negro Movement is fueled by a sense of moral superiority. No wonder that some sloshes over on the white bystander as condescension. The only effective payment for all the other kinds of condescension visited on black men over the years. Antidote indicated: humor. And not only self-humor*" (*Who Speaks for the Negro?*, 232).

6. I strongly disagree with Aldon Lynn Nielsen who, though he recognizes and admires the "constant struggle" through Warren's career with the racist assumptions of his youth, ultimately concludes that in the end Warren had "moved no farther" from these assumptions "than to a stage of radical uncertainty" (*Reading Race,* 103). Warren in *Who Speaks for the Negro?* is unambiguous about his advocacy of equality for American blacks. He *is* uncertain as to the means by which equality can best be achieved, but that uncertainty has nothing to do with racism.

7. "A Dearth of Heroes," 99.

8. James Justus calls the volume Warren's "most objective book, coming as close to being a discursive volume as anything in his canon; but in its structure, its internal patterns, and its textural 'voice,' *Who Speaks for the Negro?* speaks for Robert Penn Warren" (*The Achievement of Robert Penn Warren,* 147).

9. Despite the negative portrait of Malcolm X, Warren later expressed his admiration for the man: "He was one of the most fascinating persons I ever knew. . . . We got along fine" (Wood, "On Native Soil," 179–86).

10. James Justus offers an excellent discussion of *Who Speaks for the Negro?* in *The Achievement of Robert Penn Warren,* but I do not agree with his opinion that there is no "evidence of the blatant journalistic device of ironic juxtaposition"

(146). The juxtaposition may not be blatant, for the most part, but it is a subtle and carefully handled source of order in the book nonetheless.

11. *Chief Joseph of the Nez Perce* chronicles the betrayal of another minority group by the federal government in 1877. It was a decade of betrayal.

12. Cf. *Chief Joseph*, "For a true chief no self has" (21).

13. Jim is a victim of the sort of racial injustice Warren complains of in "The Briar Patch."

14. Aldon Lynn Nielsen does see a racial theme or disturbance in the poem: "What might it mean, for instance, that much of the plainly racist speech directed at Big Jim Todd as he hides from his pursuers is spoken to him in the ballad by a buzzard? Who might the buzzard speak for when he admonishes Todd, saying "Nigger, your breed ain't metaphysical" . . . ? The poem predates the English translations of the works of Derrida by nearly three decades, but it may prove useful to recall Derrida's identification of metaphysics as white mythology. The buzzard may then be seen as the carrier of the ostracizing power of white discourse, the trope which declares the otherness of the black and the disjunction between white and black time. . . . The use of the buzzard as spokesman for the mythology sets up a disturbance within the discourse, for it is a spokesman with whom few readers will readily identify" (*Reading Race*, 117–18).

15. According to Victor Strandberg, Warren took the couplet from an unpublished sonnet, written some forty years before, about an old man, a mule, and a cart ("Image and Persona in Warren's 'Early' Poetry," *Mississippi Quarterly* 37 [Spring 1984]: 137–38).

16. Nielsen, *Reading Race*, 118.

17. Allan Nevins, *The War for the Union: The Organized War, 1863–1864*, vol. 7 of *Ordeal of the Union*, 8 vols. (New York: Random House, 1947–71), 119–25; Shelby Foote, *The Civil War: A Narrative*, 3 vols. (New York: Random House, 1958–74), 636–37.

Chapter Six. Civil War, Nuclear War, and the American Future

1. William C. Havard, "The Burden of the Literary Mind: Some Meditations on Robert Penn Warren as Historian," *South Atlantic Quarterly* 62 (1963): 527.

2. Warren is quoting Erik Erikson, *Dimensions of a New Identity* (New York: Norton, 1974), 31.

3. Warren is quoting C. G. Jung, *The Undiscovered Self*, tr. R. F. C. Hull (Boston: Little, Brown, 1958), 13–14.

4. *Robert Penn Warren Talking*, 234.

S E L E C T E D B I B L I O G R A P H Y

I. Works by Robert Penn Warren

"A Dearth of Heroes." *American Heritage* 23 (October 1972): 4, 6–7, 95–99.

A Place to Come To. New York: Random House, 1977.

A Robert Penn Warren Reader. New York: Random House, 1987.

All the King's Men. New York: Harcourt, Brace and Co., 1946.

All the King's Men. New York: Harcourt Brace Jovanovich, 1981.

All the King's Men [play]. New York: Random House, 1960.

American Literature: The Makers and the Making. Edited with Cleanth Brooks and R. W. B. Lewis. 2 vols. New York: St. Martin's Press, 1973.

At Heaven's Gate. New York: Harcourt, Brace and Co., 1943.

Audubon: A Vision. New York: Random House, 1969.

Band of Angels. New York: Random House, 1955.

Being Here: Poetry 1977–1980. New York: Random House, 1980.

"The Briar Patch." In *I'll Take My Stand: The South and the Agrarian Tradition, by Twelve Southerners*. New York: Harper & Brothers, 1930; Baton Rouge: Louisiana State University Press, 1980.

Brother to Dragons: A Play in Two Acts. *The Georgia Review* 30 (1976): 65–138.

Brother to Dragons: A Tale in Verse and Voices. New York: Random House, 1953.

Brother to Dragons: A Tale in Verse and Voices, A New Version. New York: Random House, 1979.

The Cave. New York: Random House, 1959.

Chief Joseph of the Nez Perce. New York: Random House, 1983.

The Circus in the Attic and Other Stories. New York: Harcourt, Brace, 1947.

Democracy and Poetry. Cambridge: Harvard University Press, 1975.

Eleven Poems on the Same Theme. Norfolk, Conn.: New Directions, 1942.

Flood. New York: Random House, 1964.

" 'The Great Mirage': Conrad and *Nostromo*." In *Selected Essays*. New York: Random House, 1958.

Homage to Theodore Dreiser, on the Centennial of His Birth. New York: Random House, 1971.

Incarnations: Poems 1966–1968. New York: Random House, 1968.

Jefferson Davis Gets His Citizenship Back. Lexington: University Press of Kentucky, 1980.

John Brown: The Making of a Martyr. New York: Payson and Clarke, 1929.

John Greenleaf Whittier's Poetry: An Appraisal and a Selection. Minneapolis: University of Minnesota Press, 1971.

The Legacy of the Civil War. New York: Random House, 1961; New Haven: Yale University Press, 1983.

"Love and Separateness in Eudora Welty." In *Selected Essays*. New York: Random House, 1958.

Meet Me in the Green Glen. New York: Random House, 1971.

"The Negro Movement in Upheaval." *New York Review of Books*, 18 August 1966, 22–25.

New and Selected Poems: 1923–1985. New York: Random House, 1985.

Night Rider. Boston: Houghton-Mifflin, 1939.

Now and Then: Poems 1976–1978. New York: Random House, 1978.

Or Else—Poem/Poems 1968–1974. New York: Random House, 1974.

Portrait of a Father. Lexington: University Press of Kentucky, 1988. Originally published in the *Southern Review* 23 (1987): 33–67.

Promises: Poems 1954–1956. New York: Random House, 1957.

"Race." *The New York Times Book Review*. 8 October 1964, 7–9.

[Robert Penn Warren to Nicola Chiaromonte] *The Yale Review* 1 (1961): 474–80.

Rumor Verified: Poems 1979–1980. New York: Random House, 1981.

Segregation: The Inner Conflict in the South. New York: Random House, 1956.

Selected Essays. New York: Random House, 1958.

Selected Poems: New and Old, 1923–1966. New York: Random House, 1966.

Selected Poems: 1923–1975. New York: Random House, 1976.

Selected Poems, 1923–1943. New York: Harcourt, Brace, 1943.

Selected Poems of Herman Melville. Edited by RPW. New York: Random House, 1971.

Thirty-Six Poems. New York: Alcestis Press, 1935.

"Who Shall Overcome." *The New York Times Book Review*, 22 October 1964, 8, 10.

Who Speaks for the Negro? New York: Random House, 1965.

Wilderness. New York: Random House, 1961.

World Enough and Time: A Romantic Novel. New York: Random House, 1950.

You, Emperors, and Others: Poems 1957–1960. New York: Random House, 1960.

II. General

Beal, Merrill B. *"I Will Fight No More Forever": Chief Joseph and the Nez Perce War*. Seattle: University of Washington Press, 1963.

Bedient, Calvin. *In the Heart's Last Kingdom: Robert Penn Warren's Major Poetry*. Cambridge: Harvard University Press, 1984.

Bloom, Harold. Review. *The New Republic*, 30 September 1978, 34.

————. Review of *Brother to Dragons: A New Version*. *The New Republic,* 1 and 8 September 1979, 30–31.

————, ed. *Robert Penn Warren: Modern Critical Views*. New York: Chelsea House, 1986.

Brooks, Cleanth. "R. P. Warren: Experience Redeemed in Knowledge." In *The Hidden God: Studies in Hemingway, Faulkner, Yeats, Eliot, and Warren*. New Haven: Yale University Press, 1963: 98–103. Reprinted in *Robert Penn Warren's "Brother to Dragons": A Discussion,* edited by James A. Grimshaw, Jr. Baton Rouge: Louisiana State University Press, 1983.

Burt, John. *Robert Penn Warren and American Idealism*. New Haven: Yale University Press, 1988.

Callander, Marilyn. "Robert Penn Warren's *Chief Joseph of the Nez Perce:* A Story of Deep Delight." *Southern Literary Journal* 16 (Fall 1983): 24–33.

Casper, Leonard. *Robert Penn Warren: The Dark and Bloody Ground*. Seattle: University of Washington Press, 1960.

Chesnut, Mary Boykin. *Mary Chesnut's Civil War*. Edited by C. Vann Woodward. New Haven: Yale University Press, 1981.

Chrisman, Richard N. "*Brother to Dragons* or *Brother to Dragons, A New Version?* A Case for the 1953 Edition." In *Robert Penn Warren's "Brother to Dragons": A Discussion,* edited by James A. Grimshaw, Jr. Baton Rouge: Louisiana State University Press, 1983.

Clark, William Bedford. " 'Canaan's Grander Counterfeit': Jefferson and America in *Brother to Dragons*." *Renascence* 30 (1978): 171–78. Reprinted in *Robert Penn Warren's "Brother to Dragons": A Discussion,* edited by James A. Grimshaw, Jr. Baton Rouge: Louisiana State University Press, 1983.

————, ed. *Critical Essays on Robert Penn Warren*. Boston: G. K. Hall, 1981.

————. "Robert Penn Warren's Love Affair with America." *Southern Review* 22 (1986): 667–79.

————. "Warren's Audubon: The Artist as Hero." *South Atlantic Quarterly* 81 (1982): 387–98.

Davidson, Donald. "A Mirror for Artists." In *I'll Take My Stand: The South and the Agrarian Tradition, by Twelve Southerners*. New York: Harper & Brothers, 1930; Baton Rouge: Louisiana State University Press, 1980.

————. *Lee in the Mountains and other poems*. New York: Scribner's, 1938.

Emerson, Ralph Waldo. "Experience." From *Essays: Second Series,* in *Essays and Lectures*. The Library of America, 1983.

Erikson, Erik. *Dimensions of a New Identity*. New York: Norton, 1974.

Fain, John Tyree, and Thomas Daniel Young, eds. *The Literary Correspondence of Donald Davidson and Allen Tate*. Athens: University of Georgia Press, 1974.

Foote, Shelby. *The Civil War: A Narrative*. 3 vols. New York: Random House, 1958–74.

Freud, Sigmund. *Civilization and Its Discontents*. Translated by James Strachey. New York: W. W. Norton, 1962.

Grimshaw, James A., Jr. *Robert Penn Warren: A Descriptive Bibliography 1917–1978*. Charlottesville: University Press of Virginia, 1980.

———, ed. *Robert Penn Warren's "Brother to Dragons": A Discussion*. Baton Rouge: Louisiana State University Press, 1983.

———, ed. *Time's Glory: Original Essays on Robert Penn Warren*. Conway, Ark.: University of Central Arkansas Press, 1986.

Guttenberg, Barnett. *Web of Being: The Novels of Robert Penn Warren*. Nashville, Tenn.: Vanderbilt University Press, 1974.

Harper, Margaret Mills. "Versions of History and *Brother to Dragons*." In *Robert Penn Warren's "Brother to Dragons": A Discussion,* edited by James A. Grimshaw, Jr. Baton Rouge: Louisiana State University Press, 1983.

Harwood, Michael, and Mary Durant. "In Search of the Real Mr. Audubon," *Audubon Magazine* 87 (May 1985): 58–119.

Havard, William C. "The Burden of the Literary Mind: Some Meditations on Robert Penn Warren as Historian." *South Atlantic Quarterly* 62 (1963): 516–31.

Jefferson, Thomas. *Notes on Virginia,* in *Thomas Jefferson/Writings*. New York: Library of America, 1984.

Josephy, Alvin M., Jr. *The Nez Perce Indians and the Opening of the Northwest*. New Haven: Yale University Press, 1965.

Jung, C. G. *The Undiscovered Self*. Translated by R. F. C. Hull. Boston: Little, Brown, 1958.

Justus, James H. *The Achievement of Robert Penn Warren*. Baton Rouge: Louisiana State University Press, 1981.

———. "Warren's Later Poetry: Unverified Rumors of Wisdom." *Mississippi Quarterly* 37 (1984): 161–72.

Law, Richard G. " 'Doom Is Always Domestic': Familial Betrayal in *Brother to Dragons*." In *Robert Penn Warren's "Brother to Dragons": A Discussion,* edited by James A. Grimshaw, Jr. Baton Rouge: Louisiana State University Press, 1983.

Malone, Dumas. *Jefferson and His Time: The Sage of Monticello*. Boston: Little, Brown and Co., 1981.

Mukherjee, Bharati. "Immigrant Writing: Give Us Your Maximalists!" *New York Times Book Review,* 28 August 1988, 1, 28–29.

Nevins, Allan. *The War for the Union: The Organized War, 1863–1864*. Vol. 7 of *Ordeal of the Union*. 8 vols. New York: Random House, 1947–71.

Nielsen, Aldon Lynn. *Reading Race: White American Poets and the Racial Discourse in the Twentieth Century*. Athens: University of Georgia Press, 1988.

Ransom, John Crowe. "Reconstructed but Unregenerate." In *I'll Take My Stand: The South and the Agrarian Tradition, by Twelve Southerners*. New York: Harper & Brothers, 1930; Baton Rouge: Louisiana State University Press, 1980.

Rubin, Louis D., Jr. "Dreiser and *Meet Me in the Green Glen:* A Vintage Year for Robert Penn Warren." *Hollins Critic* 9 (1972): 1–10.

————. *The Wary Fugitives: Four Poets and the South*. Baton Rouge: Louisiana State University Press, 1978.

Shepherd, Allen. "Warren's *Audubon:* 'Issues in Purer Form' and 'The Ground Rules of Fact.' " *Mississippi Quarterly* 24 (Winter 1970–71): 47–56.

Simpson, Louis. "The Concept of the Historical Self in *Brother to Dragons*." In *Robert Penn Warren's "Brother to Dragons": A Discussion,* edited by James A. Grimshaw, Jr. Baton Rouge: Louisiana State University Press, 1983.

————. "The Ideology of Revolution." In *The History of Southern Literature,* edited by Louis D. Rubin, Jr., et al. Baton Rouge: Louisiana State University Press, 1985.

Smith, Page. *The Rise of Industrial America*. New York: McGraw-Hill, 1984.

Spears, Monroe K. "Robert Penn Warren: A Hardy American." *Sewanee Review* 91 (1983): 658–59.

Strandberg, Victor H. *A Colder Fire: The Poetry of Robert Penn Warren.* Lexington: University Press of Kentucky, 1965.

————. "*Brother to Dragons* and the Craft of Revision." In *Robert Penn Warren's "Brother to Dragons": A Discussion,* edited by James A. Grimshaw, Jr. Baton Rouge: Louisiana State University Press, 1983.

————. "Image and Persona in Warren's 'Early' Poetry." *Mississippi Quarterly* 37 (Spring 1984): 135–48.

————. *The Poetic Vision of Robert Penn Warren*. Lexington: University Press of Kentucky, 1977.

Tredell, Nicolas. "Shaman and showmen." *Times Literary Supplement,* 27 April 1984, 454.

Walker, Marshall. *Robert Penn Warren: A Vision Earned*. New York: Barnes & Noble, 1979.

Watkins, Floyd C. "A Dialogue With Robert Penn Warren on *Brother to Dragons*." *Southern Review* 16 (1980): 1–17.

————. "A National Poet." *Mississippi Quarterly* 37 (1984): 173–78.

————. *Then & Now: The Personal Past in the Poetry of Robert Penn Warren.* Lexington: University Press of Kentucky, 1982.

————, and John T. Hiers, Jr. *Robert Penn Warren Talking: Interviews 1950–1978*. New York: Random House, 1980.

Wood, Edwin Thomas. "On Native Soil: A Talk With Robert Penn Warren." *Mississippi Quarterly* 37 (1984): 179–86.

Zinn, Howard. *A People's History of America*. New York: Harper & Row, 1980.

INDEX

Abolitionists, radical, 5, 14–15, 25, 27, 132, 164–65
Absalom, Absalom! [Faulkner], 150
Adams, John, 10
African-Americans, 29–35, 60, 69, 105–6, 108, 115, 116, 119, 129, 131–60, 165, 180 (n. 12), 181 (nn. 26, 28), 183 (nn. 13, 23), 186–87 (n. 2), 187 (nn. 5, 6)
Afro-American nationalism, 131, 144, 150
Agrarianism, 9, 16, 28–36, 37, 127, 139, 150, 163, 170–71, 177–78, 181 (n. 26), 183 (n. 23)
Algiers Hotel Incident, The [Hersey], 187 (n. 3)
All the King's Men, 11, 19, 22, 24–25, 29, 45, 71, 112, 113, 122, 167, 180 (n. 19)
"Altitudes and Extensions," 97, 111
America, 1, 7, 16, 49, 51, 76, 79, 105, 111, 122, 128. *See also* United States
America: myth of, 1, 40
American democracy, 3, 4, 37, 62, 134, 144, 172. *See also* Democracy
American dream, 3, 13, 17, 18, 19, 41, 44–45, 54, 70, 95, 120, 128, 133, 150, 157
American Eden, 118, 119
American vision, 1, 4, 6, 7, 160
American West, 5, 7, 48–49, 54, 77, 104, 112–14, 117
American wilderness, 7–8, 41–42, 44,

48–55, 65–66, 79–105 passim, 113, 119–20
An American Tragedy [Dreiser], 133
Anse [*At Heaven's Gate*], 151–52
Arts, in modern society, 173–74. *See also* Poetry
At Heaven's Gate, 2, 3, 18, 19, 24, 32, 97, 148, 151–52
Atomic age, 3
Atomic bomb, 168, 169
Auden, W. H., 148
Audubon, John James, 7, 8, 13, 14, 45, 77, 79–103, 105, 107, 111, 127, 168, 184 (nn. 1, 6), 185 (n. 8)
Audubon, Lucy, 86, 87, 92, 93, 95
Audubon: A Vision, 2, 3, 9, 37, 55, 70, 75, 76, 77, 79–105, 107, 111, 114, 130, 177, 184 (nn. 1, 2), 184–85 (n. 6), 185 (nn. 8, 11); "The Dream He Never Knew the End Of," 80, 85–90, 185 (n. 8); "Love and Knowledge," 98–100; "The Sign Whereby He Knew," 89, 91–94; "Tell Me a Story," 81, 102–3; "Was Not the Lost Dauphin," 80, 82–85; "We Are Only Ourselves," 90–91, 103

Baldwin, James, 131, 140, 145
"The Ballad of Mister Dutcher and the Last Lynching in Gupton," 152
Band of Angels, 3, 4, 5, 11, 19, 21, 22, 45, 129, 148, 150, 151, 154, 156, 167, 168

Bay of Pigs invasion, 167
Beaumont, Jeremiah [*World Enough
    and Time*], 53, 71, 112
Bedient, Calvin, 76, 83, 86, 186 (n. 9)
Being Here, 111
Big Business, 163
The Birds of North America [Audubon],
    84, 96
Bitterroot Mountains, 97, 119
Black Americans. *See* African-
    Americans
Black Muslims, 140
Blaustein, Aaron [*Wilderness*], 157
Bloom, Harold, 7, 76
Boone, Daniel, 79
Bowie, Jim, 20
Boyle, Jack [*Brother to Dragons*], 76
"The Briar Patch," 29–35, 129, 132,
    139, 150, 181 (nn. 26, 28)
Brooks, Cleanth, 46, 70, 115
Brother to Dragons, 1–5, 7, 11, 13–14,
    38–78, 79, 81, 96, 99, 104, 112,
    113, 114, 122, 124, 129, 150, 176,
    177, 179 (n. 1), 182 (nn. 2, 4, 8),
    183 (nn. 12, 13, 21, 23), 183–84 (n.
    25), 184 (n. 28)
Brown, John, 2, 4, 13, 24–27, 28, 74,
    76, 105, 165
Bryant, William Cullen, 84–85
Burden, Jack [*All the King's Men*], 11,
    22, 45, 71, 112, 167
Burke, Sadie [*All the King's Men*], 11
Burt, John, 11, 180 (n. 21)

Calhoun, Jerry [*At Heaven's Gate*], 19
Calhoun, John C., 26
"Caribou," 97
Carter, Jimmy, 174
Carter, Reverend Joe, 143, 144
The Cave, 19
Cherokee Indians, 63
Chiaromonte, Nick, 181 (n. 23)
Chief Joseph, 13, 14, 104, 113–28
Chief Joseph of the Nez Perce, 2–9

passim, 55, 67, 70, 75, 76, 77, 97,
    104, 111, 113–28, 185–86 (n. 4),
    186 (nn. 7, 9, 12), 188 (nn. 11, 12)
Chrisman, Richard N., 182 (n. 8)
Civil disobedience: Warren's attitude
    toward, 28, 132, 181 (n. 23)
Civil law, 23, 132, 135, 162
Civil rights movement, 9, 28, 30, 36–
    37, 129–50, 157, 158–60, 170–71,
    178
Civil War, 5–6, 9, 12, 13, 16–17, 27,
    41, 54, 63, 67, 114, 116, 118, 122–
    23, 130, 132–35, 145, 156, 158–60,
    161–71, 180 (n. 21), 183 (n. 21);
    consequences of, 5, 17, 122–23,
    133–34, 159–60; as source of
    American history, 161
Civilization and Its Discontents [Freud],
    51
Clark, Felton, 143–44, 146
Clark, William Bedford, 23, 40, 54,
    182 (n. 4), 183 (nn. 13, 21), 184
    (n. 2)
Cody, Buffalo Bill, 120
Cold War, the, 167
Commercialism, 6, 175
Communism, 6
Confederacy, the, 162
Conrad, Joseph, 44, 50, 52, 70, 160
Conscription Act of 1863, 156
Constitution, United States, 10, 12, 15,
    17, 24, 26, 47, 134, 162, 172
Constitutional law, 12, 23, 135, 162
Cooper, James Fenimore, 15, 162
Crawfurd, Mose [*Wilderness*]. *See*
    Talbutt, Mose
Cuban missile crisis, 167

Darwinism, 93
Davidson, Donald, 30, 32, 35, 118,
    178
Davis, Jefferson, 2, 9–10, 12–13, 27
"A Dearth of Heroes," 13, 14, 19, 141
The Death of the Past [Plumb], 4

196   INDEX

Havard, William C., 164
Hawksworth, Jed [*Wilderness*], 19, 159
Hawthorne, Nathaniel, 2, 7, 15
Hayes, Rutherford B., 123
Hayes-Tilden Compromise, 5, 116, 123, 145
Haymarket Riot (1886), 54, 63
Heart of Darkness [Conrad], 44, 52, 70
Hemingway, Ernest, 148
The Hero in America [Dixon Wecter], 13
Hersey, John, 187 (n. 3)
Higher Law, 25, 27, 28, 105, 132, 183 (n. 21); conflict with civil law, 27, 132
Hiroshima [Hersey], 187 (n. 3)
Hiroshima, Japan, 168–70, 175
History, 1, 2, 12, 16, 25, 28, 39, 42, 44, 50, 54, 62–63, 75–76, 101, 103, 112–13, 117, 121, 129, 131–32, 136, 144, 156, 159, 165, 170; demise of, 4, 172; determinism and, 22, 55, 125, 145, 166, 168; Great Men and, 2, 10, 13, 14, 20, 26, 76; identity and, 4, 172; patterns of, 6, 9, 10, 46, 79, 133, 171–72, 175–76, 179 (n. 5); responsibility and, 21, 22–23, 26–27, 37, 120, 134, 137, 147, 167, 171, 178; Warren's attitude toward, 1, 2, 5, 13, 20–21, 26, 29, 39–40, 41, 68, 76, 114, 116, 117, 126, 133, 135, 145, 161, 167–68, 171. *See also* Warren, Robert Penn, as historical writer
Holmes, Oliver Wendell, 18, 162–63
Homage to Theodore Dreiser, 2, 17–18, 117, 133
Houston, Sam, 20
Howard, General Oliver O., 122
Hughes, Langston, 186–87 (n. 2)

I'll Take My Stand, 28–29, 33, 35, 170, 177

Idealism, 6, 7, 11, 19, 27, 38, 41, 46, 66, 67, 79, 85, 103, 116, 148, 150, 158, 161, 180 (n. 22)
Identity, 3, 4, 8, 10, 21, 23, 29, 36, 44, 55, 58, 62, 70, 75, 79–80, 81, 82, 89, 97, 102, 108, 110, 119, 122, 125–27, 130, 134, 135, 137–38, 139, 142, 145–47, 151, 153, 154, 155, 160–78 passim
"Immortality Over the Dakotas," 97
Incarnations, 3, 101, 105–11, 150, 174, 189
Indian, American, 5, 6, 41, 55, 63, 67, 85, 95, 113–28
Individual, 7, 9, 10, 23, 27, 28, 34, 35–36, 46, 47, 59, 77, 81, 133, 148, 171, 173, 174, 181 (n. 23); and history, 2, 3, 4, 21–22, 27, 134, 167; in the modern world, 3, 4, 106, 114, 137, 146, 149, 151, 168, 172, 178; and nature, 93, 99, 103; responsibility of, 22–23, 29, 55, 129, 137, 164, 172; and the state, 23, 27; survival of, 4, 35–36, 37, 149, 170. *See also* Democracy and the individual; Dehumanization
Individualism, 1, 9–10, 18, 44, 137, 139, 166, 178
Industrialization, 6, 29, 34, 35, 163, 170, 171
"Internal Injuries," 101, 105–11, 150
The Invisible Man [Ellison], 149
Irwin, Judge [*All the King's Men*], 11, 18–19, 45

Jefferson, Thomas, 1, 6, 7–8, 10–11, 13, 14, 27, 33, 38–78, 79, 96, 111, 116, 127, 163, 177, 182 (n. 2), 183 (nn. 13, 21), 183–84 (n. 25)
Jefferson Davis Gets His Citizenship Back, 4, 9–10, 11–13, 19, 27, 117, 123, 129, 130, 162, 167
Jeffersonian Dream, 13, 17, 54

Jeffersonian idealism, 11, 116
John Brown: The Making of a Martyr,
1–2, 4, 24, 25–27, 76, 105, 129
John Greenleaf Whittier's Poetry, 2,
14–16
John [*Brother to Dragons*], 48, 52,
58–63, 68, 71, 150
Johnson, James Weldon, 186–87 (n. 2)
Johnson, Lyndon Baines, 174
Jonathan Wild [Fielding], 18
Jung, Carl G., 172, 188 (n. 3)
Justus, James, 71, 114–15, 132, 180
(n. 19), 187 (n. 8), 187–88 (n. 10)

Keats, John, 84
"Keep That Morphine Moving, Cap,"
106–7
Kentucky, 8, 24, 36, 51, 52, 54–55,
56, 70, 72, 75, 101
Kentucky tobacco wars, 3, 24
King, Martin Luther, Jr., 13, 131,
140–41, 144, 150
Korean War, 55
Kurtz [*Heart of Darkness*], 52, 70

"Last Meeting," 153–54
Law, Richard G., 73
Law of the land. *See* Civil law and
Constitutional law
Lee, Robert E., 153
The Legacy of the Civil War, 4, 12, 17,
18, 21, 22, 25, 26–27, 68, 105, 114,
117, 122–23, 129, 130, 132, 133,
145, 146, 149, 157, 160, 161–67,
168, 173, 181 (n. 26), 183 (n. 21)
Lewis, Charles [*Brother to Dragons*],
51–53, 65, 67, 72
Lewis, Isham [*Brother to Dragons*],
46, 52, 56, 59, 182 (n. 2)
Lewis, Letitia [*Brother to Dragons*],
56–57, 67
Lewis, Lilburne [*Brother to Dragons*],

38–39, 42–65 passim, 67, 70–72,
182 (n. 2), 183 (n. 13)
Lewis, Lucy Jefferson [*Brother to
Dragons*], 39, 51, 52, 56, 58–59,
61, 65, 69
Lewis, Meriwether [*Brother to
Dragons*], 42, 45, 48–51, 54, 55,
63–67, 69, 72, 77, 96, 104, 112
Lewis, R. W. B., 115
Lewis and Clark expedition, 48
Life magazine, 134
Light in August [Faulkner], 150
Lincoln, President Abraham, 10, 12–
13, 18, 24, 27, 162, 163, 174, 180
(n. 12)
Long, Huey, 3
Louisiana Purchase, 8, 48, 49, 116
Louisiana Territory, 64, 65, 116
"Lycidas" [Milton], 130

Macbeth, 24
Maison Quarée, 47, 71, 183–84
(n. 25)
Malcolm X, 131, 140, 144–45, 148,
187 (n. 9)
Malone, Dumas, 182 (n. 2)
Manifest destiny, 5–6, 54, 117, 122
Marlow [*Heart of Darkness*], 70
Materialism, 7, 116
Mediterranean fruit fly, 6
Meet Me in the Green Glen, 22, 174
Melville, Herman, 2, 13, 15, 16–17,
18, 162
Mexico, 114
Miles, Colonel Nelson H., 115, 124
Mill, John Stuart, 171
Miller, Hugh [*All the King's Men*], 11
"A Mirror for Artists" [Davidson], 35
Mississippi Summer Project, 131, 143
Modern Age, 36, 41, 46, 55, 107,
128, 170; character of, 36, 41, 46,
55, 107, 128, 170; symptoms of,
174. *See also* Dehumanization

Modern technology, 6, 34, 176
Monticello, Jefferson's home, 47, 48, 58
The Mosquito Coast [Theroux], 176
Moyers, Bill, 4, 6, 114
Mukherjee, Bharati, 179 (n. 5)
Munn, Perse [*Night Rider*], 22, 24, 53
Murdock, Bogan [*At Heaven's Gate*], 18, 24, 32, 151
Myrdal, Gunnar, 142

Narcissism, 93, 175
Natural aristocrat, 10–11
Negro. *See* African-Americans
New and Selected Poems: 1923–1985, 111, 152
"New Dawn," 3, 37, 168–70, 187 (n. 3)
New Deal, 180 (n. 19)
New historicism, 115
New Journalism, 131, 187 (n. 3)
New Madrid earthquake, 68
New York City, 21, 142, 156, 158, 169
New York draft riots, 21, 156–57
Nez Perce War, 115–28 passim
Nielsen, Aldon Lynn, 155, 181 (n. 26), 183 (n. 23), 187 (n. 6), 188 (n. 14)
"Night: In the Motel Down the Road from the Pen," 107–8
Night Rider, 2, 3, 11, 18, 22–24, 26, 53, 54, 67, 112, 113, 167
Nihilism, 7
North, 5, 30, 32, 34, 35, 122–23, 140, 143, 154, 156, 157, 162–66, 180 (n. 21). *See also* Treasury of Virtue
Notes on Virginia [Jefferson], 33, 41, 61–62
Now and Then, 111
Nuclear War, 129, 164, 168, 170, 171

"Ode on a Grecian Urn" [Keats], 84
"Ode to a Nightingale" [Keats], 84

Or Else, 101, 111, 152, 153
Oregonian, Portland, 124

Page, Thomas Nelson, 69, 181 (n. 26)
"Pantaloon in Black" [Faulkner], 53
The Paris Review, 40
Percoon, 72–73, 184 (n. 28)
Perse, St.-John, 120
Philadelphia, Mississippi, 140, 153
Philadelphia, Pennsylvania, 41, 71
A Place to Come To, 2, 3, 19, 22, 36, 37, 45, 111, 130, 136, 151, 154, 156, 168, 174
Plumb, John Harold, 4
Poetry: diagnostic function of, 120, 130; as redeeming social force, 173–74; therapeutic function of, 76
Polis: concept of, in Warren's writing, 23–24
"Pondy Woods," 151, 152, 160, 188 (nn. 13, 14)
Porter, Katherine Anne, 2, 13
Pound, Ezra, 148
Powell, Adam Clayton, 144, 148
Pragmatic idealism, 7, 38, 41, 66, 79, 116, 161
Pragmatism, 7, 11–12, 13, 32, 33, 38, 41, 46, 66, 79, 116, 123, 161, 162, 163
"Prime Leaf," 180 (n. 19)
Promises, 9
Proudfit, Willie [*Night Rider*], 2, 54, 67, 112
"Proud Flesh," 122
Purdew, Simms [*Wilderness*], 157
Purtle, Leontine [*Flood*], 175

R. P. W. [*Brother to Dragons*], 4, 14, 38, 41–77 passim
Racism, 5, 6, 34, 41, 117, 139, 142, 143, 150, 151, 152, 155, 157, 158, 160, 165, 183 (n. 23), 187 (n. 6)

"To a Waterfowl" [Bryant], 84–85
Tobacco Association [*Night Rider*], 23
Todd, Big Jim ["Pondy Wood"], 151, 152, 160, 188 (nn. 13, 14)
Todd, Captain [*Night Rider*], 11
Tolliver, Bradwell [*Flood*], 45, 175
Tolliver, Senator [*Night Rider*], 11, 18
Tolstoy, Leo, 22
Toomer, Jean, 186–87 (n. 2)
Trail of Tears, 63
Transcendentalism. *See* "Higher law"
Treasury of Virtue, 5, 68, 122–23, 157, 159, 165–66, 172
Twain, Mark, 18
Twentieth Century, 2, 4, 36, 63, 71, 81, 171, 172

Under Western Eyes [Conrad], 160
Union: concept of, in Warren's writing, 12, 13, 24–25, 27, 28, 162–63, 180 (nn. 12, 21)
United States, 1, 7, 16, 35, 49, 51, 76, 79, 105, 111, 122, 128, 147, 164, 165, 167; army of, 8, 9, 115; character of, 161; government of, 6, 9, 24, 115, 116, 137, 145, 174
Utopianism, 6. *See also* Higher law

Vendler, Helen, 100

Walker, Marshall, 181 (n. 28)
Walker, Wyatt T., 134, 144, 187 (n. 5)
War and Peace [Tolstoy], 22
War of 1812, 172
Warren, Robert Penn: as historical writer, 2–3, 4, 14, 23, 39–40, 79, 114–15, 115–16, 117, 121–22, 124, 128, 129, 130, 134, 142, 161–78, 185 (n. 8); the individual and, 1–2; as "old Confederate," 35;

pragmatism and, 7, 11, 32, 33, 46, 79, 116, 161–63; racial paternalism of, 32, 148, 157; Southern agrarianism and, 28–37, 127, 139, 170–71, 177–78, 183 (n. 23). *See also* Civil Rights; Democracy; History, Warren's attitude toward; Individual; Individualism; Pragmatism
Washington, Booker T., 31, 34, 186–87 (n. 2)
The Waste Land [Eliot], 24, 130, 176
"A Way to Love God," 53, 99, 177
Webster, Daniel, 26, 95
Wecter, Dixon, 13, 19
Welty, Eudora, 13, 82, 184–85 (n. 6)
Western civilization, 5, 9, 36, 118, 148, 149, 150, 164, 170, 174, 178
Whitman, Walt, 163
Whittier, John Greenleaf, 2, 14–18
Who Speaks for the Negro?, 21, 28, 30, 33, 34, 101, 114, 129, 131–34, 135, 138, 139–50, 153, 155, 160, 170, 173, 183 (n. 23), 186–87 (n. 1), 186–87 (n. 2), 187 (nn. 5, 6, 8), 187–88 (n. 10)
Wilderness, 2, 4, 5, 19, 22, 60, 130, 148, 150, 156–59
Wilderness, Battle of, 54, 63
Wilkins, Roy, 131, 144
Wordsworth, William, 7, 9, 85, 103
World Enough and Time, 9, 11, 19, 23, 53, 71, 112, 129, 130, 167, 180 (n. 19)
Wright, Richard, 186–87 (n. 2)

You, Emperor and Others, 179 (n. 4)
Young, Whitney, 144, 148

Zinn, Howard, 180